Alexander the King

The Sequel to Philip and Olympias

By

Peter Messmore

authorHOUSE

1663 LIBERTY DRIVE, SUITE 200
BLOOMINGTON, INDIANA 47403
(800) 839-8640
www.authorhouse.com

First published by AuthorHouse 09/14/04

ISBN: 1-4184-5038-3 (e)
ISBN: 1-4184-5037-5 (sc)

Library of Congress Control Number: 2004094439

Printed in the United States of America
Bloomington, Indiana

This book is printed on acid-free paper.

TABLE OF CONTENTS

ARISTOTLE'S REFLECTIONS FROM A SPIRIT WORLD 1 1

CHAPTER 1
POTHOS 6

CHAPTER 2
ALEXANDER & DEMOSTHENES 17

CHAPTER 3
CONSOLIDATION 23

CHAPTER 4
DARIUS 35

CHAPTER 5
ANDRAPODISMOS 43

CHAPTER 6
DEPARTURE 48

CHAPTER 7
PERSIA 61

CHAPTER 8
CONSEQUENCES 72

CHAPTER 9
ISSUS 80

ARISTOTLE'S REFLECTIONS FROM A SPIRIT WORLD 2 87

CHAPTER 10
SOUTHWARD 91

CHAPTER 11
JEWS, EGYPT & SIWAH 100

CHAPTER 12
PURSUING DARIUS 112

CHAPTER 13
PERSIA'S HEART: BABYLON, SUSA & PARSA............... 133

CHAPTER 14
HUNTING DARIUS 147

CHAPTER 15
PARMENIO............... 156

CHAPTER 16
MORTALITY............... 165

CHAPTER 17
ROXANE............... 174

CHAPTER 18
INDIA & THE JHELUM............... 182

CHAPTER 19
EASTWARD TO THE BEAS............... 192

CHAPTER 20
JALALPUR ON THE JHELUM TO PATTALA AT THE
DELTA 200

CHAPTER 21
THE GEDROSIAN DESERT............... 210

CHAPTER 22
PERSEPOLIS TO SUSA............... 220

**ARISTOTLE'S REFLECTIONS FROM A SPIRIT
WORLD 3 .... 228**

CHAPTER 23
ECBATANA............... 231

CHAPTER 24
BABYLON 238

CHAPTER 25
DIONYSUS' EMPTY MASK 245

**ARISTOTLE'S REFLECTIONS FROM A SPIRIT
WORLD 4............... 251**

When the Persians meet one another in the roads, you can see whether those who meet are of equal rank. For instead of greeting by words, they kiss each other on the mouth; but if one of them is inferior to the other, they kiss one another on the cheeks, and if one is of much less noble rank than the other, he falls down before him and worships him.

Herodotus, *Histories* 1.134

Preface to

ARISTOTLE'S
REFLECTIONS FROM A SPIRIT WORLD

I speak to you from a spirit world. Others who were my peers in life, as well as the intellectual giants who preceded me, are here. We are men and women you still dismissively and arrogantly call pagans. However, the nature of my spiritual existence is not my subject.

Instead, I will reflect on the life of a man who shaped ancient events so significantly, that he altered forever what you call civilization. The world was different then. So different, that you may find my reflections incredible.

Alexander lived his tumultuous life with little regard of others' viewpoints. Different though our world was, humans who lived in it shared traits that I have observed in you for over two millennia. Power and a compulsive sense of destiny consumed Alexander. Men and women in your world still exhibit these qualities.

Yet, I am unable to tell the complete story. I only offer my reflections and, perhaps, can be your guide. You must learn what lessons you will from Alexander's life.

My wisdom has been centuries in the making. Insights I share were not known to me when I lived. You must also understand that my reflections have been tested and modified innumerable times since my death. I used your sad history to do this. So the tale begins. Learn of Alexander of Macedon
(whom you now call Alexander the Great).
Learn of yourselves.

ARISTOTLE'S REFLECTIONS FROM A SPIRIT WORLD

1

I begin chronologically, reflecting first about my Mieza School and Philip's Royal pages. It was a grand experiment. Educating the best young men in a nation was every pedagogue's dream. However, it ended too soon. After only three years, Philip withdrew Alexander and the other pages and closed the school. Soon after that, they marched into battle at Chaeronea.

The Mieza curriculum was heavily influenced by my mentor, Plato, and of course indirectly by Plato's teacher, Socrates. The course of study there later developed into my Lyceum, which became one of the most famous Athenian schools.

It was there, on the cool slopes of Mount Bermion that my instructional style began. I had agonized for months over the nature of the school's curriculum. Developing in my mind was an emerging model for a scientific study of everything. I was fast evolving into a fervent empiricist. Knowledge existed to be analyzed, categorized, and understood. I had long practiced, especially in Assos and on Lesbos, what I called the scientific method. In the natural sciences, the method involved collecting and testing data, formulating inductive hypotheses from the data collection, and applying a set of principles— sometimes called laws by those whose egos were bigger than their minds— by deduction to a particular condition. I had even worked on a modification of this method for politics and government with Hermias, my Persian-threatened former benefactor in Assos.

However, Macedon, King Philip, and Alexander posed a completely different set of social and intellectual conditions that threatened the free intellectual environment I had enjoyed on Assos. I knew that my freedom to teach would be limited by Philip's expectations—expectations for Macedon, for himself as an absolute monarch in a feudal society, and for his son, Prince Alexander. I could not advocate establishing a democratic middle class, protected from the excesses of a king by a constitution, while instructing the Macedonian royal pages. An academic accommodation had to be reached. I was also concerned with the ability of naive teenage boys to grasp the abstract cognitive and philosophical models with which I had grappled all of my adult life.

At last, I decided to simplify for the royal pages the universal model that swirled inside my brain. I divided the Mieza curriculum into three kinds of knowledge: theoretical, practical, and productive. I explained to my teaching assistants that theoretical knowledge was to be further subdivided into theology, the natural world, and mathematics. I termed these areas theoretical because they did not lead directly to anything. They were to be studied and understood simply for their own sakes. I never doubted that the human mind needed this theoretical foundation so that it could think without self-delusion and confusion.

I focused practical knowledge on politics, governments, and the use of ethics to guide the organization of laws, the style of monarchies and the establishment of unified nations. Clearly, there had to be some modification of this practical knowledge for Alexander, but I had ideas about how this could be done.

Productive knowledge centered on drama, art, music, and poetry. I decided to teach the pages how to analyze tragedy using the works of Aeschylus, Euripides and Sophocles. Priceless life-lessons lay in these productive works and they allowed my students to be immersed in Greece's rich dramatic heritage.

≈

I can still remember seeing the royal pages approaching Mieza from afar with Prince Alexander at their head, riding Bucephalas, his magnificent horse. Near him was Hephaestion, followed closely by the other energetic pages. I waited in the courtyard until they charged into our quiet school at full gallop. Coming to a halt, Alexander leaped off Bucephalas and stood before me.

"We have arrived, Aristotle," he said. "What do you require of us?"

I looked at the Prince of Macedon. I had not seen him since he was a much younger lad. For the first time, I examined his physical characteristics. The initial impression he gave was of being short, much shorter than his peers. Although he added some weight to his attenuated stature during the following years, he was as tall now as he would ever become.

However, the arrogant young prince had a presence about him. I was surprised at how quickly I got over the disappointment of his height and was instead captured by his eyes. They projected a disarming gaze. I felt as if the deep brown eye examined the visible part of me while the blue one probed deeper for any sign of weakness. Alexander was beardless, in contrast to the other pages who had started to show the beginnings of the hairy facial growths of which Macedonian men prided themselves. His hair was long and wavy, almost blond. I noticed that he held his head elevated and to the left, probably the result of a neck injury experienced during demanding military training or the rough games that Macedonian boys played. Even at thirteen, he carried the body of an athlete—he was muscular and lean. Despite and not because of his titular status, he was clearly the leader of the other thirty-nine youths who arrived that day at Mieza.

My first lecture concerned politics and government. I reviewed tyranny, oligarchy, and the need for a democratic middle class. Then, before going too far with the sons of Macedonian aristocracy, I tempered these views with a thesis that described a singular exception to these principles. There was only one justification for an absolute monarchy: outstanding personal achievement by a man who was widely recognized as a god among men. Every page and the prince understood that I was speaking of King Philip and, eventually, Alexander.

Toward the end of the lecture, I defended slavery, teaching that enlightened rulers and leaders should treat slaves as beasts and plants. I stated my conviction that all barbarians, especially Persians, were slaves by their very nature and nothing could ever change that. Finally, I defended private property and great wealth, explaining that poverty was as permanent, and as pervasive as inclement weather.

Every page, especially Alexander, understood that I was advocating the establishment of an enlightened monarchy—a monarchy tempered by democratic ideals and guided by philosophic principles. Abundantly clear was my contention that a just society could only be achieved when kings became philosophers and philosophers became kings.

≈

3

During the months that followed, my assistants took the pages on field expeditions up the slopes of Mount Bermion, to the shores of Lake Ostrovo, and across the Gardens of Midas to collect plant specimens. The specimens were brought back to the Mieza School, where they were analyzed, categorized, and put in our botanical museum display racks. Within half a year, every page could scientifically describe over a hundred plants found in southwestern Macedonia.

Callisthenes, my nephew, lectured the pages on the history of Greece, Persia, Macedon, and the far-reaching barbaric lands. He taught them a historical scientific method and had each student begin a historical diary, which he urged them to keep the rest of their lives.

My greatest expertise was in biology, medicine, and the natural sciences. I obtained aborted fetuses from a nearby village and carefully examined their embryonic parts. I compared the human fetus with the undeveloped embryo of a chicken and taught the pages how it paralleled the development of a seed. I imparted to them medical knowledge, as taught me by my father. The students learned how to use herbs to treat illness, how to counteract snakebites, and how different foods alter human performance. They learned simple geometry by surveying land and plotting the direction of much-needed roads in the district. I showed them the habits of bees and for over a year studied the life cycle of the Aegean mosquito. Alexander was especially interested in the mosquito.

Embankments in the countryside produced natural lodestones that were collected, taken back to Mieza, and used in simple physics experiments. Alexander was amazed when I explained the use of the lever and fulcrum and demonstrated how enormous weights could be moved using simple machinery.

The most difficult subject to teach the pages was ethics and rhetoric. Macedonians and Greeks took it as axiomatic that rulers and leaders could do and say whatever they wanted to achieve their goals. Lying had been a celebrated Greek art since Homeric times. Every educated Greek knew that even the great Odysseus had prevailed through trickery and verbal misrepresentation. That model had been the norm for centuries. With difficulty, I taught countless lessons explaining the nature of truth. The pages (and Alexander in private, epoptic sessions) were taught how the rules of logic could aid humans as they sought social, political and personal truth. An area of study that Alexander came to excel at was eristics. It required a skilled thinker, speaker, or writer to argue a position with equal facility from both a pro and a con position. I taught them that truth could only be found by understanding the extreme opposites surrounding any difficult or controversial issue.

To evaluate the success of these lessons, I modeled mental exercises, demonstrating how a speaker could hide his real feelings about an issue by showing that he understood its extremes. Only when I completed my presentation would I reveal what I really thought. If my students could not fathom my true feelings during these presentations, I had succeeded in teaching them the power of logic. Alexander mastered the technique early and enjoyed using it in the evening when the pages discussed the day's instruction in their quarters.

However, that was long ago. Alexander became king immediately after Philip's death and set out to defend and establish his new kingdom. He was insistent that he would surpass Philip's achievements. Macedonia and Greece would only see him for two more years. After that, he never returned to the land of his birth.

I returned to Athens and established the Lyceum. It became famous as the "walking school," because much of my instruction occurred as we strolled about the school's grounds. King Alexander wrote me often—more in the beginnings of his campaigns than at the end, however.

Alexander's brilliant, meteoric time changed civilization—even when I lived. My reflections will continue as you read of his life.

CHAPTER 1

POTHOS

Leonnatus brought Queen Cleopatra-Eurydice into the old Aegae palace throne room. The new King of Macedon, Alexander, awaited the quaking former Queen. She cradled her infant son, Caranus, in her slender arms. Her terrified little girl, Europa, was at her side. Leonnatus had followed his new king's command and found the ex-queen on the road to Paiko, escorted by a small group of Olympias' priests. They were only three stadia from Paiko, where they were to have been killed. Alexander's mother had instructed the priests to burn the bodies, crush their bones into pieces no larger than a fist, and then cast the remains in the River Vardar. Only Alexander's quick action the day of his father's assassination had saved them.

"Cleopatra-Eurydice," Alexander said as he walked toward the young mother and her children. "Forgive my mother's harsh treatment of you. She acted without my authority before I had recovered from my father's cruel murder. Are your children well?"

Cleopatra-Eurydice seethed with anger. Nonetheless, fear and concern for the safety of her children caused her hold her tongue. She knew that the twenty-year-old upstart who stood before her had known everything about the plot that had just robbed her of a husband and father. Robbed also was Macedon. The greatest king her country ever had was dead, killed by his former wife and his only son. She knew that Alexander was lying as he spoke to her. *Play along*, she decided. *Let him make his move.* If she could survive the next months, there were forces in Macedonia that might rescue her. General Attalus was in the Troad as co-commander of a formidable army. He hated Alexander. She also hoped, more than believed, that there might be highland uprisings against Alexander. Usurpers had always nested in Lyncestis. Her options were few. She could only be compliant until events either saved or eliminated her.

"My daughter and I were beaten by the priests during the trip, but we were not seriously injured. Praise Zeus that they did not harm my son."

Alexander moved toward the former queen and reached out to touch her baby. The boy slept serenely in his mother's arms, as Alexander caressed the infant's smooth cheek. He turned from the mother and children and walked to the throne dais.

"You think I was involved in Philip's murder, don't you. I assure you I was not. I've investigated the plot thoroughly. Pausanius acted alone, motivated by the cruel rape that Attalus caused. We've tortured the stable hands who ravished Pausanius. They confessed that Attalus commanded them to violate Philip's former lover. Attalus will pay for his actions with his life. If you must blame someone for Philip's murder, blame him. He set in motion the events that felled your husband and my father."

At that, Cleopatra-Eurydice burst into tears. Almost as quickly, she regained control, wiped her eyes with her sleeve cuff, and looked demurely at the king. "I mourn Philip with every breath and fear for my children's safety, Alexander. But anger is not in me," she lied. "I'm just numb." She saw Alexander smirk at her self-serving remark. However, she hoped it would buy her time. It was all she could think of.

"You will be taken to Pella today," Alexander said. "For a time, you must remain under palace arrest. I've given orders that no harm is to come to you or your children. When I have time, I'll send for you. We will discuss your exile."

"I'm grateful to you, Alexander," the young woman answered. "I never hated you. The fates put us in opposing roles." She couldn't bring herself to call him king, although he had held the title for two days now. "A lesser man would have had me killed, as your mother intends."

"Olympias won't harm you," Alexander shot back. "She understands her limitations and responsibilities. Go with Leonnatus to Pella. I'll speak to you when I get there."

Cleopatra-Eurydice left the throne room, accompanied by her two children.

≈

Alone, Alexander ruminated on his actions involving the ex-queen. He knew there would be no exile for the woman or her children. Her elimination was inevitable; it just had to be done at the right time. For an instant, he regretted that her infant son, only one of two potential rivals

7

to his ascendancy, must die. Then he steeled himself and forced the weak thoughts from his mind. Their removal would not happen immediately, he decided. That was how his mother thought. Other, more deadly, rivals must be dispatched first.

Is this how a king's reign starts? he thought. *With deception, lies and manipulation?* It wouldn't always be this way, he finally decided. When he had stabilized the kingdom and established himself, he could act as Aristotle had taught him at Mieza. Kingly truth would then become his life standard. Life-threatening expediency caused him to act duplicitously now. Circumstances justified it. His survival was at stake. Philip would have done the same. Zeus-Ammon, his spiritual father, would forgive these necessary sins.

≈

Over the next several days, King Alexander issued a series of commands that were his first official acts as Macedonian monarch. Swift horse messengers were dispatched to Epirus and Illyria, recalling a host of his friends who had been exiled by Philip. Among them were Ptolemy, Harpalus, Nearchus, and two brothers, Erigyius and Laomedon. Perdiccas, one of the plotters who had killed Pausanius after he had assassinated Philip, was given a high command in the army. Philotas, a longtime friend, was made temporary chief of staff.

After issuing these orders, the king sent for Hephaestion. His lifelong friend came immediately and was escorted into Alexander's private chambers. When the door was closed, the companions embraced warmly. Each man's head rested on the other's shoulder until the embrace verged on something more. Finally, Alexander pulled away and walked to an alcove couch.

"Sit with me, Hephaestion," Alexander said. "I need your counsel."

"Your need is written on your face," Hephaestion said. "Ask anything of me and I'll do it."

"I know you will. Listen to me while I think aloud. Tell me if the actions I'm considering are needed."

Hephaestion looked at Alexander. He had seen his companion go through this process before. It was the only way that his troubled spirit could ever have survived parents like Philip and Olympias. Anguishing and personal recrimination were not in Hephaestion's character, however. He simply confronted problems, made a decision and then acted. His personality manifested a direct, linear-simplicity that was nearly the opposite of Alexander's. Too much swirled in the king's prodigious brain for that. The two made a good complementary team when time permitted discussions such as these.

Hephaestion saw Alexander stretch out his short arms then run his fingers through his near-golden, wavy hair. Then he interlaced his fingers over his head and rested his arms there while his different colored eyes darted about the throne room.

"Mother seethes with revenge," he began. "I must avoid her for a while." The king buried his head in his hands, rubbed his eyes and then continued. "Within the next ten days my supporters will return. I'll then be in a stronger position to take the offensive against the uprisings that have broken out. My enemies see me as vulnerable; therefore, I must act quickly. I'll command today that Amyntas is to be put under palace arrest. He's Philip's brother's only son and could be used by those who challenge me." Alexander paused.

Hephaestion's eyes were fixated on Alexander. He had seen the same, troubled look on his friend's face when Alexander had made the decision not to oppose Philip's assassination. The king's wide-eyed gaze told him that Alexander wanted his reaction.

"I agree," is all Hephaestion said. Nevertheless, he was surprised with Alexander's leniency. It was the time-honored Macedonian custom to eliminate quickly rivals to the throne when a new king came to power. Amyntas was fortunate that Alexander didn't order his death outright.

"I've decided to let Philip Arridaeus live," Alexander continued. "Olympias destroyed his brain when he was an infant; he'll never threaten my kingship. Sometimes I pity my half-brother." Alexander didn't wait for Hephaestion's reaction on that issue.

The king continued his crisis list. "Yesterday, a son of the Lyncestian Aeropus demanded an audience with me. He acknowledged me king, and then told me of a plot involving his father and two of his brothers. I'm to be killed soon, probably on my return to Pella."

"Take them out immediately," Hephaestion said without hesitation. "They'll do it!"

"Yes," Alexander replied calmly. "How will the highland, provincial chiefs react? Will they join a revolt against me? Aeropus and his sons appear to have secret support."

"It's likely," Hephaestion said. "But you have no choice. We can deal with the uprisings as they come. But eliminate these threats now, before the plot spreads."

Alexander grew even more pensive. There was another long silence, and then he brought up another menace. "Attalus is my most serious threat. Our army can easily put down any uprisings in the months ahead. But Attalus co-commands Macedonian forces in the Troad. If he gets Parmenio to join him, Macedon will be thrust into civil war. Athens and Persia would pick the winner's bones clean."

Hephaestion thought briefly, and then reacted to his lover's last remark. "Send for Attalus before he takes any action. Command him to return, alone, to Pella. If he refuses, and he will, have him killed there. The only uncertainty is Parmenio. He was your father's oldest friend. If he thinks that you were involved in Philip's murder, he'll join Attalus against us."

"Perdiccas is already spreading word to our commanders and foreign diplomats that Pausanius acted alone. We have scribe-recorded confessions from the stable hands who raped Pausanius that he swore revenge on both Attalus and Philip. We also have the written assurance from Demosthenes that Pausanius was to have been given safe passage to Persia. Copies of these confessions and the letter have been sent to everyone that matters. That should be enough to convince Parmenio and bring him to our side."

"He may not believe the evidence," Hephaestion replied. "Those things can be faked. Parmenio has done it over the years."

"I know, but it might convince those who want to be convinced. Parmenio may have doubts about the evidence, but he also wants to be on the winning side." Alexander stood and walked toward the ancient throne of Macedon, lost in thought.

He then turned and faced his friend to announce his decision. "I'll send Hecataeus on a trireme today to find Attalus in the Troad. The assassins you trained will accompany him. If Attalus won't return, they will have orders to kill him there and return with his body. A different agent will be sent to persuade Parmenio to stay out of the mess and remain loyal to me. Pray to Zeus-Ammon that he does."

"It's a good plan, Alexander," Hephaestion said. "Attalus must be eliminated or he'll join with Athens, even King Darius, against you. You have no other choice."

"I'm grateful for your strong support, Hephaestion," Alexander said with a smile on his face. "I'll get through this and win more glory than Philip ever dreamed of. You'll be at my side as I go forward."

"I'll be there, Alexander," Hephaestion responded. The two men walked to the door and embraced intimately. Alexander gave his friend an order before he left.

"Return to Pella today. I want you in command of the army until I return in a few days. When the exiles return, I'll reorganize the army units and appoint new commanders who are my supporters. Make sure no plots hatch against me until then.

"Take this," Alexander said, handing to his friend the symbol of the Macedonian monarchy. "It's my royal seal. It will validate any actions you deem necessary. I don't want to be murdered on the Aegae-Pella road."

"There will be no army plots, Alexander. You are the gods' anointed. We will prevail," Hephaestion said as he embraced the king once more and then left.

≈

Alexander issued orders for the immediate execution of Aeropus and his two sons. He then sent for Hecataeus. The king gave him orders to travel by swift trireme to the Troad, where Attalus and Parmenio were encamped with the Macedonian and Greek allied expeditionary force. He

11

knew that word of Philip's death would have already reached the army; valuable time must not be lost turning events in his favor.

Hecataeus gladly accepted his king's orders and left with twenty of Hephaestion's trained assassins to confront Attalus. Traveling with him was a special envoy, Amyntas. Amyntas' assignment, the most delicate of all of King Alexander's agents, was to go to Parmenio. All Hecataeus had to do was ask Attalus to return and kill him if he refused. Amyntas had to reason with the venerated general and convince him that Alexander had played no role in his father's death.

The outcomes of these dangerous actions were in doubt as Alexander began to review urgent dispatches from Greece and the conquered Macedonian lands. Predictably, the Illyrians were mounting raids against Macedonian border outposts. Equally dire, the primitive, blue-body-painted Triballians began to invade Macedonian territory in northern Thrace, south of the Danube River. These same savages had nearly killed Philip with a spear thrust to his leg.

Most alarmingly, the horse-rich estate chieftains of Thessaly were in open rebellion against Macedonian authority. Philip had been given the title of archon for life, but they did not intend to transfer the title to his son—especially a son who many of them felt had a hand in his father's death.

Alexander knew that the Greek states must be taught a lesson quickly or everything that Philip had accomplished over twenty years would be lost. He spent his last days in Aegae, prioritizing solutions to these multiple crises as he awaited word from Hephaestion that it was safe for him to return to his army in Pella.

≈

Alexander used this time to commission a great tumulus that would hold the washed bones and last worldly possessions of Philip. He issued a series of commands to his royal engineers to prepare the site that would house the former king's remains. There were to be three structures at the gravesite, each without a main door. The main burial chamber was to contain Philip's afterlife accessories. His remains were to be sealed in a royal funeral chamber, which would be closed from the top with a large, wedge shaped, blocking stone. All buildings were then to be covered with enormous quantities of earth, hauled in by slaves to create an earthen tumulus. A small temple honoring Zeus was to be built atop the mound, where an eternal fire was always to be kept burning.

Alexander told the engineers that he would inspect and give final approval of the site before Philip's remains were placed in it. Before that, however, he must attend to more critical matters in Pella. Strict orders were given to keep Olympias away from the burial site.

Word finally came from Hephaestion that it was safe for Alexander's return to Pella. The king prepared to leave the next day. He decided to take his mother with him. He had deliberately avoided Olympias since the day of the murder, but now her role in his monarchy must be explained. His hopelessly headstrong mother had to be reined in. Her limitations and what she could and couldn't do had to be made clear.

Alexander spent half a morning deciding the roles he would allow Olympias to assume. Then he called for Macedon's queen mother and awaited her sitting patiently on the ancient throne of Macedon.

"You have finally learned to sit on the throne," Olympias said as she entered. She wore a half smile. "It becomes you. You look exactly as I thought you would."

"Enough, Mother," Alexander said curtly. "Macedon's in turmoil! There's no time for your annoying cuteness. We leave for Pella tomorrow. Prepare for a sunrise departure."

"I'll be ready," his mother answered. She kept the enigmatic smile on her still-beautiful face as she spoke.

"Cleopatra-Eurydice and her children were taken to Pella yesterday," Alexander said. "She's to be kept safe in the palace for the immediate future. No harm is to come to her, not now. Stay away from her! Is that understood?"

"Why do you put off what must be done, Alexander?" his mother asked. "Every Macedonian monarch before you eliminated rivals immediately after assuming power. Philip did it! You'll never be safe until all three of them are dead."

13

"Caranus, the baby, must die. On that we agree," Alexander answered. "I've not decided what to do with his mother and sister. I alone will make that decision. You're not to see her or cause her or her children harm. Is that clear?"

"I hear you, son. But you are not thinking straight. Delaying their deaths jeopardizes us both."

Alexander raised his voice to a near shout. "It is how I'll have it, Olympias. You'll do as I tell you!"

Olympias relented. There would be other chances and other times. She walked to her son, pulled him off his throne by one arm, and embraced him. "You're king now, son. I acknowledge your authority, even over me."

"That's how it must be," Alexander said. "When the army is ready, I must leave Pella and crush our enemies. Antipater will be made regent in my absence. You should like that! You couldn't have done what you did without him."

"Have you considered making me regent during your absences, son?"

"Macedonians will never accept a woman as regent, Mother. You should understand that."

"Establish a new pattern," she shouted. "You're king now; you can do what you want."

"My throne is precarious, Mother. Don't burden me with absurd requests. Even Aristotle wouldn't support such a ludicrous idea. Be satisfied with your queen-mother role. You'll have more power than Philip ever gave you. But stay away from Antipater. He has my trust and he will govern Macedon ably. I'll be in regular correspondence with him, so I'll know if you're following my wishes."

"You may change your mind as you watch me in the years to come," Olympias persisted. "For now, I'll do as you ask."

"I must stamp out all of these rebellions before I rule the world, Mother. Don't cause me problems with your wild notions. I want you as an ally and supporter, not a viper that I must watch constantly."

Alexander was tiring of this contentious exchange and led Olympias to the door. They embraced and she left. The new king spent the rest of the day studying maps of Thessaly and central Greece. The maps were the ones that Philip had made immediately after Chaeronea. Thessaly, immediately south of his threatened kingdom, must be dealt with soon after he returned to his main army. He wouldn't take years to cajole, negotiate, and bribe his path to glory as Philip had. The rebellious Thessalians would be the first Greeks to understand how King Alexander handled mutinous former allies.

≈

Alexander stayed only half a day in Pella. Both he and Hephaestion thought the capital still too dangerous. He planned a midday departure to join his vast army encamped outside the city. Before leaving, he met with Antipater, gave him the royal seal, and empowered him to rule in his absence.

"Send me regular dispatches, no matter how far from Macedon I might be," Alexander told Antipater. "Continue doing this as long as you are regent."

"The dispatches will start immediately," Antipater answered. "I'll begin training special couriers as soon as you leave. They'll use the fast steeds your father bred from Thessalian stock."

"Good," Alexander said. "Make arrangements for Olympias to correspond regularly with me. I want her perspectives on events in Macedonia. She is connected to the gods, and I want her religious counsel."

"She will have a special pouch," Antipater said. "I'll put your royal seal on it as soon as she gives the scroll to me. No one will ever read your mother's letters."

Alexander was pleased with Antipater's attitude. "Take care of my kingdom, Antipater," he said as he led his new regent to the door. "If you can keep it calm here, I'll take care of the rebellions that break out. Then I'll complete Philip's dream of conquering Persia."

"And you will do it," Antipater shot back. "You know my administrative abilities. Don't worry; your orders will be followed."

Antipater left. Alexander stayed in the throne room, alone. His thoughts covered Philip's death, how he would deal with his rebellious Greek allies and his destiny. Then he turned and walked to the ancient throne of Macedon. Constructed of strong Macedonian oak, it was beginning to show its age. He wondered if he would ever gaze on the symbol of his royal ancestors again. For the first time, he felt the burdens of monarchy. Reverentially, he stroked the old throne's arm with his left hand and sighed. "Enough!" he said loudly to himself. He turned and walked briskly to the door. King Alexander of Macedon had much to do.

CHAPTER 2

ALEXANDER & DEMOSTHENES

It was late summer when the young king, reinforced by his formidable 10,000 man horse cavalry, began to move south into Thessaly. The 30,000 force was unchallenged until it approached the vale of the Tempe River. The Thessalians occupied the narrow gorge, held nearly impregnable by the enormous slopes of Mount Olympus and Mount Ossa. Warned by Macedonian advance scouts that a frontal assault was impossible, Alexander halted his army. He took a small group of the scouts, several of his engineers, and his officer inner-circle, and walked along the shore of the Thermaic Gulf, where Mount Ossa fell precipitously into the lapping waves. A strong, humid breeze was blowing, causing the king's wavy hair to dance.

"It's just too dangerous to lead the full army along this rocky shore," Hephaestion said as the small group sought another path around the Thessalian blocked pass. "We may have to backtrack north and then swing westward toward Elimea to meet the Thessalians."

"That would take too long," Alexander replied. "There has to be another way." The king walked under the near vertical wall of rock that represented the east side of Mount Ossa. It towered high above him and projected itself outward, so that he could see no higher than twenty or thirty cubits. "We need an enormous ladder," he said. Then his blue and gray eyes lit up.

"Get my chief engineer," he ordered.

The engineer came quickly and was taken to the king. "Is it possible to cut steps into this rock?" Alexander asked as he pointed upward. "The steps would have to be wide and deep. Several thousand lightly armed hypaspists could then climb over Ossa and descend into the plain of the River Peneus on the other side. I remember the area from when we returned from Chaeronea."

The engineer walked to the vertical wall and felt its surface with outstretched hands and arms. He then took a small hammer and a chisel from a leather belt around his waist and began to chip the rock away. It was hard, but not that hard. Soon a rough stair, a cubit wide and half a cubit deep started to take shape in the rock wall's side. "It can be done, King Alexander," the engineer said at last. "With ten of my nimble assistants, I'll have stairs up and down Mount Ossa in three days. We'll only be able to work in daylight. It's too dangerous to cut stone at night from such heights. But it can be done!"

Alexander smiled. A characteristic that Philip had noticed in him was being displayed. Greeks and Macedonians called it pothos: a yearning to strive against seemingly insurmountable odds and accomplish what everyone else thought was impossible. It was the first time the young king displayed it to gain advantage over a situation or enemy. It would not be the last.

"Begin immediately," he commanded the engineer. "I'll send for your men. The work must be done quickly. If there are problems, let me know. Don't fall behind the schedule you gave me. Our army will wait at the pass's northern entrance, making enough noise to mask any rock cutting sounds. The Thessalians will never know what hit them when I come up from their rear. The pass will be ours."

Hephaestion and Alexander's officers looked in awe at the young king. If they ever doubted it, here was a man they could follow and admire. He had Philip's courage but was more resourceful. There would be no end to the worlds that they could conquer following such a leader. Most of the officers, scouts, and the king left the engineers at the beach and returned to the main army.

In three and a half days, the stairs had been cut neatly up Mount Ossa's eastern side and down its western flank. Alexander then led three thousand of his hypaspists up and over Ossa and entered the plain of the Peneus. When the Thessalians realized that they had been flanked, they surrendered without any loss of life on either side.

≈

Demosthenes of Athens had planned his boule show for days. A former officer in Thessaly's cavalry, a unit that had served with Alexander during the days after he had first left Pella, had defected to him ten days ago. He had told Demosthenes that he had personally seen King Alexander killed while leading a cavalry charge in Thrace. He further explained that the Macedonian army's victories in Illyria had been achieved under the leadership of a different Alexander, Alexander of Lyncestis. The turncoat officer had agreed to appear before the boule and repeat his story. A rich payment, drawn from Darius' bribe, had helped motivate the Thessalian.

"I was closer to him than I am to most of you," the officer announced to the boule members. "A Thracian soldier, who had been knocked to the ground and was thought to be unconscious or killed, regained his senses and allowed Alexander to ride by. In an instant, he reached out for a partially broken sarissa, stood, and then launched the spear into Alexander's back. It went through the king's chest, and he fell dead to the ground. Blood gushed from his mouth as his companions surrounded him. Alexander's killer was immediately stabbed to death, but he had done his duty. Greece will no longer be threatened by Philip's son."

There was a roar of elation from the boule members as the Thessalian finished his story. A few legislators asked clarifying questions, but the essential truth of the man's story remained unchanged: Alexander was dead.

"The gods have saved Athens and Greece," Demosthenes announced theatrically as he replaced the Thessalian on the speaker's platform. "Yet the powerful Macedonian army remains under the command of able generals. We must first spread the word of Alexander's death to every polis in Greece. Since Thebes is in imminent danger, we must send arms to help them throw off the Macedonian yoke. They won't need any of our soldiers; their hatred of the Macedonians is sufficient to spark a rebellion. All of Greece will rise up to reclaim its independence. Our time is now! Don't miss another opportunity to liberate Hellas from the northern barbarians."

Demosthenes' motion was debated for half a day and then passed. The next day, the full ecclesia supported the boule's recommendation. Athens sent the first of a series of arms shipments to Thebes and other Greek poleis having strong Macedonian garrisons. Swift horse messengers were dispatched to every major Greek city-state as Demosthenes' plan gained momentum.

≈

Alexander, Hephaestion, Ptolemy and Perdiccas sat in the king's command tent near Larissa, Thessaly. All were exhausted and dirty from a forced march back to Macedonia. Nevertheless, broad smiles painted each face and a spirit of joviality was present. The group had opened a second large cask of strong Macedonian red wine, one from the Gardens of Midas that still bore Philip's name. They were quickly becoming drunk.

Ptolemy, who was not quite as inebriated as the others were, spoke first. He had been a fellow student at Aristotle's Mieza school and was the rumored bastard son of former King Philip. "Cutting those stairs over Mount Ossa was brilliant, Alexander. Already, they're being called 'Alexander's Stairs.' They will last as long as the mountain itself." Then he grew more political. "The Thessalians knew they were whipped when we emerged behind them. Never has a Greek achieved life-long archon status without a single battle. Philip had to fight many wars before he was granted it."

Alexander smiled. Privately, he knew his legend was just beginning to grow. Filling another kantharos of wine, he grew serious. "The Greek city-states granted me hegemon of the Corinthian League because of our lightning-fast descent into central and southern Greece. It wasn't because they wanted it, but because of our army. It won't last; we will be back soon. I'll have to raze a city before Greece is pacified."

Perdiccas, Alexander's friend and an aristocrat from Orestis province, allowed silence, then changed the subject with vital news that he had just received. "Alexander, you are aware that Demosthenes has been promising Attalus in the Troad everything imaginable. Hecataeus just informed me that the offers ranged from great gifts of gold to honorary citizenship in Athens. With our unopposed moves into Greece, all of that is over. Attalus has appealed for mercy and turned over all written communications from Demosthenes to Hecataeus."

Alexander suddenly grew more sober. "Is Hecataeus bringing him back to Pella as I ordered?" he asked.

"Attalus refused to come and was killed on the spot," Perdiccas answered. "His body awaits you in Pella."

Alexander was pleased but knew that the murder of one of Macedon's leading generals was not without great risk. Most of that risk could be managed. But Philip's other general in the Troad, the venerable Parmenio, was his greatest concern. "What was Parmenio's reaction to all of this?" he asked.

"He remains loyal to you, Alexander," Perdiccas said. "He told Hecataeus that he accepts your version of Philip's assassination. He will need your encouragement and understanding as the Persian invasion begins, however. We don't want him opposing us. He would split apart our forces."

Hephaestion finally spoke. "Parmenio won't oppose us. His allegiance to Philip has been transferred to Alexander. If that changes, I will take care of him."

Alexander smiled at his friend. "We won't need your dagger, Hephaestion," he said. "Let's be patient with Parmenio—he will come around. I need his abilities as we prepare for the invasion. Leave me now. I have dispatches from Pella that must be read before I sleep."

The king's generals left and Alexander started on the dispatches. Among them was one from his regent in Pella, Antipater. He wrote that he knew of Attalus' death and was pleased. The last part of Antipater's message complained to the king that Olympias was making his regency almost impossible. She questioned every decision he made and she was reestablishing her priest spy network, one that Philip had dismantled. Using strong language, Antipater pleaded with Alexander to confront his mother upon his return. Without that action, he concluded, he would find it difficult to continue in the important role that the king had given him.

Alexander thought about Antipater's complaints. He knew well how Olympias could meddle in others' affairs. Yet, she was his strongest domestic ally. He was not about to curb her powers just because Antipater was having trouble getting along with her. *Let mother serve as a check on any ambitions that Antipater might have*, he decided. He would speak with Olympias about Antipater's concerns, but his words to his mother would not carry the sting that the regent wanted. *Let them battle it out*, he thought. *I'll decide the issues that are important.* Frankly, he wanted his mother's priest network expanded, for it would provide a much-needed source of intelligence information. Antipater's threat to resign was meaningless. The regent would just have to cope with Olympias. The king was glad that the unpleasant task of dealing with her on a daily basis would be spared him. Olympias was like fire. She could be used to light his way in life, but getting too close to her on a regular basis would singe anyone's body and spirit. It was better to have Antipater vexed than himself. He smiled and thanked Zeus-Ammon for a gift in the form of his demanding mother, who would unhesitatingly aid his ascent to glory.

CHAPTER 3

CONSOLIDATION

Alexander had been gone from Pella more than two months when Antipater received word that the king was returning victorious from Thrace and Illyria. His bravery and leadership had been stunning. It was well-received news by everyone in Pella but especially by Antipater. Alexander's victories would allow Macedon's regent to slow his hectic administrative pace. It appeared, at last, that most of Macedon's threats had been eliminated. Among the communications that the regent had spent the morning examining was one from Alexander to his mother. From its size, Antipater knew it was a brief one. It was sealed and marked on the outside with large writing: Olympias' Eyes Only.

"The courier made it clear that you alone were to read it, Olympias," Antipater said to the king's mother as he gave the scroll to her. He waited, showing that he wanted Olympias to open it in his presence.

"That will be all, Antipater," Olympias said, with a callous dismissive stare.

The regent returned the gaze, but said nothing. *So this is the way it is going to be,* he thought. As regent, he expected that all communication from Alexander in the field would come through him, even letters to Olympias. It was clear that the king was still devoted to his mother and saw her as his strongest ally. He would have to learn to live with the son-mother bond. The message probably involved some useless drivel about Alexander's Zeus-Ammon linkage and how his spiritual father was guiding him to new victories. Antipater turned and left.

When Olympias was alone, she broke the seal on the small parchment scroll. It was no larger than a man's hand. Unrolling it, she saw a simple coded message. Then, as Alexander had instructed her before he left, she went to her copy of the *Iliad*. On the third scroll segment was the key to interpreting Alexander's clandestine communication.

She opened Homer's work and began to decode her son's brief message. Then she went to a sofa and considered its significance. Alexander's decoded message contained two commands. They were written simply, both to avoid confusion and to aid his mother's limited reading ability. The first said "Eliminate Caranus now." The second read, "I'll remove Amyntas when I return."

Olympias stared across her sitting room in silence. A grim, deadly look of determination developed on her face. Then she stood up, walked quickly to her door, and shouted "Open!" Her plan was well rehearsed; her actions were sure and unwavering.

"Get Altious, now!" she commanded the waiting guard. Her most trusted priest soon joined her. When the guard closed the door, she addressed the expectant priest.

"Isolate Cleopatra-Eurydice from her two children immediately," she said with a glint in her eyes. "Use Alexander's seal as authority for your action. When she's locked in a room alone, get two other priests and bring her two children to my bedchamber. This must be done quickly," she shouted. "No one can interfere with what must be done."

The Queen Mother of Macedon released her long-awaited plan; each person carrying it out knew his role. "Tell them the time of Olympias has come," she yelled at Altious as he was leaving. "They'll understand."

Alexander's mother walked into her bedchamber and stood before a large charcoal brazier. She stirred its nearly cold coals with an iron rod until she could feel heat. Impatiently, she blew briskly on the small cluster of coals until a small patch of red could be seen. Then she added charcoal chips until a strong fire blazed. Soon, the bronze brazier bowel began to ping and pop as cool metal surrendered to the fire. By the time her guard knocked at her door, the brazier's heat could be felt halfway across the room. Olympias was ready.

She opened the door and saw her bodyguard, Altious, and two priests standing there. One held an infant boy. The other cradled a nearly asleep one-year-old girl. "Give me the boy!" she demanded. "Put the girl on the sofa in my bed chamber and leave."

The priests obeyed and left. One had a smile on his face; the other looked troubled. Altious walked silently to a corner of the bedchamber and stood there with his arms crossed. When Olympias heard the door close, she walked to the charcoal brazier and knelt beneath it holding baby Caranus above her head.

"You commanded me to do this, mighty Zeus-Ammon. It's the first action that you have ordered to protect Alexander. I do it without remorse, just as a soldier kills his enemy. I'll do it again, if necessary."

She stood slowly, repositioned an awakening Caranus in her arms and thrust the baby face-first into the red-hot coals. A muffled, high-pitched scream filled the room. It merged with a sizzling, hissing sound of human flesh being incinerated. The sound and smell filled the room. Olympias held the baby hard against the glowing coals until his spasmodic movements stopped. Then she released her claw grip and surrendered the dead infant's body to the fire.

Her bedchamber filled with the nauseating stench of burned, human flesh. It had already started to burn her eyes.

Most everyone who was in the palace that morning heard the screams. It wouldn't be long until they also smelled burning human flesh. Its odor was unmistakable.

Caranus' death screech awakened his older sister, Europa. She was crying uncontrollably on the sofa in an adjacent room. Olympias went to her and gently picked her up. She held the frightened child to her breast and soon stopped her crying. "It's all right, dear," she said. Then she walked back to the brazier with the girl in her arms and repeated the second, hideous infanticide of the morning with Europa.

Seconds later, both of Philip's and Cleopatra-Eurydice's children lay burning on the brazier. The smoke and smell in the room made the air no longer breathable, not even to a woman who had long dreamed of eliminating her replacement's children. Olympias walked slowly to her bedchamber door and ordered it opened. Her guard retched as soon as the acrid human smoke invaded his nostrils. The room was no longer tolerable to living humans. Altious burst out of the room, followed by Alexander's mother.

"Leave it open until the smoke clears," Olympias screeched viciously at the aghast bodyguard, a veteran of Macedon's many wars. "I'll be in the courtyard. Get Cleopatra-Eurydice and take her to the brazier. Show her what remains of her children. Then bring her to me."

The guard gagged on the acrid smoke, frowned, and then obeyed Olympias' command.

≈

When Cleopatra-Eurydice saw her blackened children, smoldering on the large brazier, she let out a heart-stopping scream that was heard throughout the palace grounds. Then she fainted. Her lifeless body was brought to Olympias, sitting serenely in the courtyard beneath her bedchamber window. She had heard everything that had happened in the room above.

"Put her on the bench," she commanded the guard. "Then leave us. Get those burned bodies out of my bedchamber. Take them into the country and finish the cremation. Break their bones in small pieces. Then, scatter them along the road to Paiko. No one must ever be able to identify either of them. If you fail at this you will answer to Alexander."

The guard looked with quiet contempt at Olympias and returned to the bedchamber. Then he poured a large container of water on the brazier and extinguished the fire. Using two metal thongs, he picked up the children's blackened and soaked remains and put the charred bodies in his cloak. He left quickly, after tying his cloak into a bundle so he would not have to look at the product of Olympias' vengeance.

Alone with the unconscious body of Philip's last wife, Olympias studied the limp body of her mortal enemy. She was young and beautiful, just as Olympias had been when Philip had married her. *Philip always liked large-breasted women*, she thought as she watched her rival's chest move up and down.

At last, the mother of Caranus and Europa stirred. She opened her eyes, and then remembered the terrorizing reason why she had fainted and began screaming again. Olympias helped her sit up and waited for the young woman to regain control. Then, towering over her, she gave an ultimatum.

"I act with Alexander's authority, Cleopatra-Eurydice. He ordered the death of your children and you. You will soon join them. Unlike them, you have a choice of how you can die. One of my priests will kill you, you can take poison, or you can hang yourself in your room. If you're unable to decide, I will. Give me your answer now!"

The young woman couldn't speak and merely resumed her screaming and crying. Finally, her composure returned and she stood regally to face the woman who was ending her world. "I'll do it myself; stay away from me, you bitch!"

Philip's last wife continued cursing and crying. Then she shoved Olympias out of her intended path and turned to leave. The distraught young woman stumbled, regained her footing, and then slowly began making her way toward her bedroom on quivering legs that barely supported her.

Olympias motioned for a priest to follow her. Macedon's Queen Mother walked away, studying an approaching rainstorm that was moving swiftly across muddy Lake Loudias. Her nostrils were still burning from the mordant smell of the two roasted children. She wanted to inhale the fresh wind of a Macedonian downpour. It would help wash away the small amount of guilt she felt and the pungent, oily smell of human flesh that seemed to cover her alabaster skin.

Olympias remained at the garden vista overlooking the lake until the edge of the storm began dampening her chiton. She then made her way back to the palace before the storm's fury broke, where Altious met her. Three other priests carrying the dead body of Cleopatra-Eurydice followed the priest. The storm's continuous thunderclaps were deafening and made normal conversation difficult.

"How did she do it?" Olympias yelled.

"She used one of Philip's purple sashes to hang herself," the priest answered. "We didn't know she had anything of his left. It must have been hidden in her clothing."

"Is her neck broken? She hasn't just passed out has she?" Olympias asked.

"We checked her, she's not breathing. She's dead," the priest said.

27

"Cremate her before Alexander returns. Keep her bones after cleaning so Alexander can see that no one can ever challenge him."

"It will be done," the priest answered obediently.

Olympias, now serene and fully recovered, walked toward her bedchamber. The closer she got to her bedroom the more acrid the lingering smell of the children's burning bodies became. When she entered the room, the air was still stifling.

Slaves were ordered in and the Queen Mother commanded them to begin scrubbing the ceiling, walls, and floor. Incense and expensive oils were burned that day and into the night, only slightly helping the room to return to its normal, cold-stone smell.

The room's cleansing continued for two days until finally, Olympias' bedroom suite was again inhabitable.

In the next week, Olympias offered prayers to her gods that Alexander wouldn't smell the hideous smell upon entering the palace. She wanted him in a good mood when she told him the great favors that she had done for him.

≈

"What's that obnoxious smell in here?" Alexander yelled as he entered the throne room. "Have the lake frogs invaded my domain along with the Illyrians?"

His palace attendants remained silent, looking at the pebble-mosaic floor. Before he could berate them for their silence, Olympias joined the king and his entourage. She beamed with joy at her son's return and walked up to him. Almost half a head taller than her victorious son, Olympias hugged him warmly, placing a delicate kiss on his forehead.

"We need privacy," she whispered. Her expression changed.

"Leave us," Alexander commanded his companions. "Hephaestion, I'll see you when I finish with mother. Go to Antipater and get the latest dispatches from our garrison in Thebes. They'll need our help soon."

Hephaestion followed the other companions out of the throne room, and the king and Olympias walked to a large sofa along the wall. Mother and son were united and alone. "Did you follow my instructions, mother? Is Caranus dead?"

"The boy, his sister, and their mother stopped living a week ago, Alexander." She waited for her son's reaction. It was immediate.

"I told you to eliminate only Caranus!" Alexander yelled as he leaped from his sofa. "Why did you kill the others? Have you forgotten how to read? Couldn't you figure out the code?" His face was red, his fists clenched.

"Cleopatra-Eurydice would never have rested until she toppled you, son. Don't you understand that? She had to die. My priests discovered a plot that she was hatching against both of us. Europa died because she was part of the problem. Little girls grow up to be troublesome women."

Alexander heard his mother's words but refused to be calmed. Still furious, he reasoned that she just might be right. He would soon cause the death of Amyntas, Philip's brother's last son. It probably would happen that very afternoon. His motivation would be identical to his mother's. What was the difference between what she had done and what he was about to do, he finally asked himself.

Alexander forced himself to calm down. He took a deep breath, and then stared hard at his waiting mother. "There are two issues here, mother," the king said at last. "The first is killing three people who probably would have been killed or banished anyway. That I can tolerate, though I am not pleased with you. However, the second is the affront of you disobeying my orders. Even though I'm your son, you are my subject. Kings kill subjects for disobeying direct orders! Do you understand that?" The king of Macedon was yelling again.

Olympias allowed silence to absorb her son's fury. Then she took his hands and projected an innocent, almost coquettish look of contrition. She knew it still worked on men, even on her son.

29

"Of course, you're right, Alexander. I'll never take such drastic action again without consulting you. I understand how it could cause you harm or embarrassment." She spoke softly, with her eyes averted.

Olympias' repentant response was exactly what Alexander wanted and needed. The mother knew the son. He left her standing in the middle of the throne room and walked to the balcony overlooking Lake Loudias. Two days of rain had made the muddy lake even more turbid. It was silting fast, and he wondered how much longer ocean-going triremes would be able to navigate its diminishing depths.

He allowed the late summer breeze to fill his lungs, and then returned to Olympias. "You speak one way but think another, mother. You always will. If you ever again take such foolish action without my knowledge and approval, I'll send you to a religious shrine in the hinterland. You'll never be allowed in Pella again. Is that understood?"

"It's perfectly clear," his mother said.

"I assume you had all three of them cremated. Where are their bones?"

"The children's remains have already been scattered in the countryside. Their mother's bones will be cleansed by evening. I intend to scatter hers as well."

"You're out of this ghastly mess from now on, mother. Have Cleopatra-Eurydice's washed bones brought to me before nightfall. I'll finish the episode. Leave me now! I want to be alone."

Olympias started to leave, and then looked back at her son sitting sideways on the throne of Macedon. "I'm going to the Temple of Heracles, your ancestor," she said with a serious look on her face. "Offerings will be made to protect you in the months ahead. You will wear his holy mantle as your majesty grows."

"Pray that you're forgiven for what you did, mother. My army and cavalry will take care of my majesty. Now leave!"

≈

The king sat alone in Macedon's ancient throne room for most of the morning. Scores of conflicting emotions swept over him and his spirit was troubled. Soon he would give the command to eliminate Amyntas. *How am I different from mother?* he asked himself a second time. *Only in degree,* he answered silently. He would soon leave Pella and had to be sure that his homeland problems were eliminated. There was no other choice. As he would do during the remainder of his life, he was acting out a role that had been preordained by Zeus-Ammon, by Olympias, even by Philip.

Suddenly, he jumped from the throne and called for his guard. The guard was to give Hephaestion a deadly message: "Lead an armed party to get Amyntas. Kill him immediately and then cremate his body outside the city. Ensure that no evidence of his remains will ever be found."

The king then went to the baths, where he remained while the time-honored Macedonian way of dealing with rivals was carried out. He knew Hephaestion would join him there and inform him that he no longer had any rivals inside Macedon. It had to be.

≈

Alexander's prediction didn't take long. Thebes was the first polis to rebel against the new Macedonian-dominated confederation. When two Macedonian garrison captains were caught outside the safety of the Cadmea citadel, Thebans, using arms supplied by Athens, set upon them. Both officers were killed and the city rose up against the Macedonian garrison. In days, the Cadmea was partially surrounded and a siege started. The humiliated Thebans planned to starve out the occupiers of their sacred citadel.

Other Greek city-states quickly joined the insurrection against Macedonian domination. The Arcadians in the Peloponnese raised an army with the gold that Darius provided Demosthenes and began to march toward the isthmus connecting the two parts of Greece. Riots and rebellions broke out in Aetolia and in far off Elis. Hopes of independence spread wildly throughout Greece, and patriots were heard in every agora, haranguing against the Macedonian barbarians.

Demosthenes was pleased but knew he was treading on loose earth. He knew Alexander wasn't dead. Three agents he had planted in Philip's inner circle years ago had all sent secret word to him. They related that they were with Alexander in Illyria, nearly a month after he was supposed to have been killed in Thrace. One of the agents had nearly been discovered by Hephaestion and had just fled to Athens. The traitor had been richly rewarded by Demosthenes for his efforts, and now walked with the orator in the courtyard of his comfortable home.

"What will Alexander do now?" Demosthenes asked the former Macedonian officer.

"I'm sure he'll race to Thebes. He'll not be gentle with them."

"How long do I have to rally the poleis before his army destroys them? Is his rear secure enough that he can risk a major assault into central Greece now?"

"He has done more in less time than any of us thought possible. Even Philip didn't press his army to march such distances in mere days. Don't underestimate him. I did, and it nearly cost me my life."

Demosthenes lifted his head and gazed toward a grove of trees surrounding his home. A sweet smell from their blossoms filled the air. "Is there any chance of our assassination plot succeeding, now that you have fled?"

"The network we established has surely been discovered by now. Hephaestion was closing in on me when I fled. I'm sure your two other spies have been detected and executed. Hephaestion isn't very bright, but he is completely devoted to Alexander. He won't let anyone near Alexander that he doesn't trust fully. My discovery alerted them to the plot. You'll never get to him now. Alexander will have to be killed on the battlefield. His inner and outer security circles are impenetrable."

Demosthenes was furious that his agents, men he had long cultivated and rewarded, had been neutralized. They had been originally set in place through the cooperation of Olympias, when she had planned Philip's death. Evidence from another source had just come to his attention that it was she who had alerted Hephaestion to the presence of Demosthenes' three operatives. Olympias was as much his enemy now as was Alexander. Briefly, he considered mounting an effort to kill her, but realized that she would receive as much protection now as her son. The many assurances that he had given Darius' agents in Athens that Alexander would be eliminated before the end of the year would not be received gently in Persia if Alexander remained alive. Events were getting out of hand. He knew Athens couldn't confront Alexander alone. He would be lucky if he could rally enough city-states to mount another decisive battle against the Macedonians. Soon the source of so many of his operations against the new Macedonian king could be in jeopardy.

"How can we establish new spy networks?" he asked the waiting defector. "What is Alexander's weakness?"

"Philip bankrupted the country during his reign, Demosthenes. That's Alexander's greatest problem. He's in arrears paying his soldiers. Only the spoils of sacked cities and the grubby property of primitive barbarians north of Macedonia have rewarded them. They'll not follow him long unless he finds new money. The expeditionary force in the Troad continues to drain gold from the mines of Mount Pangaeus. An engineer who spent a year in dirty Crenides told me that the mines there are almost exhausted. If you can cut off Alexander's ability to generate new sources of revenue, you'll stop him."

Demosthenes brightened. He knew little about financial matters or how gold was mined. Most of his income over the years had come from his modest arms factory and large bribes from two Persian Great Kings. However, the traitor's suggestion to wage economic warfare against Alexander was an interesting one. Athens was still a formidable economic power in the Aegean. If Alexander's military zeal could be dissipated through protracted skirmishes with several Greek poleis, perhaps he would fall from his own over-aggressiveness.

A plan started to evolve in the orator's cunning mind. He would urge Darius' agents to plead with the Great King to let Parmenio retain his precarious foothold in the Troad. The strategy would be to enervate the Macedonian economy by drawing off resources that they simply could not replace. Demosthenes would work in the boule to do the same thing with Alexander's army in Greece. If the dual economic sapping could be maintained for half a year, Alexander's power would erode. Then a resurgent Athens could lead a unified Greek army against the boy-king and drive him back to his primitive homeland.

Demosthenes dismissed his agent and left his home to visit Eubulus, Athens' brilliant Minister of Finance. He wanted to learn more about economics. His plan called for Eubulus to help him achieve what no army had yet been able to do: crush the murdering hoards of Macedonians that held Greece in their deadly grip.

CHAPTER 4

DARIUS

Persia's new Great King, Codomannus, was a huge man, a full one third of a human body taller than Alexander of Macedon. Codomannus had ascended to the peacock throne after Grand Vizier Bagoas poisoned his predecessor, Great King Artaxerxes Ochus. Bagoas had then selected Ochus' young, inept son, Arses, to rule the empire. Soon, Bagoas had poisoned Arses too and selected a little known member of the Achaemenid royal family, Codomannus, to become Great King.

Codomannus took the name Darius III. He was 45 when he ascended to the throne, only a few months before Philip was assassinated. Bagoas was certain that he could control the former satrap of mountainous Armenia. He was wrong. Darius' first act was eliminating Bagoas by poison, ridding the Persian empire of his invidious influence.

Darius was impressive, not only in personal stature and handsome features, but in his achievements. He was brave in battle and had a quick mind, despite being the offspring of parents who were brother and sister.

Even before his accession, Codomannus was aware of events in Greece and Macedonia. When he was just an able satrap, the petty squabbles of the Greeks had not been at the top of his list of priorities. Then he became Persia's Great King. When Philip was eliminated, he was sure that Persia needed only to stand by and let the Greeks destroy each other. Recent events were proving him right. Until Alexander marched into Thessaly and bloodlessly brought central Greece back into the Macedonian sphere, Darius had refused all requests from Demosthenes to help Athens confront the new Macedonian monarch.

That had changed during the last month. Through his agents, he had started moving gold into Greece. As before, Athens was the conduit for the Great King's bribery. Demosthenes personally benefited from these bribes, as did most of the boule members who had opposed Philip and now opposed his son.

However, other matters concerned Darius just as much as the twenty-year-old king of Macedon. Egypt was being pacified and the last Egyptian pharaoh removed. Administrative minutiae never ended for the Great King, despite his legions of scribes, civil administrators, and accountants to make the task more manageable.

≈

In recent months, Darius had spent most of his time supervising the construction of his royal tomb at Parsa. Whenever he could, he left the administrative capital at Susa and traveled to Parsa, Persia's ancient ceremonial and religious center.

Darius the Great had built Parsa. The city occupied a series of three manmade terraces, each higher than the other. The entire bastion was set before an enormous rock outcropping called Naghsh-e-Rostam. Its high wall was unbroken except for a double set of grand stairs that instilled in any visitor a sense of awe and Great King approbation.

Parsa's palace was made up of a series of quadrangles, containing interior halls, spacious rooms, and a central audience chamber, the Apadana. Colossal columns, twice the height of Athens' Parthenon columns, supported great wooden beams. Immense images of griffins and bulls heads decorated the columns' capitals. Deep-cut reliefs covered every doorway. Most prominent of these were several depictions of the first Darius and his son, Xerxes.

A short horseback ride from Parsa, behind and beside Naghsh-e-Rostam, was an imposing, flat rock-face that Darius the Great had chosen for his tomb site. Deep-cut squares, four in number, had been formed by the stonecutter's tools to create a monumental final resting place for the greatest of the Achaemenid rulers. Each Great King had followed Darius' example and the rock face was filled with reliefs and inscriptions of Persia's legendary monarchs. Each inscription told the story of the king's reign and achievements. The latest Darius had just returned from the site and received his architects and builders in the Apadana.

"Will mine be as impressive as Darius', when one encounters the mountain?" Darius III asked his chief architect. A group of the architect's assistants and construction foremen stood well behind their chief.

"At least as impressive, Great King," the architect responded. "Your fame will be as great as your line's originator. Your new tomb will magnify your magnificence."

"How long will it take?" Darius asked. The answer was of great importance to him. He wanted to live long enough to be able to plan the tomb's interior details, just as he was now directing its external appearance.

"That depends on how many stonecutters you provide, Great King," said the architect. "My best estimate is between two and three years. The interior should take about a year to complete, depending on the finished features you desire."

"I want the exterior done in two years or less," Darius shot back. "Get more stonecutters to meet this accelerated schedule. Use as many men as necessary. Don't fail me! If you fail to complete my tomb on time, I will bury you and your workers in the stone rubble that falls from Naghsh-e-Rostam. Leave me now! You understand your task!"

≈

The next day, Darius summoned his Grand Vizier to the Apadana. The Grand Vizier performed the required proskynesis, rose from the floor, and then waited for his monarch's recognition. As he waited, he studied the Great King's features. Darius, sitting beneath the jewel-laden golden plane tree, was near godlike in the impression that he made. He was handsome by any culture's standards, enormously tall and had sharp facial features. His face was covered with a thick, black beard. The royal barber had curled it into scores of tiny ringlets.

Even standing at two arm lengths, the beard's smell overwhelmed the Vizier's nostrils. He knew that its fragrance came from an exotic combination of rich unguents and expensive Persian perfumes. The powerful aroma wafting through the throne room signified the Great King's exalted status and masked his foul breath. The Vizier saw that Darius seemed lost in afterlife reveries, as he watched him continue to gaze across the vastness of his throne room.

Still unacknowledged, the Vizier studied Darius' clothing. It could only be described as exalted. The Great King wore a Median garment that

37

was predominantly royal purple. His chest was covered with a shirt that had long sleeves down to his wrists. Layering this was a mantle. It was beautifully sewn with intricate and abstract images of Persian peacocks. Darius' legs were covered to the ankle with multicolored, silken trousers. Precious jewels, gold, and silver were draped from nearly every part of his body. His enormous feet were booted and rested on a stool of pure gold. It had been created from gold nuggets provided as tribute to the Great King from India's Indus River. No one else in the palace was allowed to dress so grandly. At last, Darius returned to earth and recognized his Grand Vizier.

"What is my schedule for today?" Darius asked.

"Memnon of Rhodes is here, Great King," the Vizier answered. "We didn't expect him for two or three days, but he made a forced ride. He arrived late this morning. Do you wish to receive him now, or should I tell him to come back in the morning?"

Darius at first considered having his Greek mercenary general return the next day, but thought better of it. He had read all the recent dispatches from Memnon and knew that he had been moderately successful in reversing the initial gains of the Macedonian expeditionary force. However, Memnon's early arrival must have special meaning. "I'll see him now," Darius said. "Stay here with us; I want you informed of the Greek's actions."

The Vizier summoned for the guard and soon Memnon came into the throne room. He gave the required proskynesis to the Great King, lying prostrate on the blue, malachite floor. When Darius acknowledged the act of subservience, the Greek rose and addressed his royal patron.

"Honor and the blessings of the god Ahura Mazda to you, Great King," he began by speaking through a court translator. "I am here to inform you of events in Macedon and relate what our sources tell us about Alexander's intentions."

"Has he returned to Pella yet, Memnon?"

"By now, yes, Great King. He appears to have been successful against the barbarians surrounding Macedon. We expect that his next move will be in central or southern Greece. Although Thessaly was pacified bloodlessly, your Athenian bribes are on the verge of causing the Greeks to rebel against the Macedonian garrisons. Alexander may be marching south as we speak."

"Will the Athenians support the rebellions with anything more than words?" Darius asked sarcastically. "Or do they simply take my gold, without any armed resistance to the boy? I've already given them 300 gold talents. Are we influencing Athenian policy or just enriching Demosthenes?"

"We don't know, Great King," Memnon responded. "Demosthenes has taken Persian gold for years, without clear results. He plays his game of Greek politics. Athens is fomenting trouble in Thebes. She would like nothing more than to have her rivals destroy each other. She could then assume Greek leadership and resume her drive toward confederation."

"I want regular reports on Alexander's actions, Memnon," Darius commanded. "When you return to Phrygia, direct our Greek agents to keep both of us informed about the Macedonians.

"What about General Parmenio? Has he driven any deeper into my territory?"

"The contest is nearly stalemated, Great King. Before you commissioned me to confront him, he had expanded the Macedonian bridgehead ever farther south. Most of the Greek colonies in Ionia had come over to him. When I retook Lampsacus, it forced Parmenio to retreat to a secure base at Abydos. The Macedonians hold it now. If Alexander secures his Greek-mainland rear, that's where his army will cross the narrows. We must stop them not far from that spot or they'll gain a foothold."

Darius became thoughtful, and then spoke. "Return and rally the satraps of Phrygia, Lydia, and Ionia. They're brave subjects, but they need knowledge of the Macedonians' tactics. You spent ten years in Philip's court with Artabazus. Teach them how to counter Parmenio's moves.

"I'll focus my attention on Egypt while you stop the Macedonians. When Egypt is pacified, I'll take the field with you. If Alexander joins his expeditionary force, I want the Macedonians eliminated within sight of the narrows. That will end the boy's career."

"It's a good plan, Great King," Memnon answered. "It will be done. I beg to request that you consider a contingency plan, however. It may be necessary if we fail to stop their Bosporus crossing."

The Vizier looked at his Great King and knew that he didn't like what he was hearing. Both men had discussed many times what the king's subjects were really saying when they asked for a fall-back plan. It usually meant that they thought that their primary plan was going to fail. When a brilliant tactician like Memnon expressed such a concern, the Vizier knew that the Great King had better listen.

"What's your point, Memnon?" Darius asked.

"I don't want to cast doubt on your forces in Phrygia, Great King," Memnon explained. "However, if the Macedonians are not halted, drastic measures will be necessary. Philip trained his army to be self-sufficient for only thirty days. After that, they must either have a victory, forage the land they hold, or retreat. There are no other choices for such a large force."

Memnon let the gravity of his request sink in, and then he continued. "I have irrefutable evidence that Philip left Macedon deep in debt, nearly bankrupt. Their treasury has borrowed all that it can borrow. They will need a quick victory, or be forced to retreat."

"What are you suggesting?"

"If our forces can't destroy them quickly, then we should have well-reasoned plans to retreat, leaving their army only a devastated landscape. They might pursue us, but their food and supplies will run out quickly if we ravage Phrygia as we withdraw. Scorched earth gives no assistance to an invader."

"You're asking me to burn our own land?"

"Only if the invaders are not stopped initially, Great King," Memnon answered defensively. "The plan is only a contingency, a last resort."

"The satraps there will oppose anything like this, Memnon," Darius shot back. "The region is rich in farmland. It's covered with forests and game. I've hunted there myself. They won't allow it!"

"I'm asking only that you give it consideration, Great King," Memnon pressed on. "It's a remote possibility, but one that a prudent monarch must entertain. If the Macedonian phalanx and cavalry are allowed onto the broad plains of your empire, all will be lost. The stakes are enormous."

The Vizier saw Darius grimace, wipe his face with his large hand, and stare into space as he absorbed what Memnon had told him.

At last Darius spoke. "I'll consider your suggestion, Memnon. However, I don't intend to face the catastrophic situation you describe. Discuss it with the satraps when you return. I already know their reaction. Your proposal might cause them to prepare more carefully for the quick defeat of the Macedonians.

"Leave me now. I'll discuss these matters with my Susa generals, when I go there in ten days. My Grand Vizier has gold for you before you leave for your post. It's yours. Give some of it as a present to your new wife, Barsine."

Memnon gave the exit proskynesis and backed out of the Apadana, leaving Darius alone with his Vizier. After a few, less consequential administrative matters were resolved, he dismissed the Vizier and left the throne room. All of this talk about the Macedonians had ruined his day.

≈

After a light meal, Darius walked to his harem. Still troubled, he decided that sex was a way to clear his mind for the challenges that lay ahead. He selected two pretty, young girls to satisfy him for the evening and walked to his private bedroom.

However, his thoughts were far from what was required to have good sex. He wondered where Alexander was now. He wondered if his plan to have him assassinated had any chance of success. These questions were so distracting that they prevented him having an erection, despite the best efforts of his harem girls. He sent them back, crestfallen, to their communal quarters and then went to his private bath. Boiling, hot water always helped him think more clearly than sex anyway.

Steaming in his enormous royal tub, Darius' mind-clearing tactics began to work and Persia's strategic situation slowly became clearer.

Perhaps Memnon's scorched earth strategy would be necessary, he concluded at last. If Alexander couldn't be defeated outright, Persian forces could starve him into retreat. Then he would personally lead several hundred thousand soldiers into Macedon and Greece and devastate the invader's territory. He only needed a few more months to settle Egypt, and then he would recall his formidable Phoenician navy and obliterate the diminutive king from Pella.

CHAPTER 5

ANDRAPODISMOS

"How many of our officers were killed?" Alexander asked Antipater.

The king, Hephaestion, and his regent, Antipater, were standing in a tight circle outside the palace peristyle courtyard in Pella. Alexander had learned long ago that the palace walls had eyes and ears. He would allow none of Demosthenes' spies to learn what he intended to do next.

Beneath the trio's feet was an enormous, sixteen-pointed Macedonian starburst, the national symbol that impressed anyone entering the royal palace. Several hundred thousand multicolored pebbles had been used to create the work. The project had taken a hundred artists and artisans over a year to complete.

"At least three, maybe as many as five. The garrison commander is one of them," Antipater answered.

"Patronius," the king said with a lowered head. "He was one of the best. He taught me how to hold a shield. His death will not go unavenged."

Alexander walked away from the group as he laced his fingers through his wavy, auburn hair. His hands slipped to the back of his neck. His elbows met as the decision process continued. At last, he returned to his friends and issued a command. "Hephaestion, tell Philotas to prepare the army. We'll leave in two days. It will be a forced march into Boeotia; our army will hit them before the Greeks can rally around the Thebans. I'll punish them so that Greece will never forget; a severe example will be made of our former ally."

"The siege engines will be necessary, Alexander," Hephaestion said. "Thebes' walls are thick."

"We'll take most of the army and its equipment, Hephaestion," Alexander answered. "A small force will be left here to protect our rear. The Thracians and the Illyrians won't be able to mount anything against us after the thrashing we gave them. I don't intend to stay long in central Greece."

Hephaestion left, leaving Alexander and Antipater standing in the starburst center. Alexander looked at Antipater and could tell that he was glad that they were alone. "Have you talked with Olympias, Alexander?" Antipater asked. "It's becoming nearly impossible for me to perform my duties because of her meddling."

"We've reached an understanding," Alexander answered. "If she oversteps her authority, she knows that I'll banish her from the palace. We'll discuss her behavior when I return."

Alexander then changed the subject. "What's happening with Philip's burial site? Are the three tombs done?"

"The tombs are complete and earth is being brought in to build a tumulus," Antipater reported. "Only the top of Philip's burial chamber remains uncovered. When you order it your father's bones will be put in the main tomb, then it will be sealed. It will take months to bring in enough dirt to create the tumulus you want. What do you want buried with him?"

Alexander fell silent again and walked away from Antipater into the peristyle courtyard. He wanted to give Philip a respectable burial tumulus, if for no other reason than to elevate his own status. Earlier, he even had thoughts of building a pyramid. However, that would have to await Persia's conquering. Raising the only pyramid in Greece would also support his court propaganda that he had nothing to do with his father's assassination. He returned to his waiting regent.

"I want Cleopatra-Eurydice's remains included, Antipater. Make sure her bones are washed, cleaned, and consecrated. Then have them placed in a solid gold larnax. Wrap them in that royal purple robe that she always wore, the one with gold flowers and leaves. Put the gold crown she wore when she married Philip inside the larnax. Then put her chest into a marble sarcophagus. But she's to be put in the antechamber, apart from my father. I won't have them buried together.

"Philip's remains are to occupy the main chamber. I've thought for some time about what he would like with him in his afterlife. Do you remember that gilded bow-and-arrow case that he got as a gift from the Scythians? He never used it, but he bragged about it all the time."

Antipater nodded, but said nothing.

"Put the case in his chamber. I want his greaves there too. Wrap his bones in his royal cloak and then put his oak-leaf and acorn crown on top of the bundle. His bones must also be put inside a gold larnax. It must have the Macedonian starburst on its top. Then place the chest in a sarcophagus and seal both tombs. The slaves can then start hauling in the earth."

"Do you want to dedicate the burial site before it's sealed?" Antipater asked.

"No," Alexander replied without thinking. "There isn't time for that. I wouldn't do it even if I had time. When the tumulus is finished, I may dedicate the temple on its summit. We must be done with Philip and go on. These actions will honor him enough."

With that unpleasant task finished, the king dismissed Antipater and went to his bedchamber. Slaves dressed him in his commander-in-chief uniform and then left the palace.

Riding Bucephalas through the streets of Pella with his bodyguards, he wondered what type burial someone would give him if he should ever fall in battle. He quickly put it out of his mind, for he knew that the matter had already been taken care of by his mother. He was confident that his tomb would be far grander than Philip's would. It might even surpass the great pyramids of Egypt.

Young King Alexander of Macedon was about to embark on a career of conquest that would make him worthy of such a monument.

≈

Alexander forced his massive army of retribution to march almost twenty-one hundred stadia in just two weeks. Remarkably, they made as much progress in difficult mountain terrain as they did on the broad plains of Thessaly. Not even Philip had been able to get such a physical response from his men.

The Macedonians slipped through the gates of Thermopylae before any word of their arrival in central Greece had preceded them. The huge force then halted at Oncestus, a mere 166 stadia from Thebes itself. Joining Alexander's army were various contingents from other Boeotian cities, cities that had long-held ancient animosities against the tyrannical rule of Thebes. The pause at Oncestus was to give the Thebans a chance to reconsider their action and end the encirclement of the Macedonian garrison on the Cadmea.

Once they recovered from the shock of hearing that Alexander was at their doorstep, the Thebans became even more intransigent. Raiding parties were sent out from Thebes and they began to harass the advance scouts of Alexander's forces.

Alexander sent scouts who demanded that the leaders of the rebellion surrender. The Thebans replied that King Alexander should turn over Philotas and Antipater to them.

Alexander, escalating the battle of words before surrounding the city, sent word that any citizen joining him and his allies would be spared. Thebes' leaders countered with a proclamation that any Greek wanting to join them and the Persian Great King in destroying Alexander should come to their city.

The battle of words and proclamations quickly became tedious to Macedon's impetuous young king. Alexander ended the verbose posturing and moved his forces outside Thebes, surrounding it. The time for words was over.

The short battle that followed was a one-sided one, although the Thebans fought bravely for their polis. Led initially by Perdiccas, a section of their outer wall was breached and the Macedonians entered the city. Alexander led the hypaspists as other commanders led his phalanx units over the walls.

Soon, Thebes' main gates were breached and the city where his father had been held hostage was burning. Six thousand Thebans were killed outright in wave after wave of Macedonian and allied attacks. Thirty thousand prisoners were captured and arrangements were made to have them held in a brutal camp outside the city gates.

The only question about the fate of Thebes was whether it was to suffer what the Greeks called andrapodismos, the complete elimination of a polis through razing and selling its inhabitants into lifelong slavery.

≈

Within days, Alexander, acting in his role as hegemon of the League of Corinth, called a hasty meeting of League members. As Philip had first done after Chaeronea and after he had done after he subdued the uprising in Thessaly only months ago, he convened a convocation in Corinth. Athens did not attend the meeting, nor did any of Thebes' marginal supporters.

The king gave the states that had joined him against Thebes the choice of deciding the defeated city's fate. The allies' decision was predictable and to Alexander's liking: Thebes was to suffer andrapodismos. Only the ancestral homes and lands of the great poet, Pindar, and a few other Macedonian supporters were spared. Within ten days, proud Thebes was nothing more than a pile of rubble.

≈

Athens was in panic. As the polis had done during Philip's reign, she had chosen inaction and debate while a threatening conqueror marched about Greece doing what he wanted. Messages arrived informing the city leaders that Alexander demanded the surrender of ten of its leading citizens who had first opposed Philip and had been opposing his successor for the last months. Demosthenes was at the head of the surrender list.

However, the boule and the ecclesia refused to meet Alexander's demands and a dangerous stalemate followed. Finally, Alexander received an Athenian delegation and a compromise was proposed. Both sides agreed that Athens would exile a large group of mercenary officers and their men. In return, Alexander would relent in his demands for Athens' political leaders to be turned over to him. Nor would he attack Athens, if she remained at peace and supported the impending Persian invasion. It was a compromise that met both sides' needs.

Alexander then led his army north, assured that, for now, Greece and Macedon's outlying barbarian territories were pacified. He would spend the remainder of the fall and winter preparing his troops for the reason why he had been born. Persia awaited the son of Zeus-Ammon.

CHAPTER 6

DEPARTURE

"Stop talking, Parmenio!" Alexander shouted. "I wouldn't have brought you back from Abydos if I thought all you were going to do was interfere in my personal life. I value your strategic and tactical advice; I honor your long service to Philip. But speak no more of me fathering a child before the invasion. I've made up my mind. Sex with a woman right now is repugnant to me. We leave for Amphipolis in two days. Go enjoy the last day of the Pan Hellenic games. Then join our army outside the city. You will ride behind me when we parade out of Pella. That is how it is going to be.

"Zeus-Ammon protects me," Alexander continued, calming himself. "I have never doubted that and neither should you. Perform your military duties and we will prevail. Serve me, as you did Philip, and we will get along. But stop your campaign to influence those around me. I know who you have been talking to; understand that each one has been told the same thing I am telling you now.

"Greece is watching me and I will not languish in my palace waiting for the birth of a successor while Persia is ripe. Tell the guard to send for Hephaestion when you leave." The king of Macedon turned his back on Parmenio and walked away.

Philip's oldest and most trusted general left the throne room. He was furious with the young king's emotional outburst and his red face showed it. For days, he had been unrelenting in his appeals to Alexander, pleading with him to delay the Persian invasion. He had argued that it must be rescheduled, at least for a month, while the king impregnated as many aristocratic young Macedonian women as his weak, opposite-sex libido could manage. Parmenio had even met privately with others close to the king. Each of them had been urged to reason with Alexander about the vital need to produce a male successor before departing Macedonia.

Parmenio had even resorted to pleading with Alexander's inner-circle of young friends. He knew they could exert more influence on him than he ever could. Chief among these able youths was Craterus. Parmenio chose him, not only because he knew that he agreed with him, but also because he knew that Craterus and Hephaestion hated each other. It was common knowledge that Alexander's close, personal relationship with Hephaestion was the primary reason the king could not be convinced to sire one or more children before he left Macedonia. However, even Craterus' plea with Alexander had been rejected. The king had told him never to mention the matter again.

Walking north out of the palace, toward the Peristyle Courtyard, Parmenio told Alexander's personal bodyguard that the king wished to see Hephaestion. Then he headed toward the city's stadium and the wrestling competition. His fists were clenched and a scowl etched his forehead as he walked through Pella.

A mere lad, a boy a third his age, had just upbraided him. The obnoxious youth was fortunate that he had decided to throw in his lot with him. He was even more fortunate that he had not brought charges of regicide against him. He would bide his time and wait his moment. Now in his mid-sixties, Parmenio had learned long ago that impetuosity rarely succeeds in kings. Philip's greatest strength had been his ability to seek council from those around him and, most often, follow their advice. Alexander would defeat himself, Parmenio thought. Time is my friend in this contest, he concluded. Longevity was a strong characteristic of his family's history.

Arriving at the stadium, he finally realized that his character, like King Philip's, was like a wrestler's fighting stance. Keep low, retain your balance; fortify yourself for the long, difficult contest ahead. He recognized that his guile and experience supporting Alexander's father had prepared him for what lay ahead. Let the blazing meteor of Alexander's character burn itself out before it reached the earth, he resolved. He would be there to pick up the pieces.

≈

"Has Parmenio stopped his ranting yet?" Hephaestion asked as he was admitted to the king's throne room.

"I think he will now, my friend," Alexander responded as he rose to greet his closest confidant. "He knows that I've made up my mind. But Olympias will never relent, not even when we leave. Join me over here."

49

Alexander considered Hephaestion as the two walked to a nearby set of couches. His friend was not nearly as bright as he was and often said things that bordered on dullness. He frequently got angry, was often spiteful, and refused to talk to him for days. However, as with opposite-sex lovers, they always seemed to make up and reaffirm their personal devotion to each other.

In a flash of insight, Alexander realized something about his companion. He loved Hephaestion for two reasons. First, he was a beautiful, almost exquisite man. Tall among Macedonians, much taller than Alexander, his clear, fair skin surpassed that of most women. Secondly, Hephaestion was unquestioningly devoted to him. Alexander knew that he would gladly die to further his kingship and his quest for glory. For these reasons alone, the two were bonded for life.

Putting his private thoughts aside, Alexander addressed the reason that he had sent for Hephaestion. "The army leaves for Amphipolis in two days. Only you and Parmenio know the exact day. By tonight, everyone in Pella will know. Darius' agents will send word back to General Memnon. Then, the contest will begin."

As was his custom when Alexander was telling him something, Hephaestion said nothing. Nevertheless, he always listened attentively. Alexander valued the characteristic. The king continued. "My last days here will be spent trying to raise money. Philip left the kingdom deep in debt. I've been forced to sell practically all of the royal land holdings just to support our departure. At most, we have only thirty to forty days of food and supplies. Then, we must either have a significant victory or stop the invasion.

"That victory will come, but you must play your role, Hephaestion. I want you to create an unassailable, inner circle of protection around me while I manage the first difficult months of the campaign. The list of men in this inner circle should start with those who attended Aristotle's school at Mieza with us. Their names are on this scroll." Alexander handed Hephaestion a small scroll. It bore the king's lion's-head seal on it.

Hephaestion took the scroll and put it in a pocket of his cloak without opening it. "I'll begin today," is all he said.

Alexander smiled, and then continued. "This group will be called the Royal Bodyguards. They will allow me to concentrate all of my energies on the Hellespont crossing and defeating Memnon's forces there. You and my young comrades must guard my back."

"Our adventure begins, Alexander," Hephaestion said. "Put away any concerns about your safety. I seek no command now; your security is the greatest need. Later, I hope you will honor me with a unit of my own. High command would help me protect you even more."

"High command is before you, Hephaestion. Don't doubt that. But give me time to solve other problems. You know of my devotion to you."

"I do, Alexander," Hephaestion answered. "Don't trouble yourself with my personal needs. I can wait."

Alexander rose, signaling the meeting was over. The two men walked to a balcony overlooking Lake Loudias and breathed in the cool, spring air sweeping across the muddy lake surface. The lake had a familiar smell, one that reminded both men of their childhood and teenage years. They spoke briefly how they used to sail the fast-silting body of water and how much deeper it had been in years past. Now, the boys had become men and the world awaited their manhood.

The king dismissed Hephaestion after his reminisces started to become maudlin. At the door to his throne room, Alexander commanded his bodyguard to inform Olympias that her son wished to dine alone with her that night. Walking back to his worktable, he knew that his last challenge before leaving was telling Olympias her role in his kingdom. Then, he would be ready to meet his destiny.

≈

A simple wooded table covered with a brightly colored Macedonian tablecloth greeted Olympias as she walked into Alexander's throne room. Her son awaited her, sitting at the head of the table, directly beneath the ancient throne of Macedon. He was already finishing his third large cup of strong, uncut Macedonian wine.

"You're lovely tonight, mother," Alexander said with sincerity. "Come sit with me. We have much to discuss."

51

Olympias smiled and joined Alexander at the table. The throne room door slammed much too loudly and they were alone, except for two slaves waiting to serve dinner. "I know your departure is imminent, Alexander," she began. "When does the army leave?"

"The day after tomorrow," Alexander answered as he poured himself another kantharos of wine. He motioned for the slaves to begin serving the meal, and then continued. "I know that you have anticipated the reason that I sent for you. You knew that I would not leave without this private time together."

"I was not worried, Alexander. You will never forget your mother. You and Hephaestion are not the only two who are bonded."

Alexander smiled as the slaves began to serve the meal. More food than ten men could have eaten soon covered the table. The meal was mostly seafood. Eels, shark meat, shellfish, and an assortment of fresh fish were spread before mother and son. Alexander took one of each of the seafood selections. His mother contented herself with a small portion of shellfish. Alexander helped himself to several types of vegetables, freshly cut that morning from the Gardens of Midas. The room was filled with the gentle smells of the finest foods in Macedonia.

Alexander watched his mother. Olympias didn't take any of the green foods. She had often told her son that seafood gave her mental energy, while preserving her alabaster skin. When the serving was complete, Alexander dismissed the slaves. Only King Alexander and former Queen Olympias now sat in Macedon's throne room.

"I want you to correspond with me regularly while I am in Persia, mother." Alexander began. He spoke as he began to eat the sumptuous meal. "It need not be every day, for Antipater will do that. I want your insight, the benefit of your guile, and your political and religious views of what is happening in both Macedon and Greece. I trust no other person to do what you do so well."

"Thank you, son," Olympias replied. "I will do it gladly. Will we use the same secret writing system that you devised?"

Alexander finished eating half of a delicious eel, then answered. "Yes. However, instead of just using the *Iliad*, there will be four other books that will be the source of our coded communications. Each scroll will have a number. The *Iliad* will be the first. Scrolls 2 through 5 will be placed in your room tonight. Our letters will rotate through the set and then begin the cycle again with the next page of each scroll. Unless I stay in Persia for the rest of my life, there will be more than enough text for us to create unbreakable codes. You'll find simple written instructions under my seal in your room when you return. They will help you remember how to do it. Memorize the instructions, and then burn them. No one must ever discover our code."

"I remember how to use it, Alexander. There is no need for additional instructions. I'll burn your directions as soon as I return. I still may not read well, but I'm as bright as you are. My letters to you will be without error."

Alexander smiled at his mother's remark about her brightness. He knew that she was right. With that matter settled, he continued "Persia's conquest will not be easy, mother. I may be gone for years. You are to submit to Antipater's political will and not challenge him. He is regent and has my trust. He will even lead the home army against insurrections that will inevitably break out. Watch him and let him know that you are protecting my interests. But I want no direct confrontations between the two of you. Is that understood?"

"I understand," Olympias answered. She wore a wry smile that caused Alexander to doubt her sincerity.

Alexander had finished his meal, but Olympias had eaten practically nothing. He looked at her quizzically, as if to invite the words that he knew were inside her. The king was sure that his mother was about to make one last appeal for him to father a son before departing. He also knew that they would not speak privately again. If Olympias had anything to tell him, now was the time.

Olympias rose from her chair and walked to the seated Alexander at the other end of the table. She smiled her enigmatic smile as she pulled her son to a standing position. Then she began unfastening her girdle that held her beautiful, rose-colored chiton snugly around her adolescent-like waist. Slowly and deliberately, she removed the garment and let it drop to the floor. Olympias stood naked before her son.

"Remove your garment, Alexander," she said softly. "Trust me; it's necessary."

Alexander had learned never to be surprised at anything his mother did, but her actions now both amused and alarmed him. Fighting the thought, he couldn't help thinking that she was inviting sex. Was this the last desperate act of a mother who was determined that the king must leave an heir before going to war with King Darius? Their sexual union would produce a defective heir, one that would be both his son and his brother.

However, the wine had charged Alexander's libido and he was in a pixilated mood. He looked up and down at his mother. He had never seen her naked before. It was an unsettling experience. Her body's skin was even paler than her face and hands. The revealed skin appeared even more blanched when contrasted with her two penetrating blue eyes. Alexander was surprised to see that his mother wore a small, golden ring on her left breast nipple.

He suddenly lifted his eyes and regained his senses. *I'll play the game up to a point*, he decided. *I can stop it anytime*. He loosened his belt and disrobed. The king of Macedon and his mother now stood nude before each other, beside a table of barely eaten Macedonian food.

"Put your left leg on the seat of your chair," Olympias commanded. "You have an imprint there, beside your organ. I know you have noticed it; I used to watch you finger it when you were a child."

Alexander's left eyebrow rose, but he complied with the request without comment. He knew of the birthmark. Hephaestion had commented on it more than once.

Olympias then knelt before her son and moved his scrotal sack away from his high, left inner thigh. Her index finger found the birthmark and she looked up. "This is the mark of Zeus-Ammon, Alexander. I know that you have never seen it clearly because of where it is. Let me describe it. It's clearly the image of a lion's head. Even its mane is visible. Close your eyes and imagine the shape as I trace it."

Alexander kept his eyes open, sighed, but allowed his mother to trace the birthmark. He then took her by the shoulders and brought her to a standing position. "Did you have to disrobe to describe my birthmark, mother?"

Olympias smiled and then moved her son gently aside. She put her slender foot on the chair seat and slowly spread her legs apart. Then she took Alexander's hand and forced it to a spot high on her own left inner thigh. It was in exactly the same place where she had just traced Alexander's mark. "Kneel and look at my mark, son," she said. "I've seen it many times with brass mirrors. It's identical to yours."

Again, Alexander did as his mother asked. She was right. A clear image of a lion's head was there. Its abundant mane appeared even fuller beside Olympias' auburn pubic hairs. The king rose, picked up both of their robes, and smiled. While the two dressed, the king was shaking his head.

"Mother, what kind of a stunt is this? It's common for children to bear the same birthmark as one of their parents. What's your point?"

"My 'point' will dominate your life forever, son," she said. "It has been prophesied for centuries that Zeus-Ammon would father a son. That son is you."

"I know all of this, mother. You drummed it into my head from my earliest years." The king was growing impatient with his mother's mystical theatrics.

"What you don't know, Alexander, is that I deliberately mislead you while Philip lived. I let you believe that you had two fathers, one spiritual and one earthly. That was not true. Philip never entered my body to create you. A lightning bolt struck my womb the night you were conceived. I was bathing in a mountain pool, immediately after the Festival of Dionysus. No one, other than my slave, was present. Philip sired your sister, but none of him is in you. Zeus-Ammon is your solitary father—the marks prove it."

Alexander grimaced and started a frustrated walk around the throne room. His head was shaking left and right as he walked. At last, he returned to his mother and stood defiantly before her. "This is absurd. You have gone too far again. I know my heritage. You don't need to elevate me more than Zeus-Ammon has already. I'll more than meet His and your expectations."

"Don't dismiss what I've just shown and told you," Olympias shot back. "Investigate it for yourself. Consider this as well: my priests tell me that during the last two years all of the statues that I had erected to Zeus-Ammon have had identical marks appear on their inner thighs. The marks were not there when the works were created. I have signed statements of the sculptors who carved them. Issue commands for agents to travel Macedonia and Greece to verify what I say. You will find that your mother speaks his truth. You are Zeus-Ammon's only son. You cannot forget that as you seek your glory in Persia. He will not let his son fail; you cannot be defeated."

Alexander, no longer bemused, reasoned that his mother just might be right. Privately, he decided to send officers to investigate what she had just told him. If true, the events could only glorify him more. Subtly, her words even started to help him feel better about his inaction while Philip was being set up for assassination.

However, Olympias wasn't done yet. "There is another thread in the tapestry of your lineage, Alexander. My oldest priest, a man who has traveled throughout the Mediterranean, told me that there is final, conclusive proof of what I've just told you at Ammon's temple in the Egyptian desert. The place is called Siwah. He didn't tell me what the proof was, but I know that you can discover it. After Persia falls, take Egypt and discover your life's greatest mystery."

Alexander was more serious now as he listened to his mother. He rubbed his face with one hand, then answered. "Thank you for sharing that with me, mother. If the opportunity presents itself, I will go to Siwa. I too have heard of this legend. Aristotle told me that it was just a myth. Know that your words have diminished some, but not all, of my guilt-demons over Philip's death. I realize increasingly that you are Zeus-Ammon's earthly messenger. Keep his revelations coming to me when we begin our letters. They'll give me sustenance on the harsh fields of Asia."

"That is my only role now, Alexander," his mother said. "That and to help you keep your home base secure. I'll not fail either Zeus-Ammon or you."

Their private time was over, and Alexander escorted his mother out of the throne room and out of the palace into the king's gardens. Macedonian wild roses were in full bloom and they filled the cool night air with their fragrance. Alexander shared his cloak with his mother as they walked downstairs to a path high above the lake. The son would see his mother again the next day, when the army marched on parade past the palace and to its staging area, east of the capitol. However, tonight was the last time the two of them would ever be alone again. Amid the croaks of the lake frogs, there was a morose quiet as mother and son continued their walk.

Alexander drew within himself with each step they took. The secret his mother had just shared was having a profound effect on him. It explained many things: why he resented his father, why they were rivals, why he had allowed King Philip to be killed.

Finally, they completed their walk and reached the palace again. "My love is always yours, mother," Alexander said. "In many ways, you have made me who I am. My lifelong gratitude is yours. You will be in my daily thoughts during the difficult days ahead."

"I know, Alexander," is all Olympias said. Then she kissed her son and slowly started the climb up the stairs alone, back to her suite in the palace.

≈

Alone in her bedchamber, Olympias was serene and happy as she got out her snakes for her nightly devotional. Her ruse had worked. As she had done all of his life, she continued to dominate her son. That domination would continue to the farthest reaches of Asia. Her power would grow as Alexander's did.

Her latest ploy had not been too difficult. The birthmark idea had come from her chief priest; but she had extended it so that it had assumed all of the attributes of past Olympias-stratagems. The worst part had been the searing pain that she had to endure when a slave-artist burned an image of a lion's head on her thigh. The slave had then been put to death.

Now, three years later, the awful burn had fully healed and the created image looked like she had worn it all of her life. She would gladly endure the pain again. For she was Olympias, descendent of Helen of Troy, former Princess of Epirus, former Queen of Macedon, soon to be Queen Mother of Macedon and, most importantly, mother of the greatest conqueror the world would ever see.

≈

King Alexander was dressed in his most resplendent military uniform. Many of the pieces had been designed and created by the king and Hephaestion during the last months before the Persian invasion. Covering his torso was a long-sleeve tunic, light purple in color. The garment skirt fell just above Alexander's knees. A long cloak, dyed in a darker purple shade, hung nearly to his heels. It was trimmed with a yellow border and held close around his thick neck by a pure gold, lion's-head clasp.

Covering his chest and shoulders was a cuirass, a body armor made up of small metal plates. It was covered in white linen. A striking depiction of Heracles was hand-painted on the cuirass front. An intricate design, suggested by Olympias, surrounded Alexander's revered ancestor. On Alexander's head was a silver Boeotian helmet, emblazoned with a fine golden wreath on its front and sides. A pure-white, horsehair plume soared impressively from the helmet's crown.

King Alexander was ready. Now his last Macedonian act was to show the people of Pella what the coming conqueror of Persia looked like.

Alexander's horse, Bucephalas, waited restlessly for the king to mount. The magnificent steed seemed to absorb all of the energy of the world-altering events that surrounded him. It had a saddlecloth on its back covered with a panther-skin shabraque.

At last, Alexander mounted the powerful stead. Bucephalas reared and let out a mighty whinny, as if it were announcing to the world that the moment of conquest had begun. Alexander got control of the horse, and then looked up at his mother standing on the balcony of his throne room.

He considered yelling a last farewell, but changed his mind. He had said everything he wanted to say to her. It was time to leave. Instead, he gave her a last wave and lurched forward on his horse to begin the parade.

The king led his Companion Cavalry forward through Pella's broad streets, flanked by the elite circle of young men that Hephaestion had just established. The departure mood was joyous and a great air of expectation surrounded both the army and Pella's citizens.

General Parmenio, surrounded by his close supporters, followed the king's group at a measured interval. The old general's support of Alexander had been purchased at a high cost. Nearly all of the king's key army command positions were either one of Parmenio's sons, a relative, or a blood-related, ancient kinsman.

Parmenio's supporters were followed by ten percent of the soldiers in each unit of the king's 30,000-man army. The other ninety percent waited at the army's departure encampment, just east of the capitol.

Most of Pella's citizens watched the army's departure by lining the city's main streets. Rich merchants and their families stood on the roofs of their impressive houses, waving colorful Macedonian battle flags. They yelled farewells and called for the gods to look after the fighters as they encountered Darius.

Alexander knew most the affluent families of the palace district and yelled back to them as the parade progressed. "Get your storehouses ready for the treasure that I'll send back soon," he yelled. "You'll become the richest people in all Macedonia and Greece! Start making male babies for the army. When they come of age, I'll take them to the ends of the earth," he roared.

Alexander's subjects acknowledged the king's remarks as they showered him and his companions with flower petals. It occurred to Alexander that more than one of Pella's citizens might think it ironic that he had not taken his own advice and left a male heir in Macedonia before leaving.

Nevertheless, he knew that they would support the invasion as long as he delivered on his promises. The young king had lived long enough to know that wealth prevails. No matter what royalty and political leaders did or didn't do, the wealthy would continue to prosper one way or the other. That was not true of the Macedonian middle class or the common people.

King Alexander led the contingent away from the palace district and down Pella's main street past the agora, the city's commercial center. Cheering, middle-class merchants and common people filled the agora. Small groups of musicians played patriotic Macedonian songs; the moment was filled with national pride.

59

Finally, the parade exited the city and the crowds started to thin. Alexander saw small groups of slaves and common laborers working on the main road leading eastward out of Pella. The road they were traveling on was the result of Philip's massive road-building projects, started over twenty years ago. It was the main east-west artery, was over fifteen cubits wide and stood high above the surrounding countryside. Practically all of the land east of Pella was dry now, even in early spring when the rains came. Alexander's father had systematically drained the vast, swampy marshes that had almost surrounded Pella.

As he rode east, these civil engineering thoughts left the king and he started to focus his attention on Amphipolis. It was there that he would bring all of the elements of his army together. The journey would require ten days. He knew that his army could only sustain itself for just a month. The thought both excited and terrified him.

The driven feeling that the Greeks called pothos suddenly infused him. Clearly, his life-mission had started. He examined these feelings as he rode along at the head of his abbreviated army. His pothos-anxiety produced a curious sensation inside him, one that both motivated and haunted him. He continued this self-analysis until the invasion force stopped for its first night's encampment. So pervasive were his reveries that he even refused Hephaestion admission into his private tent.

King Alexander appeared the next morning, refreshed and knowing that he could not be stopped. A night of private drinking and eventual deep sleep had produced a fury in him that would sustain him as he encountered the powerful Persian empire.

CHAPTER 7

PERSIA

"I want this morning's events made into legend, Callisthenes," Alexander said. "Make a reader understand why I threw my spear from my command trireme. Let them recognize that Macedonian arms will win the conquest of Persia and Asia. Record also the symbolism of what Hephaestion and I did at Troy. Write a poetic description of how I laid a wreath on the tomb of Achilles. Explain how Hephaestion laid a wreath on the tomb of Patroclus. This story will be told five thousand years from now."

The king, his expedition historian, Callisthenes, and his chief secretary, Eumenes, sat in Alexander's tent, awaiting news from Parmenio and the army's scouts. Callisthenes, Aristotle's nephew, had been one of Alexander's teachers at Mieza. He had taught Alexander that every great king must have a sympathetic chronicler of his deeds. That was the reason that King Alexander had asked him to accompany the invasion force. Eumenes had served Alexander's father. Philip had also required that Macedon's court records must always reflect his actions in a positive light.

"We understand what you desire, King Alexander," Callisthenes answered. "Will you read our reports before we send them back to Macedonia and Greece?"

"Always," Alexander said curtly. "Both of you must write three drafts. The first one should be your initial impressions of what happened. Feel free to speak with my commanders, even common infantrymen, as you gather information. During military action, do this behind our lines. I don't want you two in the way.

"You must then write a second version. My military, political, or social goals must always be reflected in this draft. At every opportunity, you must glorify my kingship and military leadership. Is that clear?"

"I did this flawlessly under King Philip," Eumenes said. "I'll explain the style to Callisthenes. You will be pleased with our product, Alexander."

Alexander smiled, but held out the palm of his hand to the two men, showing them that there was more. "When you complete the final version, it must always be read to me. I will have final edit authority. Properly written historical records are vital. After I give final approval, destroy the first two drafts. I don't want any fragmented records confusing future historians. Do both of you understand my wishes on this matter?"

The historian and secretary nodded that they understood and the meeting was at an end. Alexander escorted them out of the tent and asked his bodyguard about Parmenio's location. The Royal Bodyguard told the king that Macedonian scouts had located the enemy. Alexander's first Persian battle was at hand.

≈

Persian forces had gathered east of the River Granicus. Led by the local provincial satraps, Spithridates of Lydia and Ionia, Arsites of the Hellespont Phrygia region, and Arsamenes, of the Cilician seaboard region, they were reinforced by 5,000 Greek mercenaries under General Memnon. Memnon's scorched Persian earth strategy had been rejected by all of the satraps, just as Darius had said it would. The Macedonian boy-king wasn't believed to be that formidable. Instead, they had elected a defensive strategy.

In a command tent that far-exceeded Alexander's in opulence, Memnon met with the Persian satraps. "It has been decided then," he said. "Our forces are aligned along the Granicus; we will bring the enemy to battle at the spot we selected. The river runs fast and deep there. The eastern bank is much higher than the other side and there is soft mud below the embankment. I rode my horse there two days ago."

Hearing nothing from the satraps, Memnon continued. "I've known Alexander since his teenage years. He's impulsive and bent for Homeric glory. When his scouts report our positions, he will make a direct, frontal assault. The Granicus embankment will become our ally. His cavalry charge will be softened; the famous Macedonian phalanx will not be able to hold formation. Our numbers will then overwhelm them."

Spithridates listened to the paid Greek general. Even though he held him in high military esteem, he didn't trust any Greek. However, his battle plan and words made perfect sense. "What are our total numbers? How do they compare to our enemy's forces?" he asked.

"We total a little over 30,000 men," Memnon replied. "Half of that is cavalry. We're not sure of Alexander's numbers. Our spies and scouts seem to think we are about equal. Importantly, our 15,000 cavalry is much stronger than their 6,000 cavalry. That will be critical. With our strong defensive position, we should win the day."

Arsites finally spoke up. "Good. Then, while Alexander is retreating to Thrace, we will launch our navy against Macedonia itself. Great King Darius has promised us that his mopping up is nearly done in Egypt. In months, a year at most, Macedonia and Greece will be ours. I have always wanted possession of those Thessalian horse estates. In a few years, I will breed the finest steeds in the world."

The satraps all laughed and the war council broke up. Each knew that they would rid Persia of the Macedonian youth in a day. Then, Great King Darius himself would lead Persia's mighty army and navy into Macedonia and Greece, forever destroying their ancient adversary. The Persian supreme god, Ahura Mazda, was watching over them.

≈

"It's a deathtrap," Parmenio shouted at King Alexander. "A direct charge by our cavalry is exactly what Memnon wants. Come to your senses! They have chosen the high ground above the Granicus for good reasons. If you insist on a frontal charge, I'll fetch your dead body downstream tonight."

Alexander glared at Parmenio, sensing that his 65-year-old second-in-command may be right. Yet, this was his long-awaited opportunity. His insatiable need for glory boiled deep inside his chest. Both he and Philip had dreamed of this moment for years. The Persians didn't know that he was the son of Zeus-Ammon. "We attack," he announced with contempt for Parmenio in his voice. "I know it's late in the day. I will prevail because none of them expects that I will do it. Go to the other cavalry units on my left. Fight a holding action while I create a gap in their center. Then, we will wrap up their wings. Victory will be ours!"

Parmenio glared back at Alexander, threw up his hands, then rode off to join the Thessalian, Thracian, and allied cavalry. "Leave the fool to his own designs," he muttered to himself as his horse gained speed.

Parmenio had just given the unified cavalry under his command their orders when he saw 1,800 of Alexander's Companion Cavalry, led by the king himself, launch their charge across the swift-moving River Granicus. He was followed by thirteen squadrons of heavily equipped Thessalians and mounted Macedonian scouts. A mighty roar emerged from the Macedonian side as the riders made it to the eastern side of the river. Quickly, Alexander and 6,000 of his men were in the midst of the enemy.

Alexander charged straight into Memnon's mercenaries, while a deadly barrage of Persian javelins rained down on the attacking allies. Briefly, the flying spears obscured the late afternoon sun. The fighting soon became hand-to-hand, but Alexander could not break through Memnon's strong line. As he continued to slash his sword, killing Greek mercenaries all around him, he looked around and saw that his forces were in danger of being driven back into the Granicus. His charge had failed in less time than it takes to drink a kantharos of wine.

"Back," he yelled to his left and right. His face reflected rage at this enormous personal failure. King Alexander's first action against the Persians had been a defeat.

The withdrawal was orderly, yet scores of his men lay dead in and beside the river. Others, badly injured, were being dragged west across the Granicus to the safety of Parmenio's protective line. Gradually, parts of the Granicus started to turn red from the dead and injured as the opposing forces withdrew to their original lines. Memnon's mercenaries had suffered few losses.

≈

Darkness fell quickly that spring night beside the Granicus. Both opposing forces lit campfires and started preparation for what would be a decisive battle the next day. Soldiers from both sides were close enough that they hurled insults across the river. "You Greek bastards don't know how to fight," yelled a Persian archer from the top of a hill beside the river. "Return to Macedonia and fight women — you may have a chance with them."

A Macedonian infantryman who had fought with King Philip returned the insult with several obscene remarks about King Darius' wife. Insulting barbs continued most of the evening. They were heard clearly by most of the fighters on both sides.

"Keep the campfires burning along our lines," Alexander told Parmenio. "Don't let the men's insults stop. I want the enemy thinking we are encamped here tonight. You were right in your advice not to charge the enemy here, Parmenio," he said. "I hate to say this, but I should have listened. It won't happen again."

Parmenio's face wore a smug smile as he nodded to Alexander. "What is our next move?" he asked.

"I've sent scouts downriver to find a better crossing point. I played into the Persians superior position and the strength of our force was dissipated. We need flat land for our cavalry charge after the crossing. I will find it.

"Tomorrow will be different. Don't doubt my leadership, Parmenio. That would be fatal. I know your attitude about me. You think it's just a matter of time before I kill myself in a hotheaded charge like today. I always learn from mistakes and come back stronger. Just because you and your friends command most of our units, don't let that go to your head. I'm still the king. Do you understand that?" Alexander asked with a vicious look on his face.

Parmenio wasn't intimidated by the king's outburst. He had seen many more terrifying situations in his life than this irate lad who was more than forty years his junior. "Learn to think before you act, Alexander," he shot back. "You have a good mind, but your spirit needs seasoning."

Alexander was furious with his father's old friend and nearly went for his sword. Quickly, however, he calmed himself. "I'm not a vegetable, Parmenio, and I don't need seasoning. My seasoning occurred this afternoon. My spirit is in Zeus-Ammon's hands. Follow my commands and we will prevail. Leave now; issue immediate commands that groups of one hundred are to begin leaving camp quietly. By morning, you may change your mind about me."

≈

65

Alone in his command tent that night, Alexander knew that Parmenio was right. A complete victory tomorrow was essential to his kingship. He knelt before his sleeping cot and prayed to his spiritual father that he would guide him tomorrow. When the prayer was finished, he left to join his scouts. By the middle of the night, he had helped them find an ideal Granicus ford. Things would be different tomorrow.

≈

Dawn painted the eastern sky and Alexander began moving thousands of men across the River Granicus. A flat plain, better suited to his forces, awaited them. With the river on his right and low foothills on his left, it was exactly what his fighters needed. He made a mental note to reward his scouts.

Alexander had changed his uniform during the night. Even in the low light of early dawn, he was resplendent. Armor that he had taken from Athena's temple in Troy covered his body. On his head, he wore a magnificent, winged helmet. It had two white plumes shooting upward from its polished, rounded surface. He knew that the Persians would spot him easily.

"Their scouts have spotted us," the king yelled at his commanders. "Form your battle lines. Perdiccas, get those phalanx units in a defensive perimeter around the riverbank. I want all of our forces across the river now! We've nearly surprised them; their advantage is lost."

If Zeus-Ammon had a military mind, he would have liked what Alexander and his army did that dawn morning. On the broad plain east of the Granicus stretched the Macedonians, Greeks, Thessalian, Thracian, Paeonians, and Agrianian fighters. To the extreme left — next to the foothills — were Calas, Agatho, and Philip, commanding the non-Companion Cavalry. Under Parmenio's overall command, these units were to fight an enemy holding action.

In the middle were the phalanx units, commanded by Craterus, Meleager, Philip, Son of Amyntas, Amyntas, and the sons of Andromenes, Coenus and Perdiccas. Their roles were to advance slowly while fighting a near-defensive action. This would allow Alexander's Companion Cavalry to launch the main attack.

On the extreme right were Nicanor – commanding the guards' brigade, Arrhabaeus – commanding the lancers and Paeonians, and Philotas – commanding the crack Companion Cavalry. Next to the Granicus were Clearchus and Attalus – commanding the Agrianian archers. King Alexander directed all of the extreme right units.

The second battle of the Granicus River exploded into open conflict. "Alalalalai, Alalalalai, Alalalalai!" roared the soldiers in the phalanx as the armies raced toward each other. The fearsome sound was their war cry to the Macedonian god of war.

Racing at the Greek and Macedonian allies from the opposite direction were 30,000 Persians. Their commanders, Spithridates and Arsites, channeled their forces toward Alexander. He was unmistakable in his garish uniform. Anticipating Alexander's cavalry charge, they moved several thousand of their elite soldiers from center to left to counter him.

It was exactly what Alexander wanted them to do. At the head of the wedge formation that his father had invented, he and his cavalry made a galloping, furious feint toward the enemy left. Memnon and Arsamenes were waiting for him there with overwhelming defensive forces. At the last moment, just before they encountered the enemy mercenaries, Alexander pivoted the wedge left toward the Persian middle and struck deep into the surprised enemy. It was the precise spot where the Persian commanders had just weakened their center by anticipating Alexander's charge.

"Hit the middle," Alexander shouted. "They fell for our pivot. Cut them down!" he screamed to Philotas.

The deadly contest was joined. Darius' son-in-law, Mithridates, countered Alexander's move by leading his own Persian cavalry straight into the Macedonian center. The noise of battle rose to such a level that voice commands were now impossible.

Bodies and horses were falling all around Alexander as he broke his spear into an enemy chest. Given another spear by Demaratus, he charged straight at Mithridates. But Mithridates saw him coming and, with all of the force he could generate, launched a spear straight at Alexander. The missile had such energy behind it that it easily pierced Alexander's shield, drove into his breastplate, but only penetrated his chest by the depth of a thumbnail. Alexander pulled out the spearhead and drove his own spear into Mithridates' chest. Its tip broke off when it hit the Persian's thick body armor, leaving him uninjured. The action left Alexander with only half of his spear.

Mithridates drew his sword and urged his mount toward the enemy king. "I'll kill you with the sword of my father," he yelled at Alexander.

Alexander was ready for the attack. As Mithridates neared, he thrust his broken spear into his enemy's face, knocking him to the ground. Mithridates' wound was mortal. Futilely, he tried to stop the blood that covered his face. But the battle soon swept over him, trampling him to death.

So concentrated was the king with this personal battle that he did not see another Persian, Rhosaces, charging at him from the side. Rhosaces swung a mighty blow onto Alexander's head with such a force that it crashed through the king's helmet, cut off one of his winged plumes, and split his skull slightly.

Blood ran down Alexander's head and face and he nearly lost consciousness. Somehow, he killed Rhosaces with his sword, but he was now fighting just to remain on his horse.

From behind the king, rode Rhosaces' brother, Spithridates. His great scimitar was raised two arms' lengths above Alexander. "You Macedonian bastard!" he yelled. "I'll have your head on a pole."

Just before his slashing sword started its downward motion that would have easily decapitated Alexander, Black Cleitus severed Spithridates' arm at the shoulder. The dark-skinned brother of Alexander's childhood nurse had saved the king's life.

Unable to remain conscious any longer, the king fell to the ground amid dead bodies, maimed horses and broken weapons. Immediately, Royal Companions surrounded him as the furious battle continued. With great difficulty, they helped him remount his horse. However, the king could no longer fight. His life hung in the balance.

While King Alexander was nearly being killed, his phalanx began pouring into the gap that his charge had created in the Persian middle. Soon, they were decimating Arsites' infantry and meaningful Persian resistance in the center disappeared. Seeing the enemy's collapse, Parmenio launched his Thessalian cavalry from the left. It was too much for the Persian forces. Their lines broke and the Persian soldiers began a desperate, unorganized retreat.

Memnon and his Greek mercenaries, seeing that the battle was lost, retreated to a small hill above the battlefield and drew up defensive positions. All that remained of the Battle of the Granicus River involved Greeks killing Greeks.

Within the hour, Alexander, now partially recovered, mounted a fresh horse. "The Greek mercenaries want you to grant them surrender rights," Philotas yelled to the king as brought his horse to a halt before the king's circle of officers. "What do you say, Alexander?" he asked.

"They have betrayed their countrymen by fighting with our ancient enemies," Alexander said coldly as he wiped blood from his eyes. "Destroy them now! Those that aren't killed outright will go to the mines of Pangaeus. I'll lead the final charge myself."

Memnon's mercenaries were surrounded and Alexander's command was carried out. More than three and a half thousand were killed on the small hill where they fought. Two thousand were sent back to Thrace after the battle where they suffered a short life mining what remained of the gold and silver of Mount Pangaeus. General Memnon somehow managed to escape. He and King Alexander would meet again.

≈

After the battle, Alexander, showing bloodstained bandages on his head, dismissed his bragging officers and commanded that Callisthenes and Eumenes join him. While he waited for them, he reflected on his great victory. All of western Persia now lay open to him. The battle result was everything that he had wanted.

Alexander decided that three hundred Persian suits of armor would be sent back for display in Athens' Parthenon. Olympias would receive all of the luxurious items that he had captured from the Persians. She would like that. Everything else of value was to be sold locally or in Macedonia to help fund his campaign.

While his economic pressures had been greatly reduced with the Granicus victory, money worries still troubled him. He would soon win another victory — this time a victory over Great King Darius himself. Then he would be able to stop worrying about money. He motioned for a servant to pour him another kantharos of a fine Persian beer that he had captured. He lowered his head and rubbed his throbbing forehead as he awaited his chroniclers.

"We have already started the narrative of your great victory," Callisthenes said as he and Eumenes were escorted into the king's presence. "It will be sent to Athens tomorrow by trireme. Sympathetic supporters will spread the magnificent account throughout Greece and Macedonia."

"Slow down, Callisthenes," Alexander interrupted. "I want to discuss events at the Granicus. How did you write it? Did you record two battles or one?"

Eumenes answered for Callisthenes, who appeared puzzled. "Two, of course: the late afternoon battle and your great dawn victory. Do you want us to read it to you?"

"Destroy your first drafts," Alexander said with anger. "Write the account with both events combined into one. I don't want to feed my enemies with my afternoon failure. Remember what Aristotle taught us: carefully crafted words are as powerful as entire regiments. I don't expect any more failures, but if they should happen, I want a positive cast put on all of my actions. Do you understand what your king is telling you?" Alexander looked harshly at both men and knew that they understood him fully.

"The first drafts will be burned when we leave," Callisthenes said. "You will have a revised version this evening. Do you desire anything else from us?"

Eumenes looked at the floor as his colleague was caving in to Alexander's vanity.

"Leave me," Alexander said as he turned his back on the writers. After they left, he called for a scroll and writing instruments from his guard. He wanted to write personal messages to his mother and Aristotle.

He had survived his first battle. Only the victory allowed his first full night's sleep in weeks.

CHAPTER 8

CONSEQUENCES

King Darius was furious. His eyes were bulging and small beads of sweat spotted his large brow. He rarely raised his voice, but everything had changed. One-sixth of his entire empire was on the verge of falling to Alexander. "Memnon warned me that the Macedonians must not be allowed to gain a foothold on the mainland," he shouted. "I thought him just a Greek alarmist."

Two of the king's eastern empire satraps stood by silently, afraid to say anything unless invited. Great Kings commonly ended lives when their anger could find no easy target. Still fuming, Darius looked at them and said, "Have your brains stopped functioning? Give me your council!"

Awkward silence continued. Then the satrap whose province was farthest from Alexander's invasion route spoke. "Memnon is our best hope during these initial battles, Great King. It hurts my Persian pride to say it, but Greek and Macedonian military tactics are superior to ours. If you give Memnon everything he requires, his moves will buy us time. Already, tens of thousands of our provincial fighting men are being assembled into a mighty army. We should end up with over 150,000 fighters. Even Alexander could not oppose such a force."

The other satrap finally joined the conversation. He had just returned from meeting with Memnon, after the fall of Halicarnassus to the Macedonians. His voice was authoritative, but his meek body movements failed to support his strong words. "Memnon and Orontobates are now with our fleet in Cos. They threaten the Greek Ionian city-states daily. Memnon has expectations that Chios and Lesbos will soon be ours."

"Expectations?" Darius asked sarcastically. "I want results, not expectations. What can you and Memnon guarantee me?"

"Memnon told me to tell you that only two things matter in these contests," the second satrap answered. "Alexander is temporarily powerful on land. We are all-powerful on the sea. If you allow Memnon to attack the Greek Ionian city-states with our 300 naval vessels, Alexander will be forced to halt his advance. After that, we can redirect our navy against

Macedonia and the Greek island of Euboea. Your provincial forces will arrive by then, and we will be at full land strength. Finally, we will maneuver the Macedonians into a battle site of our liking.

Darius walked away from the satraps, exasperated. He had thought that his gold bribes and unified support of his invasion-path satraps would be enough. But not now. Quickly, he made a decision. "I want this message sent to Memnon tonight using our fire-signaling system," he commanded. "Press the naval attack against the Ionian city-states. I want Macedonian territory to feel the sting of our navy immediately. Memnon is now commander of all Persian forces in the Macedonians' path. Once we gain initial victories, the Greeks' natural hatred of Alexander will cause them to rise up. My retainers in Athens inform me that they already have 400 triremes waiting to join an insurrection. I will no longer wait for Alexander to come to me."

Darius dismissed the two satraps and waited for them to give the required proskynesis. Sometimes he hated the time that it took for his subjects to humble themselves before him. Alone, he was filled with doubts. He was placing his empire in the hands of a single Greek, Rhodian mercenary. His first thought was this was insanity. However, nearly all of his satraps and generals felt the action was wise.

If this failed, he thought, he would take the field himself and lead the greatest Persian army since Xerxes. Then, he could return to expanding his empire by invading Greece itself. He planned to watch as Olympias was raped by several of his surly veterans. This prospect made him smile as he left for a bath and a massage by his newest teenage girl. She was a wonder-worker with her small hands.

≈

Alexander's intelligence corps had kept him informed of Darius' naval strategy of attacking the Greek Ionian colonies and the successful Persian forays into the Greek mainland. He decided to split his army to counteract these threatening Persian moves. Parmenio was sent back north with orders to clean out the aggressive tribes inhabiting the central plateau. This action removed Parmenio from Alexander's presence at a time when he was unsure of the old general's allegiance. Alexander then decided to move south, aiming to control the Aegean Sea coastal strongholds of the enemy. Their powerful and effective navy could defeat his every plan if left unchecked.

More than these military moves and countermoves, Alexander worried night and day about the near bankrupt state of Macedon. Weekly reports from his mother and Antipater attested to the deplorable condition of the Macedonian economy. Precious little of the Great King's wealth had made its way back to his troubled kingdom. He was also aware from reports of his Macedonian agents in Athens that, with his first major defeat, the Greeks would rise up against him.

After moving his army awkwardly through Lycia and Pamphylia, he met with Hephaestion privately. Hephaestion started the conversation, a rare event when he and Alexander met to discuss serious matters. "Ptolemy will settle things in Halicarnassus," he began. "It will probably take a year, but with it in our hands the Persian naval forces will be greatly weakened."

"Weakened but not eliminated," Alexander answered. "I made a grievous error when I didn't capture Memnon after Granicus. Now, he has fled Halicarnassus and the Persian navy threatens cities that we have already conquered. Only a Greek could be so wily."

Hephaestion let the gravity of Alexander's lament sink in, and then added more bad news. "Parmenio's Thracian cavalry commander, Alexander of Lyncestis, is under arrest. Parmenio informed us through a small group of scouts who made it through enemy territory. It seems that the traitor accepted a bribe of 1,000 gold talents from Darius if he would assassinate you."

Alexander was surprised but wary. "Something smells here," he snapped. "Parmenio may have invented this plot to be able to replace Alexander with one of his supporters. The emerging contest between the old man and me is approaching a dangerous stage. I still need him, but my trust level is eroding fast."

"You should move slowly on this, Alexander," Hephaestion said. "I advise you to wait until our two armies join at Gordium. Our communication lines are weakened this far south. At Gordium, you will have full authority of your army behind you, should Parmenio attempt anything."

Without further consideration, Alexander agreed. "Get word back to Parmenio as soon as possible. Issue a command under my royal seal that everyone involved in the plot is to be held under close arrest. Order Parmenio not to take any independent action without my direct order. Make sure he understands that."

"I will send the message immediately," Hephaestion answered. "Is there anything else?"

"Send for Aristander when you leave. I want to consult him about Gordium. They have an ancient legend there about what is required to conquer Asia. Aristotle spoke to me about it in Mieza long ago. Since that is what I am going to do, I must know how to fulfill the prophecy."

Hephaestion left and the king walked nervously around his spacious, private tent. Although he made daily supplications and offerings to Zeus-Ammon, he craved more divine guidance. Experience had taught him to trust his personal seer, Aristander. The mystic was an inflated bag of wind at times, but there had been too many instances when he had been exactly right about how the gods were guiding him. Now, more than ever, he knew that he must stay attuned to the gods' wills.

"You look well, King Alexander," Aristander said as the king's bodyguard escorted him into the king's tent. "But your spirit is troubled. How can I help?"

Alexander smiled and grimaced simultaneously. Perhaps the seer knew that his spirit was troubled simply because he had sent for him. It was the only time that Aristander was ever asked into Alexander's private quarters. However, even with that insight, King Alexander still needed his personal seer. "Tell me more about the legend at Gordium," he said. "What is this great knot that is there?"

"I knew that this would interest you, Alexander," Aristander replied. "I have been gathering information about the legend as we moved south. The story is hundreds of years old. Near an acropolis temple to Zeus in Gordium, there is a wagon, complete with yoke and pole. No one knows its age; it was said to be old when Midas reigned." Aristander paused, knowing how Alexander loved stories about historical events that had captured men's imaginations for centuries.

He continued. "The wagon's yoke is fastened to the pole with very long strips of bark. It seems to have the appearance of an enormous knot. The knot is so complex that it defies anyone who tries to untie it. Many have tried; all have failed."

Aristander paused again. He knew that the knot's complexity was bound to have a challenging impact on Alexander. "An ancient oracle gave a prophecy that the person who successfully loosed the knot would become supreme ruler of all Asia. It is a legend that is worthy of you, great Alexander."

Alexander had known of King Midas since his days as Aristotle's student in Mieza. He did not know the fascinating details of the knot, however, until now. His eyes sparkled and, for a brief time, his troubled spirit was buoyed. "It is a challenge worthy of the son of Zeus-Ammon," he said softly. Then he looked at Aristander and gave a command. "When I untie the knot, the prophecy will be fulfilled. Speak to Callisthenes and Eumenes before we get there. I want my actions there glorified throughout the world."

Alexander dismissed Aristander and issued orders to break camp the next morning. His plan called for him to take the Persian Royal Road north and, in late winter, meet up with Parmenio in Gordium. Asia's developing legend was eager to confront one of the continent's oldest legends in ancient Gordium.

≈

At Gordium, Alexander received welcomed reinforcements from home. Men who had been granted home-leave in Macedonia returned, along with 3,000 new infantrymen. Also added were 500 cavalrymen. The king put off any confrontation with Parmenio; the timing was still not right.

Gordium's inhabitants surrendered as Alexander approached and no Macedonian lost his life in taking the city. Now, with a retinue of his closest Royal Companions, Callisthenes, Eumenes, and Aristander, the king walked up Gordium's acropolis and approached the city's ancient wagon. It was an Alexander moment.

"The wagon is old," the king said as he circled it. "Such a knot," he said as he stopped and studied it. "Who created such a puzzle?" Alexander circled the wagon yoke and pole again, then walked beside the great knot. "There are no open ends to the bark strands," he remarked. "Both ends are buried somewhere in the knot itself. It's an enigma worthy of me."

The men in his party smiled and, individually, began to examine the knot. One by one, they withdrew, leaving only Alexander to probe its complexity.

Time passed and the king continued to examine the knot. Alexander thought he might just simply pull the wooden pin where the yoke connected to the pole. Although the symbolic simplicity of such an act appealed to him, he rejected it. The situation needed more drama.

Suddenly he pulled out his short sword and savagely began hacking at the knot. Soon, its hidden, inner ends lay exposed. Alexander stopped his strokes, found one of the knot's loose ends in the severed bark strands, and flicked it with his sword tip. "What difference does it make how I loosed the damned thing," he shouted. "Asia will be taken by my sword. That's all that matters."

Alexander turned, walked up to Callisthenes, and scowled. "A Phrygian told me that the legend's wording was vague. I always believed that Asia's conqueror must literally untie the knot. The legend can also be interpreted as breaking it up. I have chosen the latter version. Let it be known that Asia's newest lord is breaking up the old, Persian empire and establishing a new one. Record this in your history of our expedition."

With a new legend established, King Alexander left Gordium's acropolis and called for a military assessment of his forces. The pedagogues, philosophers, and court propagandists could take the mythology of Gordium to new levels in their stuffy writings and treatises. Alexander of Macedon had other worlds to conquer.

≈

Zeus-Ammon must have been watching over his son. General Memnon, fresh from successful naval raids against Macedonian and Ionian ports, began the siege of Miletus. Alexander had subdued the city a year earlier. Shortly after the siege began, Memnon fell ill and died.

Memnon's death and what the Persians must now do was the only topic on King Darius' agenda as he convened a war council of nearly all of his satraps and military commanders. They met in the king's royal hall in Babylon.

"The Greek's death was a catastrophe for us," the Great King began. "The outcome of our offensive naval moves against Macedonia and the Ionian ports is in jeopardy. I want open and honest opinion expressed about our future strategy. Let me hear from each of you. No one can leave this gathering until a sensible strategy emerges. I don't care if it takes a week!"

The Persian debate settled quickly on two possible courses of action. A semi-retired naval commander emerged as the leader of the group that wanted Memnon's naval offensive carried to the Macedonian homeland. Although he spoke forcefully and wisely, the old man clearly was no Memnon. His position gained little support from the king's active commanders. The other course of action, advocated by Darius' current infantry and cavalry commanders, urged the king to bring the Macedonians to a direct battle in a location where Persian knowledge of their land would bring eventual victory. "By then, our great numbers will win the day and the war," a young nobleman who had distinguished himself at Granicus added.

King Darius accepted the strategy of using Persian army and cavalry against Macedonian army and cavalry. Nearly unanimously, his subjects also urged him to lead the army as its in-the-field commander. "Morale will be boosted beyond imagination if our infantry sees you at their head," an aging general told the king.

The only dissenter was an Athenian mercenary captain in the king's paid service. "This is folly," he shouted. "Great King, you should stay in your capitol, directing overall strategy. You are risking your entire empire!"

Acrimonious yelling started between the Persians and the Greek. It quickly degenerated into insulting name-calling. Darius, more incensed than was necessary, grabbed the mercenary and threw him to his guards. "Execute him now!" he shouted. "These are the kind of fighters that go over to the enemy when the battles start."

The Great King committed his empire to a single strategy. They would begin the hunt for Alexander and his army. Then, they would maneuver the Macedonians into a pivotal battle that could only result in a Persian victory.

The offensive naval strategy might have worked under Memnon's generalship. Now, it was abandoned. Soon, the Great King believed, Persia's greater numbers would win the war. Darius was satisfied that it was the only way to rid his empire of the barbarian hordes that even now were moving east.

CHAPTER 9

ISSUS

"Only the Taurus Mountains separate us then," said Darius. "We are only two day's march from each other. Has it come down to this?"

"It has, Great King," answered his intelligence chief. "Alexander must be guessing which gate we will move our forces through. Parmenio's scouts check the gates that they are aware of daily. My most recent reports have Alexander waiting for us at the Syrian Gate."

"Then the fool has fallen into our trap," said the Great King showing a broad smile. "Let him wait there while I outmaneuver him. Prepare my army for immediate departure. We will sweep north, pass through the Amanic Gates, and come down on Issus. It will block his retreat and lines of communication; he will be completely surprised. What a half-wit!"

Darius' orders were issued and the Persian camp erupted into activity. All noncombatants, the Great King's considerable baggage train and most of his treasure were sent back to Damascus under heavy guard. They would only get in the way as he decimated the Macedonian barbarians.

≈

"Our intelligence stinks," Alexander lamented to his closest companions. Present were Craterus, Perdiccas, Seleucus, and Hephaestion. "We have no damn idea where the Persians are right now. They could sweep down on us from any direction. I've never felt so blind!"

"Parmenio just sent messengers urging you to return to Issus," Perdiccas said. "Our sick and wounded are still there. Establishing your headquarters there would afford you the position of most flexibility when Darius finally appears."

Seleucus agreed. "Issus' position between the sea and the mountains is of great advantage to us, Alexander. We must not allow Darius to move us onto a broad plain; his cavalry and greater infantry numbers would cut us to pieces."

"What is their total number?" asked Alexander.

"A spy just returned from a perilous trip over the mountains," Perdiccas answered. "He reports that they exceed our total number by at least 75,000 fighters. We cannot afford to lose any tactical advantage with such an inequity of forces!"

"Increase the number of our scouts," Alexander commanded after a long pause. "I want every gate checked daily for the next several days. I won't return to Issus. Parmenio is wrong; they will come through the Syrian Gate. It's there that I will wait with our main army. Everyone but Hephaestion is dismissed. Carry out my orders. We will meet again at first light tomorrow.

Hephaestion joined Alexander in an isolated corner of his command tent. Their conversation was muted so they could not be overheard. "Events are quickening," Alexander began. "With the coming battle, I want you to know something."

Hephaestion smiled, placed his hand on his companion's shoulder, and said, "I am pleased that you confide in me. What is it?"

Alexander ran his fingers through his wavy hair, looked into space, and then addressed his friend. "You and the whole camp know that Harpalus just defected to Athens. The official word is that he is a traitor and will be executed when caught. This is the surface story. It's not true. At Aristotle's suggestion, I've sent him back to gather intelligence on Athens' actions. His knowledge of economics makes him an invaluable spy. No one suspects—only he, you, and I know his real mission.

"If I should fall in the coming battle, use this information wisely. I can't tell you how to use it, but it might prove valuable in the scramble to succeed me. Do you understand?"

"I do," Hephaestion answered. "But rest assured, you are not going to be killed in this battle. You are Zeus-Ammon's anointed. Do you doubt that now?"

"No," answered Alexander. "But knowledge is power. My telling you this is only a precaution. We will speak no more of it until the time is right."

Hephaestion left and Alexander gave supplication to some local deities, asking for guidance against the illusive Persian enemy that so threatened his army's safety. Surely tomorrow would bring word of where Darius was positioned. His personal gods would see to it.

≈

A commotion awakened Alexander from a deep sleep, a sleep that was much needed for he had not slept for two days. Bursting out of his private tent, he shouted to his bodyguard. "What is it? Has Darius been spotted?"

In the distance, the king spotted the reason for the uproar. Nearly two hundred of his wounded and sick, soldiers that had been left in Issus were limping and staggering into his encampment. They were still distant but close enough that Alexander could make out that they had something black on their hands.

He ran to meet them and saw that each was handless. He approached an officer that he had known since boyhood. "What happened to you?" he asked.

The officer, weak and near collapse, told his king a ghastly story. "Darius' army is at your rear. He took Issus easily, killed or maimed most of the hospital cases you left there and did this to us. After cutting off our hands, he dipped our stubs in tar pitch to staunch the flow of blood but not release us from the pain. After the pitch dried, he forced us to tour the Persian lines where we were ridiculed. Then he sent us back here to you." Completing his account, the officer fainted.

Alexander was stunned. He had fallen for Darius' trap. The entire Persian army had outcircled him and emerged north of Issus by an unknown gate, far north of the Persians' anticipated route. Parmenio had been right again. Alexander's path of retreat was blocked and his line of communication severed. South of his position were the hostile forces of Phoenicia.

He could quickly take his army through the Syrian Gate where he had been waiting, but that would only prove advantageous to the Persians. He was left with only one choice: he must turn 40,000 men, march north, and encounter a strongly encamped enemy. The odds against doing this successfully were overwhelmingly against him.

Alexander gave orders to have the maimed soldiers given the best care and, in time, put on triremes to Macedonia. Then, he called a war council. His top commanders discussed his few options. Then the king gave orders to march north, where a Persian army of 100,000 waited for him.

≈

Late afternoon of the next day, the two armies faced each other. A small river, the Pinarus, separated them. The Persians, although they would have preferred open ground to take advantage of their greater numbers, were positioned high on the river embankment. During the last two days, they had also built earthen and log defenses where the embankment was lower.

Parmenio was on the Macedonian extreme left, immediately adjacent to the sea. His orders were to maintain contact with the rocky shore under all circumstances. No Persians were to be allowed to flank his fighters by using the beach. On the right, next to the foothills of the mountain, was Alexander with most of his massed cavalry. These were the usual positions of the allied Greek and Macedonian forces.

The battle began with initial skirmishes in which both armies sought advantage. However, these forays failed to change either side's positions. Suddenly, the Persian archers let loose their barbed missiles. The sky darkened as their arrows become so numerous that they collided with each other.

Then, with the blast of a trumpet, Alexander launched his Companion Cavalry attack, causing Darius' archers to retreat. Alexander's timing was perfect. The battle on the right took a distinct Macedonian advantage as Alexander suddenly turned on an angle and pressed toward the Persian center.

The Macedonian phalanx in the center was struggling getting across the river and surmounting the steep embankment and Persian palisades. A stalemate among allied and Persian fighters in the center soon resulted and neither side could advance more than a few feet. Parmenio was only partially successful on the allied left, barely crossing the Pinarus. Importantly, no matter what else was happening, the enemy would not flank the old general.

Having broken through the Persian troops to the right of center, Alexander now redirected his Companion Cavalry wedge toward the rear of the Persian Greek mercenaries and Darius' Royal Bodyguards. The Great King was clearly his target. Mayhem reigned as hundreds of frenzied Macedonians fought their way toward Darius. Dead horses and bodies of fighters from both sides blocked the way. The screams of dying men on both sides filled the air so that commanders' orders on both sides could not be heard. Alexander pressed the attack, furiously killing tens of enemy fighters himself as the deadly Macedonian surge neared the royal chariot of Darius himself. Alexander received a thigh wound from an enemy spear, but his relentless charge continued.

Darius and Alexander could now clearly see each other. For a moment, both men ignored the noise and confusion of the great battle that swirled around them. Darius' horses reared, stumbled and almost propelled the Great King into the enemy. However, just at that moment, despite great difficulty, one of the king's charioteers brought a lighter chariot forward and helped Darius board it. Sensing defeat, Persia's Great King grabbed the horses' reigns himself and fled the conflict. The battle of Issus turned on that single event.

Just as Alexander made the decision to pursue Darius, a scout rode up to him and shouted, "Our left and center are in jeopardy," he yelled. "They need your cavalry now!"

Alexander cursed, but he knew what he must do. He would capture Darius later. A great victory was nearly in his hands. His army needed him now. He ordered nearly all of his right wing into the center of the enemy mercenary flank and began to drive them out of the river.

The Persian cavalry commander, Nabarzanes, saw what Alexander was doing to his center. Even if he decided to aid the Persian fighters there, he would have to ride over the corpses of his own dead men. Horses needed stable footing to engage the enemy. Nabarzanes gave the retreat order and the Persian rout began.

Alexander saw that his left and center were now advancing and no longer needed him. "Come with me," he shouted to his Companion Cavalrymen as they galloped after the fleeing Darius.

However, darkness had nearly enveloped the coastal battle scene. The enemy had taken to the hills and was retreating into dark mountain passes that were unknown to the Macedonians. Alexander abandoned the chase and started the ride back to join his army, now looting Darius' base camp.

During the long and exhausting ride back, the king reflected on the day's glorious events. He had only been in Asia one and one-half years. Now the entire Persian Empire was within his grasp. Not even Philip had achieved such a great victory. But much more is possible, he thought.

Men will speak more of my pothos quality, now that I have defeated the Persians again, he reflected with a smug smile. That pothos yearning was an almost compulsive need to do what no one else had ever done. He little understood the attribute; he only felt its powerful grip inside him. He would seek the advice of new sages and religious leaders about this as his conquests continued. He reasoned briefly that the quality was unique in the world. It was a gift, or a curse, from Zeus-Ammon.

Back at his headquarters, Alexander's personal physician treated his thigh wound. He then toured what was left of Darius' camp by torchlight. Treasures beyond his imagination were spread out before the king. Entering the Great King's personal pavilion, he was astonished with its opulence. Gold-encrusted furniture was everywhere. Enormous, multicolored carpets covered the floor; rich tapestries hung from every wall. At the back of the pavilion was the Great King's personal bath. Alexander's servants had already filled the enormous tub with steaming water. It was twice the size of the King of Macedon's body. He disrobed and as he sank slowly into the bubbling water's healing depths, he smiled to himself and thought of his destiny. "So this is what it means to be a king," Alexander remarked, smiling ironically to his personal servant.

After a glorious bath, Alexander asked to be left alone. Tonight was going to be his best sleep in weeks. He had earned it.

≈

The next morning, Alexander and Hephaestion learned that Darius' royal family had been found in a tent, not far from the front lines. "Come with me, Hephaestion," Alexander said. "This is a chance to show how we will treat our vanquished enemy."

Both men were rested, scrubbed, and in an elevated mood. Each was dressed in a plain tunic, bearing no indication of rank. They entered the women's tent and found the Persian's royal women there. Among them was Darius' wife, Stateira, her face completely covered by a veil. She was the full sister of Darius, said to be the most beautiful woman in Persia. She said nothing and lowered her head as Alexander and Hephaestion entered. Also present was the Persian queen mother, Sisygambis.

Alexander was about to speak when Sisygambis rushed up to Hephaestion and threw herself at his feet. "Are we to be killed, Great Alexander?" she asked through a translator.

Hephaestion, taller and more handsome than Alexander, blushed and laughed nervously. "I am Hephaestion," he said. "I'm afraid you'll have to ask my companion here if you want an answer to your question."

Humiliated by her mistake, Sisygambis redirected her supplication and knelt at Alexander's feet. The moment was more than awkward, as she began her apologies.

"Don't trouble yourself, Sisygambis," Alexander said through the translator. "You have already lost enough. You didn't make a mistake. Hephaestion is Alexander too."

Alexander assured the women that they would retain all of their royal privileges and that what had happened yesterday was not personal. He labored, through the interpreter, to explain that an empire change was occurring, one sanctioned by great Zeus-Ammon himself. The shorter of the two men the women saw before them was the personification of god's will on earth.

Then Alexander kissed the cheeks of both women and left. Plans must be made immediately to begin the pursuit of Darius.

ARISTOTLE'S REFLECTIONS FROM A SPIRIT WORLD

2

I received secret messages from Alexander every other month, until his invasion penetrated deep into Persia. He sent them back to Pella on a medical evacuation trireme from the nearest seaport wherever he found himself. From Pella, Antipater then sent a trusted courier south to bring them to me in Athens. Since each message bore a discreet, secret coded number, I knew that no one ever intercepted any. I sent my messages to the king in the same manner.

During the first few months of Alexander's campaign, the Greek city-states were quiet. They expected that Alexander's impetuous personality would result in his early death. Then, at just the right moment, when all was in turmoil and leadership was uncertain, they would rise up. After Granicus, however, everyone began to take him more seriously. Darius and his mercenary general, Memnon, had slowly begun to bribe their way into Greek affairs. I became alarmed and wrote Alexander about this developing crisis. Left ignored, these homeland events could lead to his downfall.

Then came his great Issus victory. All of Greece knew that their Macedonian adversary was not going to eliminate himself. Greek unrest, some of it violent against Macedonian forces, became common. I decided to take drastic action. I wrote Alexander that he must send someone back that the Athenians trusted. I suggested a fake defection so that the individual would receive immediate acceptance from his enemies. The man's mission would be to assess what was happening politically, economically, and militarily in Greece, especially in Athens. Those fields are not in my areas of expertise and I felt that a spy with specialized knowledge was needed.

The king sent Harpalus and it was a brilliant choice. Within weeks, the most influential political leaders in Athens, even Demosthenes, confided in him. They never suspected that he was still loyal to Alexander. In time, he was able to discover their most secret designs. I assume that he had developed some way of preempting Greek moves and communicating those actions to Alexander. I could never have accomplished what the astute treasurer did so cleverly.

Only once, when I traveled to Pella to meet with Antipater, did I talk with Olympias. She didn't trust or like me and told me so in a most rude fashion. I informed her that Alexander trusted me and there was no reason why she should not. Nevertheless, she remained aloof toward me. I was never able to discover her feelings about her son's campaign or what was happening in Greece and Macedonia. I soon gave up on her and let her pretend that she was ruling Macedonia.

Without question, it was only through Antipater's wise and courageous actions that Macedonia was able to remain stable during the first difficult months of Alexander's campaign.

When Alexander took Tyre, I knew that Egypt was next. He needed her for her political influence and for her vast food production capacity. That he was aware of her value was clear to me.

I had taught him everything I knew about Egypt during group and individual lessons at Mieza. Alexander and Ptolemy used to debate long into the night about Egypt's value. Alexander grasped immediately Egypt's considerable importance. I share no small part in his decision to absorb that ancient nation into his emerging empire.

My last message to him before he left Gaza was to find out as much as he could about Egyptian history and traditions that were confusing to Greeks. I wanted to know about their impressive medical practices. I also wanted to know about their herbs, drugs, and medical operating procedures.

I pleaded with him to send back to my Lyceum school as many samples of plants and animals as he could find in Egypt. Greeks believed, perhaps erroneously, that Egypt had horses with two heads. Many of my Lyceum teachers wondered how that was possible. I wanted all of the new knowledge he could gather.

≈

I knew what would interest Alexander most in Egypt: his mother's ridiculous teaching that he was the son of God. We often talked of his supposed deity when he was my student.

More than once I explained to him that all religious mysteries operated on three levels. Outer mysteries were simple stories, meant for children and immature adults. This level featured beautiful legends and highly symbolic stories. The stories were never meant to be taken literally. The outer mysteries' purpose was to prepare the intellectually curious and elite members of society for deeper spiritual understanding.

I taught Alexander that the second spiritual level was the inner mysteries. Here, religious myths were revealed to a limited number of humans as spiritual allegories. This level featured explanations and life-examples of the encoded religious stories that could help a spiritual searcher achieve closer communion with the higher power. After my first lesson with him on the inner mysteries, I knew that Alexander would reject further spiritual teaching.

The last mystery level involved esoteric, spiritual teaching. It was here that the spiritual seeker discovered knowledge of himself. After that great personal achievement, the God within each seeker was revealed.

I was never able to convince Alexander that the first mystery level was just a series of highly symbolic, life-improving metaphors. After he left Mieza, and for the rest of his life, he never grew beyond the literal, outer mystery level.

Had his spiritual growth evolved, almost everything he did would have been different. However, Olympias had corrupted his brilliant mind from childhood with the absurd belief that he was the son of God. In so doing, she rendered any deeper spiritual growth impossible.

For centuries, I hoped that humans would realize the purpose of religion. Now however, over two thousand years later, I am convinced that humankind will never progress beyond literal religious beliefs while they live.

≈

My last request was for him to find out what he could about the civilization of Atlantis. Plato had spoken and written of it; all educated Greeks wanted to know more about it. Supposedly, it lay beyond the Pillars of Hercules. However, *which* Pillars of Hercules was he referencing? Was it those at the western end of the Mediterranean or at the more meager cape south of Athens? I asked for clarification.

I have come to believe that Atlantis was just another metaphor of an ideal society and that humans interpreted Plato too literally. Humans love to chase a dream. They will always seek certainty in the midst of uncertainty.

Since these legends had originated in Egypt, I knew that someone there would know the answers to these questions and could teach Alexander.

I asked King Alexander if I could visit Egypt after he conquered Persia. I knew that he would return to Macedonia and Greece after he had defeated Darius. The Great King's empire was vast, but I wrongly believed that it was not so vast that Alexander would spend much more than an additional year or two there. I even requested that he and I visit the ancient land together. I didn't understand then that I would never see him again.

≈

I envied Callisthenes' first-hand access to Alexander. What wondrous worlds must he be encountering? My students kept busy cataloguing my nephew's many scientific reports. They were priceless sources of new information in changing our view of the world.

I wondered during my life if we were just like Plato's insignificant cave-prisoners, sitting around the Mediterranean, full of societal delusion and intellectual self-importance. It seemed to be an innate characteristic of human kind.

Yet, civilization grew because of Alexander's hubris-filled odyssey. I hoped, while I lived, that humans could learn from the experiences of those that went before them. My worst fear continues to be, after the passage of centuries, that your kind will never change or make meaningful social and intellectual progress. I have observed occasional examples of elevated human behavior, but most of you have not appreciably changed during my time in this spirit world.

CHAPTER 10

SOUTHWARD

"What is Darius' offer?" Alexander asked the two Persian envoys who met him in Marathus. "Know at the outset that I will settle for nothing less than his entire empire."

Darius' two representatives, both of whom, like Great King Darius, spoke Greek fluently, looked at each other. A Macedonian barbarian that wouldn't even listen had just negated their mission. "Hear our offer, King Alexander," one of them said. "It is more than attractive."

Alexander sat in Marathus' temple narthex, accompanied only by Hephaestion and, at a distance, his Royal Bodyguards. A cruel leer painted his face. "Proceed," is all that he said.

The senior Persian stepped forward, cleared his throat, opened a scroll sealed with Darius' royal seal on it, and began reading his Great King's words. "If you agree to sign a treaty of friendship and cease all military actions against the rest of the Persian kingdom, great rewards will be given you. First, a rich ransom is yours for the return of my wife, my mother, my children and the remainder of my royal family captured at Issus. I know of the serious economic conditions in Macedonia. This ransom offer alone will solve all of your domestic problems."

The envoy continued reading Darius' offer. "Second, I will cede to you, upon treaty signing, all of my lands and cities west of the Halys River. West Asia would be yours from Cilicia to Sinope. I know factually that this is the extent of Asian territory that your father, King Philip, ever wanted to conquer."

"I am Alexander, he was just Philip," Alexander interjected sarcastically. Then he motioned for the envoy to continue.

"Finally," the envoy said cautiously, concluding his Great King's offer extemporaneously without reading any more text, "King Darius wants eternal friendship between Persia, Greece, and Macedon. War as a permanent condition between us must end."

Alexander noted that Darius' envoys had listed Macedon last. He was about to correct him and tell him that Macedon and Greece were one political unit, but thought better of it. He had already rejected Darius' offer mentally; more discussion would be a waste of time. "I have heard Darius' offer, Persians," he snapped. "Give the scroll to me. Leave and wait here in Marathus. You will have my answer in three days."

≈

Alexander faced a dilemma. He did not intend to accept any of Darius' ridiculous offers. His destiny was to become the lord of all Asia, not just a vassal of Darius. From this point forward in his conquests, he would surpass Philip's every dream. However, he was obligated to present some form of the Persian offer to his war council, for Macedonian kings did not rule absolutely. The council did not need to know the offer's details. Alexander had learned long ago that kings could, and often did, alter facts to achieve their goals.

"Get me that captured Persian scribe who served Darius' family," he told Hephaestion. "Send him to me immediately. We are going to rewrite Darius' offer to one more of my liking. I think you know what I mean."

Hephaestion gave his friend a knowing smile and left the king alone. Alexander was already mentally dictating an altered Darius offer. The changed document was insulting in tone and laced with condescending Persian expletives. Critically, Alexander's version had Darius making no territorial concessions. Alexander knew what his war council's reaction would be to this fake peace proposal. Smugly, he waited for the scribe, knowing that the battle against Darius would continue.

≈

The next day a near-perfect substitute version of Darius' scroll had been created. The scribe who produced it was killed and his body thrown in the trash heap of Marathus. Alexander's war council overwhelmingly rejected Darius' offer and supported the war's continuance.

Alexander addressed them after the vote of support. "Here is my plan, men. I know that Darius wants us to chase him across Asia. That is another one of his traps. We know little or nothing of central Asia. We don't even know how far it is to the Great Sea. Aristotle taught me that it is only a month's journey, but I suspect that he was wrong. Darius would like nothing more than to bleed us in scores of small, deadly skirmishes. I won't have it.

"Instead, we will wait for Darius. There is plenty for us to do along the coast and southward. The Persian navy can still threaten us; I want our coastal rear and Egypt settled before we meet Darius again. We will give him time to raise the largest Persian army that he can muster. Then, we will defeat him for a third and final time. That is my plan."

The officers in his war council erupted with a rowdy show of support for their king's words. "Let's skin the bastards," and "On to Persepolis," were heard from his top commanders. Alexander let the shouting continue, and then held up his arms for quiet.

"Take this decision to our men today," he said. "I want full knowledge of our military intent shared with each of our fighters. Tell the men that even more bounty will be coming to them. Explain that, in time, they will become rich. They will support our moves."

Alexander left the meeting and joined Perdiccas, Seleucus, and Craterus for a meal. As they were eating, a messenger informed him that Ptolemy had just captured Damascus, Syria. Darius' complete baggage train had been seized and the city's enormous treasure was now in Parmenio's hands. The message also informed Alexander that Greek ambassadors for Athens, Thebes, and Sparta were also being held in protective custody.

Fascinating to Alexander, was the last part of Parmenio's message. Barsine, widowed wife of Memnon, Alexander's greatest adversary to date, had been captured. She was on her way to Marathus, under armed escort, and would arrive in about a week. Alexander lifted his eyes and remembered Barsine. She and her father, Artabazus, had lived in his father's Pella court for years. The king remembered that she had received a first-class Greek education, was the daughter of a Persian nobleman and a royal blood mother, and was trilingual. His last conversation with her had been after she had taught him a lesson in basic Persian. He had been eight; she had been eighteen.

He looked forward to seeing how time had treated her.

≈

It took ten days for Barsine to arrive in Marathus. After she had gotten a good night's sleep in the sumptuous guest-tent that Alexander had prepared for her, she enjoyed a morning bath in Darius' great bathtub. It was one of the few captured Persian treasures that Alexander had decided to take with him. She then sent word through a slave that she would see King Alexander when he was available.

Royal Bodyguards escorted Barsine into Alexander's private quarters. The king's first impression of her was that she was a younger version of his mother. Barsine's clothing and hairstyle were almost identical to how Olympias had looked when Alexander had last seen her. Her lavender peplos, Greek in style, reached to the ground and surrounded her like a burst of morning sunlight. Around her neck, she wore a filigreed, golden necklace. A large lion's head hung from the chain.

"You have grown into a handsome man, Alexander," Barsine said as she walked toward Alexander. "I saw that potential when you were young."

Alexander smiled, a little embarrassed. He was amazed at how some women could immediately make first encounters personal, almost intimate. It was as if she had forgotten that he had become king since they last saw each other. Nevertheless, her mature beauty excused her behavior. She was lovelier than he had imagined.

Alexander's attitude toward women was nearly always one of indifference. He treated them with politeness, but intimate relations with them rarely entered his mind. "Sleep and sexual intercourse remind me of my mortality," he had told his male friends more than once.

"It is good to see you again, Barsine," Alexander said. He meant the words. Did Parmenio treat you well?"

"He was the perfect gentleman," Barsine answered. "I thank both of you for that." What are your plans for me, my king?" she asked, getting right to the point.

"I would like for you to stay with me for a time," Alexander surprised himself by saying. "My army is going south, not eastwards toward Darius.

Your knowledge of this fact alone means that I cannot let you leave my encampment until all is secured along the coast and in Egypt."

"I would never betray you, Alexander," Barsine shot back. "I have always had a personal interest in you."

There she goes again, Alexander thought. *Is this the beginning of her seduction attempt?* Alexander decided to get to the point. "Do you know that I prefer men over women, Barsine? It isn't that I dislike women; it's just that I'm always with men and I have grown to love them. Can you understand that?"

"I do, Alexander," Barsine answered coyly. "Nevertheless, you may want to reconsider your sexual preferences. It will make you into a more complete monarch. Philip understood the power of uninhibited sexuality." Barsine waited for what she knew would be a strong response from Alexander.

"Unlike my deceased father, I never have, nor will I ever rape young boys!" he shot back. "If that is normal male sexuality, count me out!"

"I apologize, Alexander," Barsine said, lowering her head. "I had in mind something else altogether." Then raising her head and her eyebrows a bit coyly, she ventured, "Have you ever had real, total sex with a woman? I'm talking about rich sexual experiences with a practiced, mature woman."

Alexander calmed himself, smiled, and answered. "Mother once arranged to have an Athenian courtesan spend the night with me. I explored the woman's body but sexual intercourse didn't occur. Perhaps she wasn't as experienced as you," he said with a wry smile.

"I heard of that story," Barsine answered with a knowing look on her face. "You must understand that good sex starts with a common set of personal experiences. You and Callixeina never had that. Olympias just thrust the two of you together like animals in heat."

Alexander reasoned that Barsine was right. Perhaps he should give her a chance with his woman-virginal body. "You come on strong with your seduction," he said. "I will consider you as a lover. You could never have

95

all of me, like every woman wants. Sexuality is only a small part of who Alexander is and strives to become. Do you understand that?"

"I will take whatever part of you that you can offer," Barsine answered. "I cherish the opportunity to be the first woman to give you a male child. Every warrior king must have a son."

Alexander rolled his eyes and ran his fingers through his wavy hair. *Not another lecture about how I should have a son*, he thought. The king walked up to Barsine, embraced her, fondled her firm backside, and then dismissed her. A military strategy session was about to begin for the attack on Byblos and Sidon. After those victories, he would invest Tyre, the impregnable fortress farther south. He would consider sex with Barsine after these more important matters were underway.

≈

Byblos and Sidon surrendered without a fight to Alexander's increasingly powerful army. One night prior to moving on to Tyre, Alexander was feeling especially pleased with himself. He sent Hephaestion ahead to scout Tyre's defenses. Then he gave orders to have Barsine brought to his private tent.

Barsine had prepared for this moment for weeks and was ready, but she could hardly believe her good fortune at the king's timing. She was determined to become pregnant that night. She knew that her body was ripe for conception and that the couple could not stop with a single act of copulation. For the first time in his young life, Alexander achieved sexual coitus with a woman. He was twenty-four.

The next morning, she awoke to watch Alexander stumble out of his tent, sleepless and exhausted. She smiled, remembering that she had ravished him four times. He had been a willing partner. She placed an ornate Persian pillow under her buttocks and pressed her legs close together to keep the king's sperm deep inside her. Contented, she pulled Alexander's blanket close to her nose to breathe in his scent. Slowly, she fell asleep.

Later that morning, Barsine awakened a second time. She knew, as Olympias had known the night of her wedding intercourse with Philip, that she was pregnant. Everyone would know in nine months that Alexander had a son. Her life was back on track. Her dream of becoming queen of Alexander's new Asian empire was beginning. She curled her body on Alexander's large bed, continuing to hold her legs tightly together. Completely satisfied, she knew that what lay inside her was more valuable than gold.

She waited two days before she bathed again in Darius' tub. Alexander's seed rested inside her; all was well.

≈

Alexander stood on a rocky promontory in Old Tyre, looking down at the port of Tyre. Its citadel was located on a rocky island, just over four stadia from the shore. He had just learned that water in the channel separating the island from the mainland was over twelve cubits deep. Tyre's fortress, easily the most important Persian-sympathetic commercial and naval port between Cilicia and Egypt, was formidable. On the land side, the city's walls were over ninety cubits high. It would be Alexander's greatest siege challenge to date.

"They killed our men and dumped them into the ocean from the battlements," Alexander shouted. He was at a staff meeting in his Old Tyre encampment. "I might have negotiated a settlement with them, but not now."

Every staff member shared his king's indignation. "What is your plan?" asked Ptolemy. "Without a navy, we could spend years trying to starve them out. Already, they have received three re-supply ships on the island's ocean side."

"I had a dream last night," Alexander said. "I saw my ancestor, Heracles, standing on Tyre's walls. He was beckoning me onward. I am being presented with a labor, just as Heracles was. There is only one way to take the city. We will build a mole, a temporary road across the channel. We will tear down Old Tyre and use the stones to fill in the channel. It will take our best effort, but it can be done."

His men were speechless. Was there no end to the innovative strategies that this young conqueror would devise? He was a driven genius.

"Hephaestion, you are in charge of obtaining food and water," Alexander continued. "I never want to stop military actions because my men are thirsty or hungry. Perdiccas, you and Craterus are in charge of overall operations here. I know that we must have a navy to conquer Tyre. When word of our Issus victory spreads throughout the Mediterranean, there will be Persian naval defections. Already, I have had contacts from Rhodes and Lycia offering ships. More vessels and their crews will be coming over to us.

"I will take this city; we cannot go on without it being secured. Go now to your duties."

≈

Soon, Darius sent a second, more attractive peace offer. "What does he propose now?" Alexander asked Parmenio.

The old general, fresh from a meeting with Darius' newest envoys, opened the scroll containing the Persian king's translated terms. "The ransom for his family has doubled, from 10,000 to 20,000 talents," Parmenio summarized. "Territory ceded remains as before: everything west of the Halys. He now adds that he will give you the hand of his daughter," Parmenio said with a wry look on his face. "He warns that eventually you must emerge out onto the steppes of central Asia and that you will be vulnerable there."

"I have or can eventually win all that he offers me," Alexander answered with contempt. "The Persians must understand that I will not stop until I have conquered Persepolis and all of Darius' eastern provinces. Reject his entire offer. Tyre will be ours in a few months."

≈

Six months later, Tyre fell in a bloody, final assault. It had taken all of Alexander's army, a newly developed navy of over 250 ships and every deadly siege machine that his engineers could devise to topple the city.

The King of Macedon then made plans to march deeper south, where he knew that a curious group of people lived in an obscure, theocratic-nation called Israel. They called themselves Jews. Their chief priest, a man named Shimon the Pious, had refused to give Alexander direct aid during

Tyre's long siege. Shimon did invite the king to come to their holy city, Jerusalem, and be honored. However, their capitol was well inland from the army's path of travel.

Alexander was intrigued by their odd belief in a single god, but still angry about their refusing him aid. He had already proved that cities did that at their great peril. At last, he sent a message to Jerusalem, demanding to meet Israel's chief priest beneath a local mountain on the path of his army's march south. The mountain was towering Mount Carmel. The rest of his army would go on to Gaza without him, where another long siege was likely. He could join them after he attended to these quaint Jews.

Reflecting on the Jews, it was obvious to him that if they believed in one God and he was the son of that God, then they should worship and honor him. What could be more logical? He would convince them quickly of this then move on to Gaza and Egypt.

CHAPTER 11

JEWS, EGYPT & SIWAH

"I'm going to say this again so listen to me this time," Alexander said to Israel's priests through a translator. He stood with a group of Israel's religious leaders in a cool, shaded grove beneath Mount Carmel. Each of the Jews, except for the chief priest, was dressed in full religious regalia of fine, white linen. "You believe in a single god. I believe in a single, supreme god: Zeus-Ammon. They are the same god with different names. Egyptians call him Ammon-Ra. Persians call him Ahura Mazda.

"Educated and common people throughout Greece and Ionia acknowledge me as the Son of God. Zeus's lightning bolt impregnated my mother when she bathed in a stream. Therefore, you should worship me. What could be clearer?"

Shimon the Pious, dressed in his chief priest's garments of purple and scarlet, smiled and frowned simultaneously. On his head was an impressive miter with a golden plate that bore an abstract inscription referring to the Jews' god. "We agree on just the first part of your statement, Alexander. There is but one Supreme Being. We show our highest respect to him by not saying his name. But we will forever disagree about any human being the son of the mighty one."

Shimon was on dangerous ground with such a remark. Others had been killed for even suggesting that Alexander was not Zeus-Ammon's son.

"If I weren't in a hurry to join my army at Gaza, I would go to your holy city and reduce it to rubble with all of you inside it," Alexander shot back. "Would your god stop me?"

"He could, Great Alexander," Shimon answered softly.

Alexander was irate. His every instinct called for him to order the killing of these silly excuses for religious leaders. However, in the back of his mind he recalled a dream that he had had in the Macedonian city of Dios. An identically dressed priest had appeared in that dream and assured him that he would dominate over the Persians.

He calmed himself, realizing that dreams were messages from Zeus-Ammon himself. At last, he regained control. He didn't need any more hostile peoples to his rear as he moved westward into Egypt. "This is what I demand, Shimon: you must erect a statue of me in your holy Jerusalem temple. I want to see it when I come back through this miserable land."

Shimon looked toward the heavens, uttered a brief, untranslatable prayer to his god, and then answered Alexander.

"Great King Alexander," the chief priest said slowly. "Our ancient prophet, Daniel, gave us a prophecy about the one who would destroy the empire of the Persians. He wrote that it would be a Greek. Perhaps our god is using you as his instrument."

Alexander was pleased with Daniel's prediction. The prophecy and his Dios dream started to soften his heart. "I am the conqueror who will destroy your ancient oppressor," he answered emphatically. "But this changes nothing. I still demand that you place a statue of me in your holy temple."

Shimon lowered his head, forcing silence as he thought. Then he answered. "Great King, a statue made of metal will eventually rust; one made of wood will rot; a stone image will soon be covered with pigeon droppings. None of this would honor you. I propose a more meaningful, longer-lasting honor."

Alexander liked the priest's little play on words. It reminded him of Aristotle's word games. *These Jews are no fools*, he thought. He motioned for Shimon to continue.

"Allow us to name every Jewish boy born this year to be named Alexander. Such an honor will endure for eternity, far longer than metal, wood, or stone."

Alexander smiled. The substitute honor appealed to his vanity. He knew that he was being duped, but he liked it. "You Jews must be known for your cleverness," he said. "I accept the honor.

"But I tire of this. I leave now to rejoin my army. Keep my peace here or you will see me again in your land. We will not be talking about the supreme being in this shady grove then."

Shimon gave the king a half-bow, bade him good-journey, and wished him success against Israel's oppressors. As he watched the king and his entourage mount their horses and gallop off south along the coast, he gave thanks to his god. Part of the thanks was based on the knowledge that little remained of the current Jewish year. He would keep his word to Alexander, but only a limited number of Jewish boys would ever bear the Macedonian king's name.

≈

Gaza's siege lasted two months. Like the Tyrians, the city had a nearly impregnable fortress, one that had not been conquered for centuries. Alexander's siege towers bogged down in the vast sand dunes that surrounded Gaza's citadel, and the fighting was furious. During the initial fighting, the king was shoulder-injured by a well-placed arrow fired by a sling device. His wound caused a considerable loss of blood but it was not life threatening.

While he convalesced, Alexander directed that a mound should be built around Gaza's citadel. Only then was he able to bring up his deadly catapults and launch the final attack. Gaza's entire male population was killed when the Macedonians at last entered the city. All women and children were sold into slavery and the city was repopulated as a Macedonian garrison. The king of Macedon now could move on to fabled, ancient Egypt—a land that stirred the mystical reveries of every Greek and Macedonian in Alexander's army.

≈

"This culture makes us look like children," Alexander remarked to Hephaestion. He stood in the ancient Temple of Osiris, gazing in awe at the great, white-walled, old Egyptian capitol in Memphis. "A priest told me that the city is 3,000 years old. They have written records to prove it. I will write Aristotle and Olympias about this tonight."

Hephaestion had met Alexander at the Nile delta and together they had sailed south to Memphis on one of the great river's many arms. The king had entered Egypt via Pelusium and Heliopolis. His army's quick, exhausting journey through a landscape nearly devoid of water had taken just a week.

While Hephaestion had waited for his king, the too-long Persian-dominated Egyptians welcomed him enthusiastically. Especially grateful for the Persians' ejection from their land was the Egyptian priesthood. In gratitude and religious conviction, they informed Hephaestion about an event that was to mark the beginning of a profound change in Alexander's character. Hephaestion decided not to tell his friend about it until he reached Memphis. It would be a splendid surprise.

But now, the time had arrived for Alexander to learn of the coming ceremony. "In two weeks you will receive your greatest honor yet," Hephaestion announced. "In this very temple, they will install you as Egyptian Pharaoh. In their belief system, this will mean that you will become both god and king of their land. It is a fitting honor and fulfillment of what Olympias has always told you. You are in your highest glory."

Hephaestion saw Alexander's face display astonishment, observing that he was nearly moved to tears. His friend and king stood in the temple, choking down emotion, staring across the broad Nile. Hephaestion knew that Alexander's every dream had been surpassed. Philip had foolishly aspired to become the thirteenth Greek god. Now his son was soon to become god incarnate of Egypt, ruler of both the upper and lower Nile. Alexander could not speak.

Hephaestion smiled but respected Alexander's emotions. He knew that this was a time of greatness, and it deserved silence. Then, as Alexander regained control, he grasped both of the king's arms and held firm the battle-hardened forearms. "More glory will come to you, Alexander. This is just the beginning."

Alexander, composed now, returned his friend's embrace. "This will change my life, Hephaestion," he said. "Egypt has much to teach me. I can afford to spend a month here. Darius can wait. We control the entire Mediterranean Sea. I may even go to Siwah. Great spiritual insights await me there.

"Leave me alone here. I want to watch the sun set across the Nile. This is a sacred time. I'm afraid that even you cannot share it, my dear friend." A sudden burst of cool wind shot up from the river, as if to punctuate the king's remark.

Hephaestion knew that Alexander was right. Nothing would ever be the same after this. He left the temple, arranged for six all-night bodyguards for his king, and then began meeting with Egypt's chief priests to plan for the Pharaonic installation ceremony. It would occur late in the month of Maimakterion. God, as Alexander, was truly among them.

≈

After a magnificent installation ceremony, Alexander organized a festival for athletic games and literary competitions. Great athletes and literary figures were brought in from all over the Greek world, and his tired but proud army reveled in the rest and celebration. Then he sailed north on the Nile, letting the south-to-north flow of the great river carry him slowly through his newest empire.

It was a gentle trip as he watched great Egypt unfold before him. Farmers tilled the rich farmland as they had for hundreds of years. Simple but effective devices, called shadoofs by the Egyptians, lifted water out of the Nile and dumped it into an elaborate system of canals. The centuries-old machine, consisting of a water bucket suspended on a weighted rod, allowed the farmers to irrigate their fields and produce two crops per year. The irrigation technique fascinated Alexander. Egypt would become his breadbasket as his conquests continued. He made a mental note that he might use the shadoof when he reached the arid lands of Persia.

He spent a day at the Giza plateau, touring the Great Sphinx and the great Pyramid of Cheops. Already, it was recognized as one of the wonders of the world. Despite his healing shoulder wound, Alexander and Ptolemy managed to climb to the top of Cheops' great structure.

"The Egyptians call this pyramid Khufu," the king said. "Neither Greece nor Persia has anything like this," he said to his climbing companion. "If I die in battle," he said as they rested at the pyramid's apex, "I want an even bigger structure built as my necropolis. Promise me that you will do that"

Ptolemy nodded agreement but refused to talk any more of his king's death and changed the subject abruptly. "Herodotus wrote that everything is different here," he offered. "Egyptian women are said to urinate standing up while men pass their water while sitting. I haven't seen these things yet, so I don't know if the historian got it right or not."

Alexander smiled and looked at the man he believed to be his half-brother. Ptolemy had disappointed him more than once, but he had many laudable qualities that any king would find valuable. He was unassuming yet steadfast in his military duties. Alexander had never known him to be anything but cautious and in full control of his emotions. His only vice was his relationship with the wildly sexual Thais. She was an Athenian courtesan who had accompanied Ptolemy on the expedition.

Neither Alexander nor Ptolemy suspected that, one day, this bastard son of King Philip would become pharaoh of the land that stretched below both of their feet.

≈

At last, the king's entourage arrived at one of the arms of the Nile delta where the great river emptied into the Mediterranean. From there Alexander traveled west and found a site that pleased him. It was opposite the island the Egyptians called Pharos. "I will establish a great city here," the king said. "Tyre is destroyed and the Mediterranean must have a new commercial seaport.

"Send for Deinocrates, the Rhodian architect. He is the best, and I am serious about the future quality of this new city. It must have straight and wide streets. The strong sea breezes here will make it a pleasant place, even in summer.

"It will become a place of commerce. Perhaps more importantly, I want centers of learning established here. Civilization will grow in new directions because of what will happen in this place. I am issuing an order today for a great library to be built here, facing the Mediterranean and our homeland. I want every book ever written anywhere in the world to be kept here. It will also become a center for science and research. I will seek Aristotle's advice on this. The city will be named Alexandria."

After staking out the city's plot lines himself, he turned over the rest of the city-building tasks to civil engineers. Then Alexander called his inner circle of commanders together for an announcement that surprised most of them. Present were Hephaestion, Ptolemy, Perdiccas, and Seleucus. Callisthenes and Eumenes also attended to preserve the historical record.

"In two or three days, I will leave for the great desert oasis at Siwah," the king began. "My spiritual destiny awaits me there. Only fifty men and Ptolemy will accompany me. No one else is going. Ptolemy is going because he has nearly mastered the Egyptian language.

"Each of the men accompanying me has proven his toughness in the most trying conditions. While the rest of you wait here, your tasks are to build our Egyptian garrisons and organize a system of grain production that will support our army. There must never be an interruption of Egypt's grain supply."

"I have heard of Siwah, Alexander," Hephaestion spoke up. "It's almost 2,500 stadia from here. One of the worst deserts in the world surrounds it. You risk much by going there."

"Don't question my decision, Hephaestion," the king answered angrily. "I cannot continue with my conquests until I hear Zeus-Ammon's Siwah oracle. A supplicant can ask as many questions as he wants and answers from god himself will be given. I will not miss this opportunity."

Alexander dismissed his friends and then started a series of meetings and treaty negotiations with city and tribal representatives from all over Northern Africa. Each had come to acknowledge Alexander's divinity, assure him that peace with the new Egyptian Pharaoh was their goal and agree to supply foodstuffs to his army. It was just as Alexander wanted it.

≈

Alexander spent the next two days attending to administrative matters and meeting with local Egyptian officials. At last, a strong need emerged in him to share his spiritual reveries with his mother. Late one night, he wrote a letter to Olympias. It was shorter than others he had written. It read:

'Mother, I have come far and achieved much. However, tomorrow, I begin the most important quest of my life. I know that it will change me forever. Zeus-Ammon's oracle, at Siwah, is in the Great Desert, southwest of where I am now. You spoke of his temple there during our last night together.

The Furies still haunt me about Philip's death. Terrifying nightmares about his elimination are rarely absent from my sleep. I know that guilt about Philip is the reason I have increased my drinking. Until now, none of this has affected my leadership; our great victories attest to this.

Only you know of my torment. You must never reveal this to anyone. Mention it only to Zeus-Ammon in your private devotions.

I know that our actions against Philip do not trouble you. Demons never have invaded your sleep, nor will they. I envy your peace of mind. Yet, I know that without your actions, I would not be alive. I continue to thank you for that.

At Siwah, I will ask the oracle if I must forever be harried by guilt. Egypt has ordained me as a living god and pharaoh. My men adore me. Darius' entire empire will soon be mine. However, I am never at peace. I know that this is the source of my pothos-driven actions. Other men consider my behavior as just a manic part of my personality. It is much more than that.

This message will not reach you for weeks, even by our fastest trireme. By then, I will be back on the campaign. Pray to Zeus-Ammon that I will find peace through his oracle.

Your son, Alexander'

The king reread his letter just once. Then he used their secret code system to encrypt it. No eyes but his mother's would ever read the letter. He then burned the original draft, rolled up the finished scroll, and double-sealed it with his royal signet ring. His correspondence left the next morning, just as he began his perilous journey toward the great oasis that was Siwah.

≈

Alexander's small party stumbled into the Siwah oasis. They were dirty, covered with sand, and had countless lip-sores and sunburned skin all over them. Their three-week journey had almost ended in death when they ran out of water and became lost. An unusual rainstorm saved them, and they struggled on. Then their guides became lost and death once again was close. Miraculously, a flock of crows appeared and guided them southward toward the oasis and the last miserable part of their trip.

Alexander gave all but a few of his men leave, then through an interpreter announced to a priest of Ammon that he was ready. There would be time to rest and bathe later. God's son was ready to converse with his true father.

Soon, a different priest came to him. He was a scrawny, older man, fluent in Greek. The priest bowed and greeted him warmly as the son of God. They walked to a wooden bench, sat down, and started the consultation process. They were alone, in a shady grove of palm trees. Indeed, the grove was made up of thousands of palm trees fed by Siwah's underground springs. Close by were countless other trees growing pomegranates, olives, lemons, and olives. A sweet, dry fragrance hung in the air. In the near distance, Alexander saw the stark, ominous desert lurking. Here, however, it was a paradise: a miracle of Zeus-Ammon himself.

"Take me to the oracle now," Alexander said impatiently to the priest. "I have waited for this moment all of my life."

The priest smiled but shook his head to the king. "I must explain first what will happen, Great Pharaoh Alexander," he said. "Ammon's image is kept in a symbolic wooden boat. When you approach it, priests will hoist it on their shoulders. You should then direct questions to Great Ammon. If the answer to your question is yes, Ammon's image will sway up and down; if the answer is no, his image will sway left and right. Do you understand?"

Alexander stood up, waving his arms and shouting. "I have not come all this way to view your stupid theatrics, priest. You have just acknowledged me as Egyptian Pharaoh and the son of Ammon. Now get moving and take me to the temple's inner sanctum. I demand a private audience with the oracle. I will write my questions and you will give me written answers. Anything less than this and I will return with my army to destroy this place. Do *you* understand?"

Shaken, the priest said that he did. "Allow me to go to the Rock of Aghurmi before you. Follow me up the path, through the gate, and into the Temple of the Oracle inner chamber. No one must accompany you beyond that point."

"Get on with it," Alexander shouted with a dismissive wave of his hand.

The king, Ptolemy, and two other companions waited until the timid priest had disappeared, and then they walked up the path to the temple entrance. Ptolemy led the others to a shaded area beneath a great mud-brick wall and started a vigil.

Alexander walked away, ducked his head to get into the low door, and disappeared into a darkened room. The king's companions heard the door close. Each settled down for what would be a long, sweltering afternoon.

$$\approx$$

Alexander found himself in a tiny room. It was dark and dank. He saw a torch mounted on the wall providing minimal light. Its smoke disappeared into the ceiling. A small wooden stool rested in the room's exact center. A leather cord, five cubits long, hung down from a hole in the ceiling. The ceiling was obviously false. Alexander guessed that one of Ammon's priests waited there. He had seen the arrangement before. "Proceed!" Egypt's new pharaoh said to the ceiling.

A deep voice from above him said, "Great Pharaoh Alexander, son of Ammon, write your questions on the small scrolls beside you. Then, tie the scroll to the string you see hanging. I will give your questions to the oracle. I speak and write Greek; communication will not be a problem."

Alexander's first question had already been answered. Every priest he had met in Siwah had greeted him as the son of Ammon, but this was where he would begin. He wrote, "Am I the son of Zeus-Ammon, the god you Egyptians call Ammon-Ra?" He quickly rolled up the small scroll, tied the leather cord around it, and said, "I am done."

The scroll disappeared into the hole and Alexander waited, sitting humbly on the small wooden stool in near darkness. He thought the oracle would take forever, but his answer came down through the hole before long. He opened the scroll and read the oracle's answer from Zeus-Ammon. It read simply, "You are the son of Great Ammon."

109

A broad smile spread across Alexander's face. Olympias had been right. From his childhood, she had assured him that his single father was Zeus-Ammon. At this moment, the most revered oracle in the world confirmed his deity. He was ecstatic.

Alexander spent the rest of the afternoon writing questions to the oracle and reading the answers. Each response made the questing Alexander more joyful. When he asked if his father's murder had been punished, the oracle wrote back that the question would not be answered, since Alexander's father was Ammon and he was not mortal. Pleased with the answer but still insistent, Alexander rephrased the question and wrote, "Have all of former King Philip's murders been punished?" The oracle answered that "Philip's death had been sufficiently avenged." Hugely relieved, Alexander wrote more questions and read other answers.

The oracle assured Alexander that other oracular prophesies he had been given from Delphi, Didyma, Xanthus, and Gordium were true. He would become lord of the entire world. His last question about the eventual viability and success of his newly established city, Alexandria, received just the answer he wanted: "It will become the foremost city in the known world" was the reply.

Finally, with eyes aglow and a strange aura of invincibility around his face, Alexander left Zeus-Ammon's inner sanctum and emerged back into the blinding light of late afternoon Siwah. Calmly and slowly, he walked down the path to where Ptolemy and his other companions were waiting. Clutched in his hands were the small scrolls containing the holy answers from the oracle.

"What did you learn?" one of his men asked.

"Are the prophesies favorable? Are they to your liking?" another inquired.

Ptolemy remained silent and let Alexander decide what he wanted to announce.

Alexander held out the palm of his hand to his friends. "The answers are only for me," he said. "I will only tell you that the experience has warmed my heart. I am immensely pleased. Our difficult journey was worth it. We will never fail in anything we attempt. I am truly the son of Zeus-Ammon."

"I will tell our men how you looked when you came down the path," Ptolemy said at last. That will be enough."

≈

Alexander and his men stayed at the oasis just two nights and then left Siwah. Before leaving, Alexander burned the oracular scrolls, after having reread them countless times. The king's small group returned by a different route, crossing the Great Western Desert due east of Siwah.

Each night of the return journey, Alexander wrote segments of a letter to his mother. He described the dangerous journey to and from Siwah. Withheld, however, were the oracle's answers to his questions. 'I will relate the profound and inspiring answers to you personally, when we meet again' he wrote. Some things must never be written for others to see and judge.

Alexander resolved that no one but his mother must ever be allowed to discover the details of what he had been told in the Egyptian desert. Only she had made him the son of God.

CHAPTER 12

PURSUING DARIUS

Alexander waited for Harpalus in Tyre. The king had been gone from the once-powerful seaport for almost a year. Egypt was now completely his. He was pleased that the breadbasket of the Mediterranean had come to him without major military difficulties. Before leaving, he had divided the ruling power there among distinct groups of local leaders, Upper and Lower Kingdom governors, and Macedonian military commanders. The ancient society was firmly established as the western cornerstone of his growing empire. In time, he knew that his newly founded city, Alexandria, would become the commercial, cultural, and intellectual jewel of his empire.

However, as self-affirming and character changing as his Siwah spiritual experience had been, he continued having nightmares about Philip. His heavy drinking resumed and he often woke up hung-over from an all night session of uncontrolled consumption of uncut, Macedonian wine. Anguishing to the point of daily turmoil, he decided to give his troubled spirit more time. Future conquests and Darius' defeat would help him live with any demons that would not leave him.

Eumenes finally announced Harpalus' arrival. "Do you want additional bodyguards during this meeting?" he asked his king. Neither he nor anyone else in the king's camp knew the real reason for Harpalus' supposed defection to the Athenians.

"No," answered Alexander. "My meeting with him is secret. Keep the normal guard. When we are done, I will tell you what to write in the record. You may be surprised."

Harpalus entered the command tent, limping as always from a childhood illness, and approached his monarch. A broad smile stretched across his face. "Greetings and glory to you, Alexander," he said enthusiastically. "Word of your great conquest of Egypt has spread throughout Greece. It solved many problems for us."

"Yes," Alexander answered. "Nothing satisfies Greek souls like the chance to become rich on someone else's efforts. Sit with me and tell me how serious the rebellions are. Must I delay pursuit of Darius and take care of the situation myself?"

Harpalus showed a self-satisfied expression, then began to allay his king's fears. "Allow me to summarize my mission," Harpalus answered. "When you sent me, I had grave doubts about success. I had believed Aristotle and your other retainers in Athens to be wrong. Nor could I believe that Hephaestion had developed a constructive dialogue with Demosthenes. However, it was all true.

"After your nearly bloodless Egyptian conquest, only King Agis and a group in Thrace are now revolting. Everyone else, including Athens' leaders, is either undecided or fearful what would happen if you return to Greece. I'm pleased that you took my advice about the one hundred triremes. Once they sail for the Peloponnese, the Spartan threat will all but be over.

"Antipater, in Pella, can handle the ground battles. You chose your regent well. He is extremely able. He does need more money, however."

Alexander did not respond to the money request.

Harpalus continued. "I recommend that you release all Athenian prisoners captured at Granicus. It will create an immense amount of good will."

"I agree," Alexander said tersely. "It will be done today. Is there anything else?"

"Don't worry anymore about matters in our homeland. Go get the bastard Darius."

"You have done well, Harpalus," Alexander said. "Tomorrow, I will reinstate you as my treasurer and quartermaster. I will tell anyone who needs to know of your successful mission. Your actions have been worth 5,000 cavalry to me; I want that known to our officers. Any anger about what they believed was your defection will vanish. Keep up your brilliant fiscal work on my behalf. I will greatly reward you when Persia's treasure is mine.

"Later, we will discuss establishing mints in several of the conquered cities. I have several likenesses of myself in mind that I want used. I'll show you some drawings when I get time. Most of the designs are based on my Siwah experience. Men will value these coins for thousands of years. I want it done right."

Harpalus agreed and told the king that he would begin establishing the mints immediately. Before leaving, he gave Alexander personal messages from Aristotle. They discussed the awkward position in which his former teacher found himself. "He is respected for his intellect and the quality of his school, the Lyceum," Harpalus said. "However, he is rejected by many Athenians because of his support of you."

"I know this," the king said peevishly. "We correspond regularly. It's a burden he will have to learn to live with. I have mine as well."

The men spoke of older, simpler times when they were boys in Macedonia. Then Alexander rose, signaling that the meeting was over. He bid Harpalus goodbye, escorted him to the tent entrance, and asked Eumenes if anyone else was waiting to see him.

"Barsine comes here daily," his secretary answered. "I have used every excuse that I know why she cannot see you. Nevertheless, she's insistent. Should I send her away again?"

Alexander rubbed his eyes, sighed, and then ran both hands through his wavy hair. It had grown long during his time in Egypt and now nearly covered his shoulders. "No, send her in. Is she pregnant?

"She is not," Eumenes answered. "She wants to be, but she is not."

Alexander had not given Barsine any thought since their nightlong intercourse session and he was surprised. How was that possible? He motioned for his guard to bring in Barsine.

Barsine floated into the king's presence and greeted him. "Zeus-Ammon has smiled on you, Alexander," she said. "You radiate his glory."

Alexander, pleased with her remark, walked to her and gave her a half-hearted embrace. "A gift of a son would have pleased me," he said, getting right to the point. "I thought your body was ready that night."

"My body was ready, Alexander," she said without hesitation. "Perhaps it was your body. Men always assume that something is wrong with women when conception does not occur."

Alexander grimaced and was irritated. "I am the oracle-declared Son of God, Barsine. When Zeus-Ammon is ready, I will father a child. It won't come from you insulting your king."

"It was not an insult," Barsine replied apologetically. "I spoke the truth. I have given birth to children before. I know my body—it is in perfect working order for birthing."

Alexander was growing tired of this tedious exchange and was about to dismiss his troubling mistress. However, Barsine wasn't done.

"While you were in Egypt, Alexander, I consulted several physicians. Some were Greek; some were local Ionian doctors. They will never reveal their identities for fear of your retribution, but each one feels that the problem is yours. More than one told me that your sexual potency has been reduced by excessive drink. Persian women have centuries- long traditions and special knowledge about men's virility," she added with a knowing expression on her face.

Alexander was now furious. "Get out of here," he yelled. "How much I drink is my concern. If you ever speak of this again, I will have your womb torn out and fed to the lions. Do you understand?"

Barsine realized that she had gone too far. It had been a calculated gamble. "I did not mean to offend you, Great Alexander," she said demurely. "I am trying to give you a son. You could be killed in the final battle with Darius."

"Get out!" Alexander shouted a second time.

Barsine left. Never again would she be intimate with Alexander, although she never gave up trying. Alexander found sexual pleasure and relief with Hephaestion and local eunuchs. These men-women would never trouble him with matters of conception. For now, that was all he needed.

≈

Great King Darius would have liked to have six more months to prepare for Alexander, but now his enemy was moving. The day Alexander's army left Tyre, Darius knew it one day later. The Persian fire-signaling system was still functional even if his army was not. The Macedonians were currently moving north through Syria. The Great King's provincial agents informed him that they were expected to cross the Euphrates River and charge straight south towards Babylon.

It was there that Darius' vast army waited. It was mid-summer and Darius counted on the sweltering heat of the Mesopotamian plain as an ally in the coming battle with the heathen invaders. It was a battle that must be won. The Great King and every Persian fighter knew that national survival was at stake.

"Where will they cross the Euphrates?" Darius asked his intelligence chief.

"We don't know," the officer answered. "When he makes the crossing, we will know it almost immediately. Our forces are well situated; we expect the enemy to reach Cunaxa in an enervated condition. The battle should be quick and decisive. Cunaxa's plain is ideal for our 34,000 cavalry units and hundreds of chariots. That's five times what we think Alexander has. Our total forces exceed 100,000. We think that our number is twice that of the enemy. All we must do is wait for their foolhardy rush south and the battle will be ours, Great King."

Darius recalled an earlier Cunaxa battle. Xenophon, a Greek invader, had met a disastrous defeat at the hands of the Persian Great King, Cyrus. Xenophon's book, *Anabasis*, had been required reading for every Persian leader and commander ever since. He wondered if the barbarian Alexander had read it. Perhaps he couldn't even read.

"Who watches the invaders on the ground?" Darius asked his commander.

"The satrap of Babylon, Mazaeus, is there, Great King. He has 3,000 cavalry but has orders not to encounter the enemy. He understands that he is just to observe their movements and report to us. We get daily reports from his scouts telling us of their actions. It seems that a pontoon bridge is being constructed now across the Euphrates at Thapsacus. After the crossing, we expect them to then move south along the river and fall into our trap."

Darius was pleased with the report but was still troubled. All of his battle strategy depended on Alexander moving due south and attacking his army's unassailable position. "I want to meet with you daily," he said to the intelligence chief. "Make it more often than that, if it's necessary. Inform me of any change in Alexander's movements. If he is as impetuous as he was at the River Granicus, we will have him this time."

Darius dismissed his commander and walked to an open balcony window that afforded him a sweeping view of magnificent Babylon. The great city was Persia's economic heart. Anyone who defeated a Persian army outside Babylon would effectively win his entire empire. Babylon was the doorway to Susa, the Persian administrative capitol. Persia's southernmost capitol was Persepolis. It was the empire's religious center and burial place for Persian kings. If the Persian forces failed to annihilate Alexander, all of this would be within the barbarian's easy grasp.

Darius kneeled and uttered a mumbled prayer to the Persian great god, Ahura Mazda. "Let me not be the one who loses all of this to a coarse hoard of uncivilized Macedonians," he said. "Give me wisdom and strength against these godless invaders. Make me a mighty leader; empower me as I command our forces and defeat the heathens. You have stood with your chosen people for centuries—we need your great power now."

Darius rose and walked slowly to his baths. Hot steam and water always cleared his mind. He was ready for Alexander.

≈

"The asshole thinks I'm going to charge right into his trap," Alexander exclaimed. "When I have him at my feet, I'll tell him that I keep *Anabasis* with my other books in his casket that we captured at Issus. Leonidas, my first tutor, made Cunaxa's defeat required reading for me. Xenophon's disaster won't be repeated."

"We are observed from a distance by his advance scouts," Parmenio said. "A defector informed us that Mazaeus plans a scorched earth policy

117

and then an orderly retreat to join their forces outside Babylon. You're right, Alexander. The Persians are trying to pull us into a trap."

"We're heading northeast, Parmenio. They don't expect it. I want to cross the second great river before we encounter them. What is its name?"

"It's the Tigris," Hephaestion answered. "I built a bridge over the Euphrates; I can do it again over the Tigris."

"We will draw them north, out of their excellent defensive positions near Cunaxa," Alexander said. "It's cooler there; we won't be withered in the summer heat as they want. I can barely breathe here. Let the summer pass — along with their advantage. Our supply lines will be more established there as well.

"I want better maps of where we are going, Parmenio. Have the Persian defector create one from what he recalls. Once we pull Darius north, I want to know where he might go. They may slightly outnumber us by the time of battle. I even want that. It will result in a more crushing defeat when we win this final battle. Persia will be ours by late fall."

≈

Fatefully, Darius left his unassailable defensive position northwest of Babylon to pursue Alexander. He chose what he considered another site that would afford him the best chances of encountering the enemy, near the ancient city of Arbela. Close to the small city of Gaugamela, he began leveling the anticipated battleground to give his cavalry and scythed chariots maximum fighting advantage. It wasn't as good as Cunaxa, but Alexander would still be at a disadvantage.

Macedonian scouts detected the Persian's move north, and Alexander reacted quickly by crossing the Tigris River northwest of Mosul. It was now early fall and the heat of summer was slowly subsiding.

A month later, the two armies made scouting contact with each other and initial skirmishes resulted in Alexander's forces gaining the hilltops above Gaugamela's battlefield. Alexander spent days observing and counting his enemy's disposition As best he could tell, the Persians forces exceeded 100,000 — mostly in cavalry. His allied Greeks and Macedonians numbered only 47,000.

Alexander had underestimated Darius' ability to raise new recruits. A new Macedonian battle plan was now essential, a plan that modified Alexander's usual battle tactics to counter the enormous Persian numerical advantage.

Alexander rested his army while he worked on a new strategy. Facing him was a challenging set of military requirements. Failure would mean death and humiliation for him and his fighters. The stakes were enormous.

Days passed during which the king rarely saw his officers. Each of them knew that their leader must come up with a new model of tactical creativity that was different from past formations that he had employed at Granicus and Issus. Somehow, the Macedonians and Greeks had to convert a numerical weakness into a strength.

≈

Just before the battle, Darius made a third and final attempt at a negotiated peace settlement. Almost in desperation, he offered all Persian territory west of the Euphrates, 30,000 talents for his wife, mother, and daughter, and Alexander's marriage to one of his daughters. Finally, he offered to let Alexander keep his son, Ochus, as a permanent hostage.

"He doesn't know that his wife just had a miscarriage and died," Alexander said wryly. "It was the second time I had tried to impregnate her. She may have been the most beautiful woman in Asia, but she clearly wasn't mothering stock."

Alexander's companions laughed knowingly. More than one of them had been intimate with poor Stateira. Several believed that it was they who had made her pregnant, not Alexander. Some, like Parmenio, thought that both miscarriages had been the result of Barsine's actions. No one knew the truth.

"Allow one of Stateira's eunuchs to escape and make his way to the Persian lines," Alexander said with a pitiless look on his face. "I want Darius mourning when we meet."

"You must take Darius' new offer to our war council," Parmenio said. "It's attractive. If I were Alexander, I would accept."

"So would I, if I were Parmenio," Alexander shot back. "The offer will go to our war council this afternoon, but I already know their decision. The die is cast. Tomorrow, we will meet Darius for the final time. Their offer is insulting and worthless."

≈

Parmenio sat on a sturdy field stool with his head lowered. He was more than frustrated. Meeting late in his private tent with his son, Philotas, and his son-in-law, Coenus, the trio evaluated Alexander's behavior the night before the great battle.

"I will never see my homeland again," Parmenio lamented. "He aims to conquer the entire world. That was never our mission. Neither Philip, the Corinthian League, nor most Macedonians would ever have supported this insanity. I think he is afraid of returning to Macedonia. His demons are strongest there. He lives for the intoxicating elation that comes from incessant, nearly impossible conquest."

"Give him one more victory, father," Philotas said. "Perhaps then he will slow down and let some of us return. He needs you now, but once he stops moving east, others of us can take your place. I must admit that I am thrilled by the victories."

Coenus was more critical of Alexander's most recent actions. He considered his rejection of Darius' offer of great Persian land tracts and gold to be folly. "His nightly drinking is clouding his judgment," he said. "He's also experienced a personality change. He became a different person after Siwah. Back home, the Assembly of Fighting Macedonians would never tolerate his manipulation of facts and events. We are but toys to help him achieve some mystical destiny that his mother pounded into his head. Already, unrest is starting in the phalanx ranks."

"I will not support him forever," Parmenio said ominously. "He knows that. He has started removing my relatives and supporters from key command positions. You two are immune, right now, because of your heroism and leadership. That could change if his disregard for our needs continues."

"Father, you grow more alarmist with the years," Philotas said as he rose and put his hands on Parmenio's broad and powerful shoulders. "Things are not as bad as the two of you think. Let's get through this next decisive battle. Then I will approach Alexander and reason with him. His brilliant mind always responds to reason."

"We've said enough," Parmenio said as he rose and walked his relatives to his tent's entrance. "Speak to no one of our feelings. We could be killed for what was said. I will help him win tomorrow, as I always have. We'll give the situation more time. Events sometimes saved Philip. Perhaps they will save us. I will see you both on the battle line. Rest well."

Parmenio couldn't sleep. He realized that his options were few. Not a religious man, he managed a short prayer to Zeus asking for not only victory but also for wisdom in dealing with an increasingly difficult monarch. Just before sunrise, he fell into a dreamless sleep.

≈

Alexander did not finalize his battle plan until the night before the battle. When he did complete it, he was at peace with himself. Then, with haughty self-satisfaction, he drank himself to sleep.

He awakened late the next day and lingered in his bed. He knew that the act showed bravado and supreme confidence in his plan. The impression it left on his men was one of confusion. His absence forced Parmenio to go to the king's bedroom to make sure he was up. Finally, Alexander emerged, bright and full of energy.

Standing on a small hill, well back from the front lines, he exhorted his commanders. "Everything I know about tactics has gone into this plan," he began. "It shows that great leaders must accept what the gods give us and make it work. That is what I have done. My first challenge was to minimize the numerical advantage that Darius has over us.

"Here is how we will do it: It's going to be a battle of wings, theirs and ours. I want our line to appear weaker than it really is, inviting an early Persian charge of their more numerous cavalry. Look at this map. Here, and here, I have strengthened our wings. Both wings will be slanted back at a forty-five degree angles. Our cavalry units on the right wing will hide

121

a massed group of mercenaries. More than we have ever allowed in past battles, Greek mercenaries and infantry will protect our rear.

"The battle will begin with an invitation to exploit our seeming weakness on the left and right wings. Everything is based on us absorbing their initial charge. We will even let great numbers of them through. This will let them think that their charge will be decisive. As I have done before, I will wait for a gap to occur. It always does. Timing and patience will be critical, so every commander must wait for my signals. Flags will give some signals; others will come from trumpets."

Alexander's commanders were spellbound as they watched and listened. Their king's plan involved a series of brilliant, high-risk tactics, but it would probably work. No one doubted that he had out-strategized the Persians again.

The king then addressed only his Corinthian League and Thessalian troops. His Macedonians didn't need pre-battle motivation; they were ready for the killing to start. He told the fighters that eternal glory was about to be theirs. Riches beyond their imagination were about to make them and their families wealthy.

Aristander gave the ceremony a favorable prophetic cast and all was ready. Everything depended on Darius becoming impatient and making a premature charge. Alexander was confident that Zeus-Ammon would force the Great King to take the required action.

≈

The battle started with both armies moving sideways, like a crab. Each commander knew the other's oblique advance tactics and they would not be drawn into battle before their formations were ready. However, this positioning soon worked to Alexander's advantage. Both sides' battle lines were moving toward rougher and higher land that Darius had not cleared.

The Great King, sensing loss of field advantage for his cavalry and chariots, launched the Persian attack. Bessus, the satrap of Bactria, charged his massed cavalry against Alexander's advancing right wing.

It was an anticipated and much-welcomed action. Desperately, Alexander fought a holding action against Persian forces that greatly outnumbered his own, while keeping an eye on the Persian center.

Darius then launched a scythed chariot attack as a diversion, but the Macedonian phalanx handled it easily. Loosed next were all of the Persian cavalry on both flanks. The mayhem of battle exploded into full conflict as fighters on both sides screamed and began the process of tearing apart enemy bodies. Horses were falling all around and the air was filled with arrows and javelins from both sides.

At last, Alexander spotted a weakness in Darius' left-center. The predicted gap always occurred when the enemy launched his full assault.

"Form the wedge," he shouted. With a fury that reflected his personality, Alexander led his Companion Cavalry straight into the weakened left-center. Remarkably, the tide of battle shifted in just a few minutes.

Bessus looked around and saw what had happened. He was out of contact with Darius and feared that Alexander's wild charge would swing around, encircle him, and destroy his cavalry units. He sounded the retreat and led his forces away from the battle scene.

Because of Bessus' withdrawal, Alexander's infantry and cavalry charge was close to encircling Darius. Persia's Great King suddenly gave up the fight and fled. He had done the same thing at Issus.

Alexander's wedge continued its deadly charge and was about to pursue Darius when a rider galloped up to him and told him that Parmenio's Thessalians were in jeopardy. "Indian and Persian cavalry have penetrated his line!" the scout yelled. "He needs you, now!"

Alexander took most of his cavalry and fought to their left. Parmenio was right; his situation was grave. "Don't let them circle back into Parmenio's fighters," Alexander yelled as they advanced closer to Parmenio's line.

However, the Persian's wild charge, under Mazaeus' able command, did not circle back against Parmenio. Instead, they keep riding at a breakneck pace until they entered Alexander's baggage camp, fifty stadia beyond the battle line. There, they began killing, looting, and freeing what Persian prisoners they could find. Soon, they were driven out of the camp, and they headed back to what they thought was a stable and soon-to-be victorious Persian battle line.

Charging straight at them was Alexander and his cavalry. Fierce, hand-to-hand combat started and killing ruled on both sides. Alexander nearly received a mortal blow more than once, but slowly, the tide of this encounter flowed to the Macedonians' side.

Mazaeus saw that both Darius and Bessus were in full retreat and broke off from the pursuing Alexander and Parmenio's recovering Thessalian fighters. It was nearly over.

"Wrap up here, Parmenio," Alexander yelled to his second-in-command. The old man had fought valiantly. Without his superb defensive efforts, the battle could not have been won. "I'm going after Darius," the king shouted. "I'll get the bastard this time."

≈

Darius fled, once again, into his empire's eastern provinces. Bessus and his Bactria cavalry soon joined him. Only 2,000 Greek mercenaries and some stragglers from the Great King's Royal guard accompanied him.

Gaugamela was a staggering Persian defeat. Darius' army had suffered 53,000 killed. The rest were either enslaved or in flight.

Alexander lost just 1,000 foot soldiers and 200 cavalrymen.

Ancient Babylon awaited the new Lord of Asia.

Ruins of Pella, Macedonia – Greece
Photograph by the author

Peter Messmore

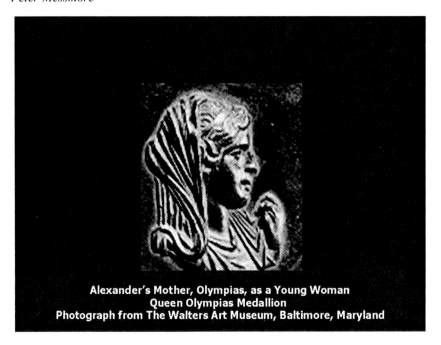

Alexander's Mother, Olympias, as a Young Woman
Queen Olympias Medallion
Photograph from The Walters Art Museum, Baltimore, Maryland

126

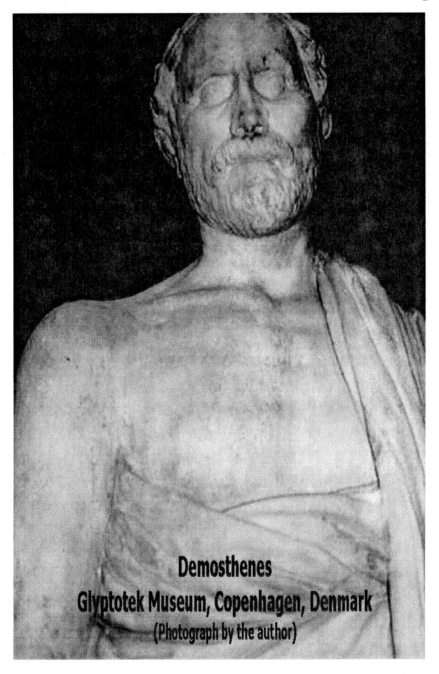

Demosthenes
Glyptotek Museum, Copenhagen, Denmark
(Photograph by the author)

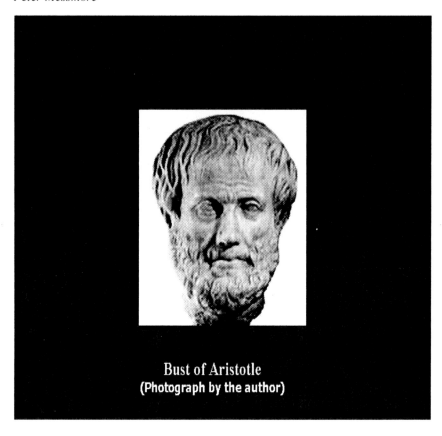

Bust of Aristotle
(Photograph by the author)

Aristotle's School at Mieza (Near Naoussa, Macedonia)
(Photographs by the author)

Alexander the King at Issus
He was twenty years old
(Photograph by the author at the National Museum, Naples, Italy)

Alexander as Pharaoh, Temple of Luxor, Luxor, Egypt

(Photograph by the author)

The Apadana in Persepolis (modern Iran)
Photograph by Monsur San: *The Land of Mehrmah. Used with Permission of Photographer*

CHAPTER 13

PERSIA'S HEART: BABYLON, SUSA & PARSA

"Stunning! Beautiful! The city is a prize worth dying for," Alexander said as he and his army approached Babylon. His forces were in full battle formation, fearing treachery from Mazaeus, the Persian satrap of Babylon. "Don't relax our battle readiness, Parmenio," he commanded. "I fear a trap."

Imposing Babylon lay before them. Its great walls created a rough square, each side nearly 125 stadia. The horizontal surfaces of the city's prodigious outer walls were so wide that two chariots, pulled by four horses each, could travel side-by-side. Even from this distance, Alexander could see that the walls were made of mud-brick, held together with the strange, black substance about which he had just learned. It was bitumen.

As Alexander waited, assessing the magnificent city's possible dangers, he heard the sound of trumpets and cymbals. Then, led by Mazaeus himself, a procession appeared from the main gate. Behind Mazaeus were groups of Babylon's leading citizens, a dour group of Chaldaean priests, and an unarmed squadron of the Great King's royal cavalry.

The Babylonian entourage turned out to be peaceful. Through a translator, they offered King Alexander the city. He boarded a royal chariot, still under heavy guard by his Royal Companions and personal bodyguards, and entered Babylon through the Processional Way. Its tall walls, built by Nebuchadnezzar, were made of deep blue, fire-glazed bricks. Covering the walls at regular intervals were ornate, highly stylized bulls and dragons. At the end of the Way was the Ishtar Gate, standing before a large square.

Alexander looked up as his chariot went under the Gate. He saw hundreds of impressive lapis and gold inlaid tiles and smiled. Above the Gate were Babylon's citizens cheering their new conqueror and showering him with a blizzard of rose petals. Piles of rich spices smoldered in small, richly decorated alters along the procession way. The air was filled with exotic smells and fragrances, causing Alexander's senses to soar. He and his Macedonians had never experienced such a scene.

"They know what happened to Tyre," Alexander remarked to Hephaestion riding at his side. "A victory like Tyre causes more surrenders without any loss of life on either side. I'll have Callisthenes develop this story more as we move east."

At last, the conquerors' came to the city center where trumpet blasts increased to a deafening crescendo. Alexander raised his arms, accepting the acclaim. Slowly, he turned inside his chariot in a series of full circles.

Parmenio, still riding on horseback behind his king, frowned.

The trumpet blasts finally stopped, and Mazaeus walked before Alexander. Speaking through a translator, he raised his hands and began. "Great conqueror, Alexander, Pharaoh of Upper and Lower Egypt, beloved of your great god Zeus-Ammon, I give you the city of Babylon."

Babylon's citizens issued a muffled cheer. Alexander noted that it was far more subdued than the wild acclamation he heard upon entering the Ishtar Gate.

Mazaeus continued. "All of your officers and most of your men will be honored by the citizens of Babylon. Starting tonight each will be a guest in a private house somewhere in the city. You will drink our wine and taste our native food. I know that you have never had such an eating experience as what awaits you. As many women as you desire will present themselves for your pleasure. Nine months from now Babylon will begin to have both a Macedonian and Persian population."

There was a roar of laughter after the translation, and Alexander felt that the reception was genuine. Nevertheless, he was still cautious. "Place units around the perimeter of the city," he quietly commanded Parmenio as both men walked toward the center of the square. "Rotate them regularly, allowing all of our men to revel in what appears to be a full Babylonian capitulation."

Mazaeus continued. "Come with me, Great Alexander. Babylon's wonders await you. We shall first visit our Hanging Gardens. I know the Greeks have heard of them. They were built for a Persian king's wife who longed for the dense forests of her native Iran."

The new ruler of great Babylon started the tour like any wide-eyed diplomat from the east. What could be more wonderful than possession of this stunning city, he thought. How could he ever surpass this grand personal achievement?

The triumphant day continued, and every Macedonian in Alexander's army knew that every sacrifice they had made had been worth it.

≈

Alexander enjoyed the tour for most of the day, and then told Mazaeus what was really on his mind: Babylon's monetary treasure.

"The royal treasury must be turned over to me immediately," he told Mazaeus. "My men have sacrificed everything. Soon, I will reward them with more than wine, food, and women. Babylon's entire treasure will go to them. Gold means little to me, except for its power to continue my conquests."

"Babylon's riches await you, Alexander," a surprised Mazaeus said. "Here is a written account of our treasury. The city's riches, plus what you will seize at Susa, will make you the wealthiest man in the world. Not even the combined Greek city-state treasuries can approach what you are about to receive."

Alexander examined the clay tablets showing Babylon's vast treasury balance. As a Persian scribe made oral account to him in Greek, he smiled and knew that his economic troubles were over.

He was now at a crossroads in his campaign. After Susa's occupation, he knew that Parmenio and many of his Macedonian supporters would consider the campaign at an end. Territorial stabilization, then eventual return to Macedonia would be their demand. Clearly, he must take immediate action that would alter that demand.

"I am impressed with your actions, Mazaeus," the king said. "Inform your citizens that I intend to honor your ancient religious heritage. In time, I may even restore Babylon's ziggurat and the Esagila Temple honoring your god. This will depend on my future success, but nothing can stop that now."

135

Mazaeus bowed and smiled. "You are gracious in victory, Alexander," he said. "Respecting our religion will mean everything to Babylon's citizens. The priesthood will be the last group to serve you, but this decision is a good start."

Alexander continued. "You will retain your position as satrap of Babylon," the king told Mazaeus. "But your full duties will be reduced. There will be a Macedonian garrison commander here when I leave. A Macedonian finance officer will direct the collection of taxes. If you violate these arrangements, I will remove and execute you. Is that clear?"

"Perfectly," Mazaeus answered solemnly.

Alexander dismissed Mazaeus and sent for Callesthenes. His command to him would delay the scholar's personal enjoyment of Babylon's alluring temptations.

≈

"I'm told that the Babylonians have astrological records that go back 31,000 years, Callesthenes," Alexander said to his chief historian. "Is that possible?"

"It appears so, Alexander," Callisthenes answered. "I am just beginning to organize and group the artifacts now. It's not an easy task because none of us knows how to read their strange orthography. Full examination of the records and translation into Greek will take years."

Alexander grew pensive and suddenly realized what he had conquered. Persia's empire was more than gold, treasure and the Great King's vast lands. Persia had a cultural and intellectual history that was far deeper than either he or Aristotle ever dreamed. That profound realization swept over him and caused continued silence.

"Send the records back to Macedonia, then on to Aristotle in Athens after your survey is complete," he told Callisthenes at last. "They are too valuable to take with us on the rest of the campaign. Who knows what priceless knowledge is contained in them."

"It will be done," Callisthenes answered. Then, he changed the subject. "I have the first draft describing your latest victories. I would like for you to read them while we enjoy Babylon."

"I will," Alexander answered. "Future written records must be carefully done, however. Some of our men, chief among them Parmenio, think we are nearing the end. We are not.

"I want a rationale developed why we must continue east. I will write some reasoning points for you to consider. Work them into your draft. We will write the final record together. I don't want any homesick feelings adversely affecting morale. Do you understand me?"

"I do, Alexander," Callesthenes replied. "Send me your ideas and I will expand them. I will support the concepts you want included. This expedition is the opportunity of a lifetime for me. No other scholar may ever have this chance to gain and categorize so much new knowledge."

Alexander grasped Callesthenes' shoulders and thanked him for his service. The two left the luxuriant Babylonian audience room together.

The king then called for Hephaestion. It was time for them to see what this striking city was really like.

≈

A month later, in late fall, Alexander moved on to Susa. It was the Persian Great King's principal residence and administrative center. Here, the Royal Road ended. It was also the location of Darius' court.

Alexander had sent Philoxenus ahead to Susa after the Gaugamela victory, while he waited to move south to Babylon. Philoxenus' orders were to demand the city's surrender and secure its treasure. Nearing Susa, Alexander received good news.

"Philoxenus has obtained Susa's surrender," a scout announced to his king. "Persia's national treasury is safe and under Macedonian guard." The scout handed Alexander a scroll that confirmed his verbal report and rode off.

"They won't all surrender as easily as Babylon and Susa," Alexander told his riding companion, Craterus. "Enjoy this while it lasts."

Nevertheless, Craterus roared with laughter and rejoiced with his king. "I want to tell my phalanx fighters about this, Alexander," he said. "They need good news. Most are questioning why we continue deeper into Persia."

Alexander was irritated with his friend's remark. His men's growing unrest was not news to him. "I don't want my officers speaking of this, Craterus," he shot back. "Soon, Persia's entire treasury will be mine. Then I will make our fighters an offer that will quell any dissatisfaction. You must keep morale high until I can make my move. Don't say anything about this. Parmenio must be kept guessing."

Craterus frowned, and then answered Alexander. "The only thing that will improve morale is to make your fighters rich, Alexander. They demand more than women and victories."

"That's enough, Craterus," Alexander commanded sharply. "Leave me! Have Harpalus join me. I'm formulating a plan and I want his assistance. Before long, I will handle your concerns. Speak to no one about this conversation."

Craterus rode off to seek Harpalus. He knew that his king was up to the challenge of his army's growing unrest. For now, he would be silent.

$$\approx$$

Abuleites, the satrap of Susa, met Alexander at Susa's gate and escorted him to the city center. "Secure the city," he told Parmenio. "I'm going to the palace and the treasury. Gold matters most now. Harpalus, come with me."

Each of the Great King's palaces seemed to get more luxurious. Alexander strode arrogantly through the great hypostyle corridor, covered with rich wall coverings of glazed brick. Eventually, he entered the treasury itself. What awaited him would change everything.

"Give me an accounting," he commanded Abuleites through a translator.

"There is over 40,000 talents of gold and silver," the satrap began. "The gold Darics number more than 9,000."

Alexander and Harpalus looked at each other with broad grins and expressions of astonishment. Never in their dreams did they imagine the immense value of the Great King's gold and silver hoard.

"How could one king have acquired so much?" Harpalus asked. "I wonder if there is more in Parsa."

Alexander stood in the middle of the treasury vault with his hands on his hips. He was ecstatic. "Is there more?" he finally asked Abuleites.

"Great King Xerxes appropriated many priceless objects and treasure from Greece during his invasion long ago, King Alexander. It's all in the next room. No doubt, you will want to send it back to your homeland."

"What else?" Alexander asked with a glower on his face.

"The treasury has another room," Abuleites answered. "Additional gold furnishings, silver and gold plates and personal jewelry the king and queen rarely wore is kept there. Do you wish to see it?"

"Show it all to me," Alexander said with impatience.

Gradually, he was beginning to understand what he had won. The monetary value of Persia's treasure meant little to him personally. The unlimited purchasing power that the hoard represented, however, was beyond value. *How much more will I be able to achieve now?* he asked himself. The treasure validated him. Beyond anyone's doubt, he had already surpassed his ancestor Heracles' and Philip's achievements. The achievement was worthy of Zeus-Ammon's son.

"Is that all?" he asked again.

"The Great King's throne room is a priceless, national treasure, King Alexander," Abuleites answered. "May I take you there?"

"Lead the way," Alexander answered.

"Remain here, Harpalus, and make a Greek accounting of this cache. We will meet tomorrow to decide how to use it. Darius didn't understand that money must be used, not hoarded. It perpetuates a king's reign.

"Think about what just happened. Darius is running for his life while his vast treasure sets here, useless to him. That will never happen to me."

The king left with Abuleites. Harpalus sent for twenty of his fiscal assistants. It would take them the rest of the day and most of the night even to begin the task that Alexander had set before them.

≈

Darius' throne room was indeed a Persian national treasure. Entering it, Alexander's first impression was of the great beauty of the blue, glazed-brick tile reliefs on both end walls. As he walked about the great room, he strolled on a shinning floor of malachite and marble. A forest of granite columns lined both sides of the entry corridor. The conquering king glanced left and right as he continued his way toward the throne. Each column he passed was trimmed in malachite and gold. Persian bulls, unicorn-like animals, horned lions, and winged griffins were inlaid into each of the columns. Alexander saw cords of white and violet flaxen attached on one end to the columns. The other ends supported silken canopies that covered the chamber's ceiling. They gently wafted in a light breeze and resembled clouds.

At the end of the chamber was the empty throne, beneath the magnificent golden plane tree. Alexander smiled and knew that the throne was waiting just for him.

He strode confidently up to the throne and, with some difficulty, seated himself on its seat. It was apparent that Great King Darius was a much taller man than the conqueror who now occupied the seat of Persian power. Alexander's feet dangled in the air, not even coming close to reaching the solid gold footstool beneath them.

An alert Macedonian page saw what had happened and saved the embarrassing moment. In a swift, two-step move, he jerked up the golden footstool and replaced it with a small table. Now, the King of Macedon, Pharaoh of Upper and Lower Egypt, and son of Zeus-Ammon had a solid resting place for his royal feet. It all seemed like a fitting omen.

≈

The Persian satrap, Ariobarzanes, thought that he had figured out Alexander's next moves. Any sane general would go into winter quarters at Susa, consolidate his position, and rest his troops. It was the beginning of a bitter winter, and Ariobarzanes knew the territory around Susa well. He intended to use the towering Zagros Mountains, adjacent to Susa, as his ally. Even in a worst-case scenario, he could slow down Alexander's advance.

"They will wait in Susa until spring," Ariobarzanes told his commanders as he pointed to a map. "Then, they will move in one of two directions: either northeast to Ecbatana or south-east toward Parsa and Pasargadae."

His commanders smiled and saw immediately what their leader was proposing.

"I now have 25,000 infantry and 700 cavalry. When he moves, we will fortify the Susian Gates and engage him. He is now in our land; I know how to use it against him. I will not repeat past mistakes.

"This delaying action will give Great King Darius in Ecbatana more time to raise additional fighters. The coming third battle with this barbarian is going to be different. We will have their Greek asses this time."

His officers roared with laughter and shouted their approval. Each left the meeting in high spirits. They knew that their great god, Ahura Mazda, would be with them when Persia's national existence was at stake. They could not fail this time.

≈

Alexander did not winter in Susa. Nor did he do what Ariobarzanes predicted. He sent Parmenio southeast toward Parsa while he led a smaller group of more lightly armed fighters over the Zagros Mountains to encounter Ariobarzanes at the Susian Gates. The king knew that the Persians would never expect this division of his forces.

Five days later Alexander's forces were at the Susian Gates. Initially, Ariobarzanes beat back the Macedonians and inflicted heavy casualties.

141

Bloodied but undaunted, Alexander abandoned his direct assault tactics. He left Craterus at the Gate, then led a smaller group of commandos over a little-known trail and came up behind the Persian defenders. The rest was a massacre. Ariobarzanes escaped with only 700 of his cavalry and retreated to Ecbatana, where Darius waited. Once again, the Persians had failed to react to Alexander's unpredictable tactics. Their time was running out.

≈

"They call it Parsa," Alexander said as he toured the most holy city in the Persian Empire. His army had now been there a week. "Aristotle called it Persepolis. Let all records from now on refer to it by the Greek term. It's gentler to my ears."

The holy city, north of the narrowest part of the Persian Gulf, had been long known to the Greeks as the most beautiful on earth. "It's an honor that is well deserved," Alexander remarked. Walking through the Apadana with his close inner circle that included Hephaestion, Craterus, Coenus, Erigyius, Perdiccas, and Leonnatus, the king was in a jovial mood.

They paused in a shaded area covered by great beams of carved cedar. His men formed a circle around the king and listened to his latest concern.

"I've already met with their priests and they are impassive. I told them that I'm aware of their new year's festival called Akitu. I hinted that they should include me in it, since I am the new Great King."

"What did they say?" asked Perdiccas.

"I received silence," Alexander answered. "Not a protest, not a lecture, just silence."

"Did you kill any of them?" asked Hephaestion. "Death always gets Persians' attention."

"They would die happily," Alexander answered. "Besides, that isn't what I want. I want them to recognize me as the chosen of Ahura Mazda. I explained that this had already happened in Egypt. It made no impression on them. They're acting like the Jews I met south of Tyre."

142

Craterus spoke up. "The common priests and the hereditary caste the Persians and Medes call the Magi make up this opposition group. I've learned that their astrology and mythology predict the arrival of a horned beast, one who will conquer their land. They are all convinced that you are the beast, Alexander."

Alexander lowered his head and sighed. His anger was building, and today he felt like a beast. Since the capture of Babylon and Susa, he had held back his troops from ravaging any of the populations. That restraint was part of a developing plan that called for peaceful domination of the Persian Empire. "I'll give them seven days," he said at last. "Get word to their leaders that I must be acknowledged as the beloved of their deity. I won't settle for less. Tell them I will turn my men loose on Persepolis if they don't comply. They haven't had a good rampage since Gaza. I won't give the Persians another chance."

≈

The priests of Ahura Mazda and the Magi remained silent. Alexander fulfilled his threat. On the eighth day, he unleashed his men. All day and into the night private homes were invaded, adult males were killed, and women raped and mutilated. At the end of the rampage, Macedonians were fighting each other for treasure that they would eventually carry back to their homeland. Only the Great King's palaces and the royal treasury were off-limits.

When the looting subsided, Harpalus and Alexander once again inspected more national treasure from conquered Persia. Persepolis' reserves were even greater than Susa's. "What is the tally, Harpalus?" Alexander asked his treasurer.

"I'm aghast," Harpalus said. "We have discovered 120,000 talents, some of the coins are very old. Darius didn't think he needed it against you. The king's bedroom alone yielded 8,000 golden talents. The palace furnishings and personal jewelry nearly equal the other two sources. Combined, it is more than Athens could have taken in for hundreds of years during her empire days. I can't believe our good fortune."

Alexander smiled a nervous smile. He was now the richest man in the world. For the first time since he had left Macedonia, deeply in debt and embarking on a nearly hopeless mission, he no longer feared having enough money to do what his destiny demanded. The treasure's vast sum also allowed him to launch a plan that he had been developing for some time.

"When the time is right, Harpalus, I'm going to reorganize my army," he began. "Commanders at every level will either be sent back home, reassigned, or eliminated. I will also allow any of our Macedonians, Thessalian, or Greek league fighters to return home. I will use Persia's treasure to buy support from now on. Those that stay with me will be enriched. However, if they take the money, they must continue east without protest. This is a critical time in my reign, and I want the reorganization done without trouble."

Alexander could see that Harpalus wasn't surprised. He had hinted at this action before. "When will this happen?" Harpalus asked.

"Soon," Alexander answered. "Only you and a few others know about it. Keep it that way. Timing is everything.

"I want you to estimate what amount we will be able to pay returning infantry and cavalrymen. Infantry should receive one-sixth what the cavalry gets. Calculate the numbers and let me know what's possible."

"It will take some time, Alexander, but I understand your plan," Harpalus answered. "How long do I have?"

"The army will go on to Ecbatana when the time is right. Have a report ready for me by then. Arrange also for the treasure to be taken out of Persepolis. Soon, it will no longer exist."

With that cryptic comment, the king and Harpalus parted. Alexander had much to do.

≈

"This is your most outrageous act yet," Parmenio shouted at Alexander. "Burning Persepolis is destroying your own property." Parmenio saw that Alexander was furious and watched his hand move toward his dagger. Just as quickly, the king's hand relaxed.

"Xerxes burned Greek temples," Alexander shot back. "What is the difference?"

"If you can't see the difference between a few temples of Macedon's Greek tormentors and this beautiful city, then I pity you," Parmenio said. "You will never be acknowledged as the Persian spiritual leader if you do this." Parmenio's eyes were bulging and distinct veins stood out from his neck.

"That's enough!" Alexander yelled. "I didn't have to tell you. It will happen tonight at the banquet. Go to our troops around the city and make sure that they know this is their king's actions and not an enemy attack."

Parmenio glared an ugly stare at Philip's son. *Why in Zeus' name did I ever support this little shit's accession,* he asked himself silently. *I had my opportunity then. It's too late now. I'm getting too old for all of this,* he concluded silently. He decided to appeal to Alexander's personality.

"History, a subject that you love, will never forgive you for this, Alexander," he finally said. "Calm down; give it more thought. More than the city will burn if you destroy Persepolis."

"Don't threaten me, Parmenio," Alexander shot back. "Get yourself to our men. The decision has been made. Remember your place. Every man in my command structure can be replaced, even you!"

Parmenio had endured as much of the overbearing youth as he could stand. He left Alexander and rode to join his men. The air was clearer there, and he knew that most of them adored him. That knowledge would sustain him a little longer.

≈

That night Alexander got very drunk at the banquet.

Late in the evening, Ptolemy's mistress, Thais, shouted a garbled challenge to Persia's new Great King. "What a good idea it would be if King Alexander burned down what remained of beautiful Persepolis. Every Greek will honor you for it," she muttered drunkenly.

The king hadn't put her up to it, but he seized the moment. He called for torches and then led a procession of over twenty fellow-drunks through the Great King's royal palace. Amid the playing of flutes and banging of cymbals, he and the others casually lit silken drapes and wooden doors. Flames spread quickly and soon, the enormous, carved cedar beams from far off Lebanon had started to burn.

The igniting procession lasted until well after midnight. At last, the king's drunken entourage was forced out of the palace by threatening, palace-eating flames. The king's rowdy group then fled to the desert and watched as the raging fire consumed the ancient city.

The spiritual center of Persia for several millennia was soon engulfed in a mighty conflagration. The fire was seen for hundreds of stadia.

≈

Parmenio stood with his men watching the palace's destruction. Most of them cheered, but the old general was saddened. None of this was necessary. Alexander's new command style was fast becoming one of revenge and vindictiveness. The old general knew that he would not be protected very long from the king's developing fury.

A deadly contest had started between the two and he intended to see his family again in Macedonia. Like Alexander, he had much to do.

CHAPTER 14

HUNTING DARIUS

"Here's my plan, Harpalus," Alexander said to his treasurer. "Persia's wealth allows me to now have mostly paid soldiers. I'm disbanding all Corinthian League troops. Cavalrymen's severance bonus will be 6,000 drachmas; each infantryman will get 1,000. This is in addition to their regular pay.

"Seleucus, get all of this organized. I want all of Parmenio's supporters out of camp by week's end. Give them an escort to the Mediterranean coast.

"Nearchus, leave today and assemble enough ships to take them back as far as Euboea. They can make their way home from there. I expect them to be a stabilizing influence throughout Greece and Macedonia. I already informed Antipater of these actions."

"Are they all going?" Ptolemy asked. "These men comprise our core fighters; they helped us get where we are."

Alexander frowned, then responded to Ptolemy. "I will encourage any man who is not known to be a supporter of Parmenio to reenlist as a soldier of fortune. Those that do will receive 18,000 drachmas. That should insure their allegiance to me. Nevertheless, those who have sided with Parmenio in recent months are leaving. Only his sons, Philotas and Nicanor, will continue to hold command positions."

The king forced a prolonged silence and then continued. "Parmenio is bringing Darius' treasure here in the next several days. I'm ordering him to remain in Ecbatana as the area's regional commander. Some local pacification there is still necessary. He's seventy now and will not be able to keep up with us as we chase Darius. I will appoint a new chief of staff before our departure."

The meeting ended, and only Hephaestion and Alexander remained in the king's command tent. "Hephaestion, this is what I have wanted since becoming king. From now on, I will control everything. Darius' capture will be the culminating moment. I will demand that he declare me Great King of Persia and may even let him live."

"Your actions were taken just in time," Hephaestion said. "Parmenio's plots were getting harder to discover. His supporters have become more secretive in the last months. This will end all of that."

"You've done well to keep him in check, Hephaestion. Tell no one of these plans. Know this too: Parmenio must be eliminated before long. I can't have him at my rear or even in Macedonia. His military skills would overwhelm Antipater.

"Enough of this! Let's get drunk the way we did after Chaeronea."

Alexander called for slaves to bring more wine as he and Hephaestion started a long evening of mind-numbing drinking. Swallowing a huge gulp of his father's favorite blend, Alexander gave his friend a command. "Watch for a situation while I'm chasing Darius that will allow me to remove Parmenio. I want it done in a way that Philotas and Nicanor will not lead a rebellion against me. Both of them are strong leaders and have supporters in my army.

"You're good at these intrigues, Hephaestion," Alexander continued. "Observe events and let me know when it is time. Tell no one what you are doing," he said a second time. "When I capture Darius, we will discuss your recommendations. Everything must be done with care. No blame can be placed on me. I want an event that will put Parmenio in a hopeless situation, one from which he cannot escape. Do you understand?"

Hephaestion smiled. Alexander was right: he was good at this sort of thing. "I understand perfectly," he answered. "I'll set it up. You won't be disappointed."

The two friends continued drinking until the middle of the night, and then fell asleep beside each other on the king's huge bed. Alexander had left orders with his bodyguards that they were to be awakened at dawn. The King of Macedon had a deadly mission ahead of him running down the Great King of Persia.

≈

Darius looked like an enormous, emaciated skeleton. Since Alexander's invasion of his empire, he had lost half of his body weight. None of his royal robes or uniforms fit him, and he had recently started wearing field uniforms borrowed from his generals. His face was pockmarked with acne scars and his hair had started to thin prematurely. At times, he wondered if his great god would take him before Alexander did.

"Why didn't those damn reinforcements arrive?" Darius shouted to his top commanders. They were gathered in a small encampment, five days ahead of the pursuing Alexander. "I wanted one last chance at Alexander. Now, all we can do is run.

"If we can make it through the Caspian Gates, I'll order the destruction of all land we pass through. By the time we move along the Caspian Sea into Bactria, Alexander will encounter nothing but burned wasteland as he pursues us. I know that he has completely outrun his communication and supply lines. It is our only hope."

The Great King examined his generals and commanders. Most looked as bad as he felt. Two groups of subordinates had developed during the Great King's ragged retreat from Alexander. One was lead by the Bactrian satrap and general, Bessus. He was of royal Achaemenid blood and was a natural leader of men in battle. The aging Artabazus, supported by the still effective Greek mercenaries, led the other group. Artabazus' group was still loyal to Darius.

Bessus' followers were wavering in support of the Great King. Darius' cowardly retreat now precipitated them to act. Nabarzanes, one of Darius' grand viziers, revealed his true allegiance by rising and approaching his monarch. Not a scintilla of proskynesis was given as he walked boldly before the human shell that was Darius. Only in this time of national catastrophe would he ever dare to approach the Great King and make a proposal such as the one that emerged from his lips.

"Great King, Bactrians, and my fellow Persians," he began. "Darius has lost what little leadership ability he ever had. Alexander has defeated him three times. If we follow his limp retreat strategy, he will be defeated a fourth and final time. We are all going to die."

Tension in the group was palpable but Nabarzanes continued. "Only Bessus can save Persia. Look at Darius! He is completely demoralized and can only flee."

Darius could take no more. With all of the strength that he could gather, he drew his royal scimitar and launched a vicious attack at Nabarzanes. "You traitorous bastard," he yelled.

At the last possible moment, men from the opposing groups surrounded the king and stopped the assault. The fury that had provoked the attack subsided and superficial calm returned.

A half day later, the Persians finally agreed that Darius should still have their support, at least for now. Leaders and men from the opposing camps swore allegiance to Great King Darius, avoiding a fatal split in their forces.

Their desperate, fragile agreement did not last long.

≈

Alexander and sixty of his finest horsemen had been riding at a furious pace in pursuit of Darius for days. Only the fittest of his men, like Alexander himself, would have been able to survive the relentless pursuit. Because of the oppressive heat, they rode only during the nighttime and early morning hours. What little sleep they got was in any shaded area they could find to protect them from the enervating heat of the eastern Iranian summer.

At last, on a sloping mountainside ten stadia from his riders, Alexander's keen eyes spotted a small covered wagon and a few hundred Persian soldiers. "It's them," he said. "Our spies were right. Let's get them!"

≈

Bessus and Nabarzanes saw Alexander approaching and made a quick decision. Darius had been their chained-up prisoner for the last several days, after they had broken the agreement to remain loyal to the Great King.

"Come with us, Darius!" Bessus shouted. "I'll unlock your chains and we can begin again in Bactria."

Darius looked up and said nothing. His eyes were vacant and his movements were lethargic.

"Speak, you miserable wretch," Bessus yelled contemptuously. "Either come with us or die here. Decide now!"

The specter that was former Great King Darius finally uttered his last words. "It's over," he muttered. "I'll no longer run like a rat. I choose to die here with dignity at the hands of Persia's new conqueror. You two traitors continue alone. Alexander will soon run you down."

Bessus was furious and done with words. He leaped off his horse, grabbed a spear, and stabbed Darius repeatedly in the chest. Quickly, Nabarzanes joined in the bloody assault. Each understood that Darius could not fall into Alexander's hands. The Macedonian would then use him to legitimize his claim as Persia's new Great King.

Both men and their ragged troops then split up and fled the fast-approaching Alexander by different routes. Each knew that Darius had been right in one thing: their lives were now at stake.

≈

"I've found him," Polystratus yelled to Alexander. The king had paused astride his horse high on a mountain path above him. The grizzled soldier waved his arms until Alexander saw him, and then returned to the crude wagon where Darius lay nearly dead.

The Great King, still bound in chains, had two broken spears protruding from his blood-soaked chest. A starving, mongrel dog was his only companion. Polystratus lifted Darius' head and listened for any final words. He heard only a death rattle from Persia's last Great King and watched as Darius' soul departed to join his ancient god, Ahura Mazda.

Alexander made his way down to the wagon then brought his horse to a halt. *Is this how kings end their days?* he thought as he leaped off his mount. He approached the wagon and saw Darius' dead body sprawled on the wagon's floor. "Great Zeus-Ammon," he cried out. "This is an abomination!"

Alexander removed his royal cloak and placed it over the top part of Darius' body. The sixteen-pointed star of Macedon covered the great king's head. Below it, Darius' last blood slowly started to stain the star's points. The symbolism of the moment was not lost on Alexander.

"His own men did this," Alexander said angrily. "I'll have their heads on poles for this." He turned to the soldier who had found Darius and gave him an order. "Take his body to our encampment. I want him returned to Persepolis in stately procession. He will be buried with his ancestors, in the tomb he was preparing before our invasion. I hope that someone does as much for me when it is time."

He stopped his morose lamentation, leaped on his horse, and gave a new command. "Come on, men. I want Bessus. We can't give up now and allow him to raise another army to fight us again. Another chase like the last one will eliminate their leadership threat forever."

Alexander saw his exhausted men roll their eyes, but knew that they would follow him. They always had.

However, Bessus' lead was too great and the mountain passes were hopelessly complex. Alexander had no idea where to continue the pursuit. Angry but resigned, he gave up the chase and returned to a miserable village called Hecatompylus. Even he needed rest and time to consider what had happened.

He had been so close to ending it all in that dusty mountain valley where Darius had been murdered. Now, more decisive battles lay ahead. The gods had decreed that life for him.

≈

Hephaestion was the first to greet Alexander as the exhausted king returned to his army's main camp, now established in Zadracarta. "Are you ill, Alexander?" he asked with a concerned look on his face.

Alexander, dirty, unshaven, and worn out from the breakneck chase of Darius, answered his friend. "I'm heartsick, Hephaestion," he said. "Not only did I fail to get Darius alive, it repulsed me to find him murdered by his own men. His body is back there in a wagon. Go look at it. I don't ever want to be seen that way."

Before viewing Darius' corpse, Hephaestion told Alexander of a group of senior Persian officials who had surrendered days before. "Old Artabazus is with them," he added.

"He still lives?" Alexander quipped. "I knew he was tough when I first met him years ago. Barsine will be pleased to see her father again. Treat him well; I may need him in the future."

"I'll see to it," Hephaestion said as he left to examine Darius' body.

Alexander's inner circle of young commanders approached their king and greeted him warmly. After fawning congratulations and male boasting of having finally subdued Darius, Ptolemy told Alexander of another Persian surrender.

"Nabarzanes came into camp this morning," he announced. "His surrender is unconditional. He brought great riches and gifts with him. He wants to present them personally when you are ready."

"First, I'll bathe and rest," Alexander said wearily. "Order slaves to fill Darius' tub with the hottest water. Then, I must sleep. I'll see Nabarzanes tomorrow."

"It will be done," the king's half-brother answered as Alexander turned and went to his private tent.

Ptolemy failed to tell his king that one of Nabarzanes' gifts was human. His name was Bagoas. The beautiful boy was a eunuch and he had been a lover of Great King Darius. Ptolemy was not the only one of Alexander's inner circle that was concerned with this potential temptation of their king. Every officer knew that Hephaestion would be devastated if Alexander found the youth appealing. However, Ptolemy had learned long ago that crises presented opportunities. The coming days would be interesting.

≈

At midday the following day, Alexander emerged from a night and morning of needed sleep. For once, his sleep had been natural, without any need for the stupefying effect of strong, uncut Macedonian wine. Waiting for the king were his top commanders, Aristander, Callisthenes, and Nabarzanes. The beautiful eunuch, Bagoas, stood behind Nabarzanes, out of sight of Persia's new supreme ruler.

Alexander smiled as he walked into the middle of the group. For the first time, he was no longer dressed as a Macedonian-Greek but as a Mede. Covering his freshly scrubbed and rested body were mostly Persian clothes. The king's legs were covered to the ankle with silken, multicolored trousers. His robe was white with Persian purple on its edges. On his head, was the royal crown of Darius, resplendent in blue and white. His shoes were no longer the rough leather of a Macedonian battle commander but the elegant, bejeweled slippers of his defeated, former enemy. Four of his ten fingers had large, jeweled rings on them. Each had stones that were found only in the orient. His transformation presented a stunning change to everyone waiting. Alexander knew that his appearance had the effect that he wanted as he approached Nabarzanes.

"Darius is dead," he said to Nabarzanes through a translator. "I am Persia's new Great King. Do you acknowledge me?"

Nabarzanes kneeled, prostrated himself in the loose dirt before Alexander, and gave the expected proskynesis. Then, from his lowly, horizontal position, he spoke. "You have won Persia by the spear, Alexander," he said. "I recognize you as Persia's Great King."

"Get up, Nabarzanes," Alexander commanded. "For this recognition, I give you your life. It remains to be seen what I will do with you."

Nabarzanes rose, dusted off his clothes, and began his presentation of gifts to Alexander. First, was the lovely eunuch Bagoas.

"His name is Bagoas," he began. "Look at his skin. No woman in Persia has such a flawless complexion. If he appeals to you, he is yours."

Alexander was taken immediately by the young boy's remarkable beauty and showed it. He walked over to him and stroked his luxuriant hair and smooth face. "Your skin is smoother than Hephaestion's," he said ominously. "I'm pleased with this gift, Nabarzanes. The boy alone will ensure a hopeful future for you."

Nabarzanes started to present his remaining gifts but was stopped by Alexander. "Later," the king said. With that curt remark, he took Bagoas' hand and walked him to his private tent. No one would see the new Great King of Persia for the rest of that day and evening.

≈

That evening, accounts of the day's events spread through the Macedonian camp like dust from an Afghan sandstorm. Alexander's altered appearance was ridiculed first. Many asked if they had risked their lives for four years so that he could give up his Macedonian identity. Then there was the eunuch. Did it mean that Hephaestion was out and Alexander's oriental conversion had been so complete that even his sexual preferences had turned Persian? Some mid-level officers even asked if they would now have to perform proskynesis every time they wanted an audience with Alexander.

At the same time, over a hundred soldiers, mostly Parmenio supporters, started to pack wagons for the 33,000 stadia trip back to Macedonia. In their minds, the reason they had started the invasion had been achieved. Many had become affluent, compared to their neighbors at home. Philip and Alexander's great cause was behind them. Alexander could stay in Persia and play oriental despot if he liked.

These events were only a few of the many storm clouds that were gathering in eastern Iran, so far from Greece and Macedonia.

CHAPTER 15

PARMENIO

"We'll rest here on the shores of Lake Seistan," Alexander said. "The new army needs orientation before we continue. I want each commander to teach the new command structure to the mercenaries and Macedonians who have signed on again. Craterus, you will now be chief of staff in matters that deal with our Macedonian and Greek troops. Hephaestion, you will be chief of staff in dealing with Persians and other conquered groups."

Gathered with the king in Drangiana were Craterus, Hephaestion, Erigyius, Perdiccas, Coenus, and Leonnatus. Important decisions were being made, decisions that would determine the course of the rest of their lives.

Conspicuously absent from the gathering was Philotas, Parmenio's remaining son. The brash and brilliant cavalry commander had just returned from his brother Nicanor's funeral. The meeting would determine his fate.

Alexander continued. "No one outside this group must know what I am going to tell you now. This conquering way of life that we have been living for the last four years will become permanent. I will never return to Macedonia. Neither will I rest until the entire world is under my domination. Each of you will become rich and powerful. Never forget who your king is as we project our might."

Craterus reacted first. "We feel the same as you, Alexander," he said. "That's why you selected us. If you ever doubt anyone's allegiance to you and your mission, eliminate him. I think I speak for everyone here."

The other men concurred. Each was smugly pleased that he would become one of the rulers of the greatest empire the world had ever known. Their youthful confidence and arrogance were just what Alexander needed as his quest for glory continued.

"I've just gotten wind of a plot among the new royal pages," Alexander said, abruptly changing the subject. "It may involve Philotas."

Hephaestion, who had informed Alexander of a possible murder plot against him, spoke up. "One of the pages, Cebalinus, was asked to join the pages' conspiracy but he refused. As he should have, he reported to Philotas that the conspirators' intentions were to assassinate Alexander in three days. But Philotas told no one about it."

Alexander used silence to punctuate Hephaestion's report. Then he told the group that he had confronted Philotas with the matter that morning. "He claims that it's just a petty squabble between jilted male lovers. I let him leave, allowing him to think that I had accepted his explanation. I haven't.

"I spoke with Cebalinus and his brother after Philotas and I talked. He repeated his story. I think both men are credible. In my bones, I feel that there is a conspiracy afoot. Philip used to say that one or both of your ears would ring when a plot develops. Both of mine haven't stopped for a week. Give me advice on what I should do."

"Cebalinus named Dymnus as one of the plot leaders," Hephaestion said. "When I went to arrest him, he fell on his sword. He died before we could extract any more information. He wouldn't have killed himself unless there is something to this."

Craterus had heard enough and was ready to pronounce Philotas' death sentence. "Both Philotas and Parmenio must be eliminated, now!" he said. "They may have failed in this plot, but you will never be safe with them around, Alexander. Do you want me to do it?"

Alexander absorbed pensively what his friend said. He knew he was right, but much was at stake. "The army's old guard supports both Parmenio and Philotas," he said. "If this is done too quickly, without evidence, there will be an insurrection. At best, it would split our army into two opposing groups. We would no longer be an effective fighting force."

Coenus, Parmenio's son-in-law, could see where events were moving. Unless he said something, immediately, he might be implicated in the plot by his marriage relationship. "Arrest Philotas and let us torture him. If there is a plot against you, Alexander, we can extract the information. Then you can have a trial and charge the conspirators with high treason. It will send a powerful message."

157

Everyone agreed with Coenus.

Alexander stood, signaling that the meeting was nearly over. "Craterus and Hephaestion stay; the rest of you join your men. Speak to no one about this. I'll invite Philotas to a banquet tonight. It may lull him into thinking that all is well. He is always the first one to get drunk at banquets and his defenses will be down. When he returns to his quarters, I'll have him arrested. The three of us will work out the details."

≈

Never, since Alexander had become king and during his long march of conquest into Persia's empire, had such a scene as this occurred. Gathered in parade formation were ten thousand Macedonian troops. Under ancient Macedonian law, they were the only ones who could hear evidence of high treason and pass final judgment on someone accused of this most serious of crimes. Four battalions of 2,500 men each formed a human square with a large opening in the middle. The king's parade observation tent had been set up in the gathering's center. Its sides had been removed so that everyone could see the officers inside.

Alexander deliberately kept the assemblage waiting and his men were starting to grumble. In the cool, autumn morning air, a light rain started to fall and the soldiers' moods became as cold as their damp uniforms. "Let's get this mess over," one of them yelled. However, no one appeared in the tent.

Finally, Alexander walked through the ranks and mounted a small dais set up inside the tent. He was dressed in a common Macedonian tunic, without any indication of his rank. His role was now that of the prosecutor. He slowly rotated his body looking into the eyes of his fellow fighters, commanding silence with the move. Everything was ready for the trial.

"A traitorous conspiracy has been discovered in our midst," he began speaking in the rough, vulgar speech pattern that was the Macedonian patois. "This trial will prove that it started with General Parmenio himself. It soon involved his son, Philotas, and spread like a Persian venereal disease to my newest pages. I was to be assassinated today."

The formations of Macedonian men exuded a collective gasp as Alexander named Parmenio and then they grew silent. The old man was venerated by most of them; they could not believe what they were hearing. These were serious charges, and the king had better have compelling evidence.

Alexander then motioned for Dymnus' body to be brought before the group. The conspirator's corpse was placed in the mud, directly before the king, as he continued reciting the charges. "Dymnus fell on his sword when confronted with his treason," Alexander continued. "But there are others who warned of this plot," he added.

"Bring in Cebalinus and his brother," the king commanded.

Quickly, Alexander's bodyguards rushed the brothers before the king. They stood waiting beside Dymnus' body as the rain became more intense. Both had been told what their testimony must be.

"Tell these Macedonians how you tried to warn Philotas of the developing plot against me, Cebalinus. Take as long as you like," Alexander said, standing in his dry tent.

Cebalinus wiped cold rain off his face and started his statement. "A group of the new pages were involved in this plot," he began. "My brother was in love with the dead man you see here. Dymnus invited him to join the plot against Alexander. But he refused and told me. He will explain these events in his own words after my testimony.

"As was my duty to my king, Macedonia, and to each of you, I went to Philotas and warned him of the plot. He assured me that he would inform King Alexander. After days of asking Philotas about what must be done, I realized that he never intended to tell our king about this conspiracy. I had to take direct action and not follow our chain of command. I got word to the king secretly and the full plot that you are hearing about was revealed. That is what happened."

Alexander had Cebalinus' brother confirm the plot details, and then the two men were dismissed.

"We arrested Philotas last night and he has been questioned," Alexander continued. "Soon, he will have a chance to tell his side of the story. Before that, here is the most damning evidence of not only a plot, but of Parmenio's complicity in it."

The king held up a scroll letter and turned in a tight circle so that all of the Macedonians could see it. "Listen to what Parmenio himself wrote," he shouted sarcastically. "These are his words: 'First, look out for yourselves, then for yours: for thus we shall accomplish what we have planned.'

"These words, written in Parmenio's own hand, refer to the discovered plot," Alexander added quickly. "More evidence and testimony will be presented to you, but this letter alone is enough to convict Parmenio, Philotas and the pages."

It was damning evidence but more would be needed to convince the skeptical Macedonians that a plot to murder Alexander was afoot.

Written testimony from Philotas' mistress was introduced next as evidence. It showed that Philotas and Parmenio had frequently criticized Alexander and had often said, in mixed company, that they were personally responsible for most of the king's greatest military achievements. However, her testimony fell far short of confirming treason.

At last, Alexander called for a still robust Philotas to appear before the Macedonians. Philotas came forward, mounted the dais platform, and stood there with an arrogant stance.

Alexander looked at him contemptuously then continued the attack. "Philotas, I know in my heart that you are a damned traitor." Alexander stood face-to-face with his brilliant cavalry commander. "Nevertheless, our tradition allows you to speak at any trial bringing serious charges against you. I know that you won't speak in our Macedonian tongue, so I refuse to stay and hear you. After you have insulted our good men's ears with Attic Greek, I will return. I have already been injured enough by your actions; I will not stand here and listen to your snobby-assed remarks."

With those pejorative words, Alexander stepped down from the dais and left Philotas under the tent. He stood alone with his hands tied behind his back.

Philotas waited for Alexander to leave and then, with a glower on his face, began to speak. "There is no evidence here." His voice was confident and his demeanor was superior. "If you ignorant men choose to believe this drivel, then I will gladly die. You know that I am unfairly being singled out for elimination. Alexander has been waiting his chance to purge me."

His strong remarks and self-assured manner started to find sympathy with pockets of old-line supporters of his father.

Philotas' forceful words were not what Alexander's supporters wanted to hear. Suddenly a newly appointed general, a man who had been promoted from the common ranks of Macedonian fighters, came forward and shouted down the crowing Philotas. "You bastard!" he yelled contemptuously. "You won't even speak to us in our mother tongue. Why don't you explain why you threw out common soldiers from the house they captured to make room for your personal prizes of war? They slept in snow that night, while your treasure remained warm and dry inside."

Other common soldiers supported the general's attack with barbed shouts as the Macedonians shifted their mood again. At last, Parmenio's brother-in-law joined the fray, walking before the prisoner and charging him with treason. He charged treason not only to Alexander but also to his family. "I should stone you myself," Coenus said as he reached down and picked up several large rocks.

The incident nearly started a riot. Shouts of "Kill him right here" and "I've never liked the snooty turd" came from the men. Only the return of Alexander brought back uneasy calm.

"That is enough for today," the king shouted. "We will reassemble tomorrow. My Royal Companions will question Philotas again to see if he is as innocent as he claims. You men will decide his fate after we get more information. As it has always been with fighting Macedonians, the final decision will be yours."

The king turned on his heel and left the trial.

He soon gave orders to Coenus, Hephaestion, and Craterus to torture Philotas and get a written confession. He also wanted written testimony from Philotas that Parmenio was involved in the plot. Like the River Granicus battle, this was a fight that he intended to win at all cost.

≈

The next morning Philotas had to be carried to the second trial session. Wounds covered his body. One of his arms was broken, and his left eye protruded from its socket. With great difficulty, as two of the king's bodyguards held him up, he uttered a mumbled confession that only the front ranks of the Macedonians could hear.

"I plotted with my father to have Alexander killed," he said softly. "Alexander has my written confession. I'm ready to meet my fate. May the gods pity us." He spat out a mouthful of blood, and then collapsed.

Quickly, two of Alexander's bodyguards carried his limp body away from the gathering.

Alexander walked slowly to the tent dais. It was time to ask his men for a verdict. The king looked down and then surveyed the eyes of the massed Macedonians. "Philotas has convicted himself from his own mouth," he began. "Parmenio's guilt is also established beyond doubt.

"You must vote now. I will name two names. Each of you will vote with your swords. If innocence is your verdict, raise your sword high in the air. If you think the man guilty, cast your sword in the mud."

Alexander heard the sound of 10,000 swords being unsheathed by his fighters. All was ready. "Philotas," he shouted.

In a near-simultaneous action, practically all of the Macedonian fighters thrust their swords into the mud. A low, growling roar and numerous shouts of profanity accompanied the rippled gesture.

Scattered among the mass of men were Alexander's inner circle of young officers. Their job was to note the men who did not vote for conviction. In the days ahead, the dissenting men would either disappear or be put on the front line of some hopeless charge against an entrenched enemy. King Alexander would not tolerate democratic descent.

The most crucial vote came next. Alexander spoke in a loud, caustic voice to his men before starting the process. "I know that many of you love General Parmenio," he began. "He served my father with distinction and brilliance. Early in our campaign, he also served me. Nevertheless, treason is treason. His own son has implicated him in the plot. A letter in Parmenio's own hand implicates him. Any other king would not even put this matter to trial. Do what is right by our fighting code, men. Raise your swords."

Alexander shouted "Parmenio!" The downward cast of thousands of swords into the mud took longer this time. Nor was it a unanimous gesture. Some men stood there with their swords high above their heads; others let their swords drop limply at their sides. However, the great majority of the fighters cast their swords aggressively into the soggy ground. Shouts of "The old bastard has lived long enough!" and "Kill both of them!" were heard, and Parmenio's fate was decided. He would die with his son.

However, Alexander wasn't done yet. He brought forward an old challenger to the Macedonian throne: Alexander of Lyncestis. The pitiful remnant of a once-proud man was given the chance to speak but his long imprisonment had affected his brain. He managed only a few, incomprehensible mutterings that no one could understand.

Without even being asked, the Macedonian fighters collectively cast their swords into the mud. "Get rid of him too," someone in the ranks shouted.

The accused started to resist, but one of the king's guards carried out the verdict and killed him on the spot with a spear.

Alexander left the trial in the hands of Craterus, who knew what was expected of him. Old enemies of the king and men with questionable loyalty were presented for verdicts. Some were found guilty; others were found innocent and escaped death. A few were permanently exiled from ever serving with Alexander again or even returning home to Greece and Macedonia. The purge was nearly complete. All that remained was Parmenio's execution.

≈

Polydamas, one of King Alexander's Companions, was chosen to deliver Parmenio's death warrant. He selected two Arab guides, dressed as they did, and then embarked on a breakneck ride using the fastest desert racing camels. Their destination was Ecbatana, where Parmenio waited.

Eleven days later, Polydamas and the Arabs arrived in Ecbatana in record time. He went to Parmenio's second in command and presented him with the old general's death warrant. Cleander, understanding what was happening, decided to cooperate. There had been a trial and Parmenio had been found guilty. The old man must die.

The next morning Cleander and several of his officers found Parmenio resting in a serene garden. It was a well-watered spot where flowers covered the walls and decorated the many pathways. Under the guise of presenting letters from his son and Alexander, Cleander waited while the old general happily open the first one from his son. Then he drew his dagger and thrust it into Parmenio's ribs. Other killers joined the attack with thrusts to Parmenio's throat and back. King Philip's old friend and most trusted confidant, a man who had survived innumerable battles and court intrigues, died exactly as his king and life-long friend had. It was the Macedonian way.

≈

A near insurrection occurred when Parmenio's soldiers discovered what had happened. Quickly, Cleander showed Parmenio's men signed documents from Alexander. The documents described the trial and summarized the evidence showing that their general had participated in the plot against Alexander. At last, an uneasy calm returned to the Macedonian forces.

After days of tension and contentious meetings with soldiers and officers of the old general, it was decided that nearly all of Parmenio's body would be buried, with full military honors, in Ecbatana.

Before burial however, his head was removed and sent to Alexander as proof of his death. It was Parmenio's sad fate that his mortal remains would rest in two separate places, so many thousands of stadia from his provincial homeland in Macedonia.

CHAPTER 16

MORTALITY

"He's blind and speechless," Alexander's physician reported to Hephaestion. "The rock that hit him in the head and throat would have killed a lesser man."

"Is his life in jeopardy?" asked Hephaestion. "After all he's been through I can't believe that the gods would end his life like this."

"He must have strict bed rest," the physician answered. "If he doesn't improve in ten days, the injury may be permanent. Don't allow him to do anything during that time. His life is in your hands, Hephaestion."

Hephaestion dismissed the physician and walked back into Alexander's quarters. He approached his bed and saw his friend sleeping fitfully on the huge field bed that had belonged to Great King Darius. Alexander's short body seemed lost in a sea of silk, peacock-embroidered sheets, and opulent Persian blankets.

Gently, so as not to disturb his friend's sleep, Hephaestion pulled away the royal blue silk sheet that covered the king's leg. Not only had Alexander suffered a possibly life-threatening head and throat injury, he had been shot in his leg. The arrow had shattered his leg bone. Hephaestion examined the leg splint, saw that it was properly positioned and free of infection, and then recovered Alexander's leg.

He then left and sought out Ptolemy, now a member of the king's Royal Bodyguards. "No one other than me, his physician, and the slaves that feed and care for him are to be admitted into the king's quarters," he told Ptolemy. "The next few days will decide his fate."

"Craterus and I will share command of the army until he recovers," Hephaestion continued. "The whole army needs rest and recuperation. Alexander's illness will serve that purpose for us all. Protect him with your life, Ptolemy. Dispel any rumors that our command structure is weak. Let me know if you hear anything and I'll deal with it. Traitors will not be tolerated!"

"This is not his end, Hephaestion," Ptolemy answered. "The king's seers examined the signs. Each assured me that he will recover. They examined the entrails of a thousand sheep and goats yesterday. There is not a negative sign among their organs."

Hephaestion frowned and pursed his lips. He was not a religious man and believed in little other than the invincibility of Alexander. However, if others took meaning from butchering animals, it didn't trouble him. Besides, there was a remote, mystical chance that it just might help in the king's recovery. These matters were far beyond his limited intellect and he knew it. All he could do now was to protect his friend so that no more harm could come to him.

Ptolemy changed the subject. "Dispatches have arrived from Pella and Epirus, Hephaestion. Do you want to read them?"

"I'll read Antipater's," Hephaestion answered. "They may contain something that requires immediate action. Only Alexander reads Olympias' messages. I've asked him more than once about her letters and he always got angry. Besides, they are written in a secret code that only the two of them know how to decipher."

Ptolemy knew that Olympias corresponded regularly with her son but was unaware that their communications were encoded. "She still sees him as her little boy, even after he has nearly conquered the world," Ptolemy said. "I suppose mothers never change."

The two men smiled and then went their separate ways.

Hephaestion knew that perilous days lay ahead as he held Alexander's army together, waiting for his recovery.

≈

"Give me mother's scroll," Alexander said to Hephaestion nine days later. His raspy voice was two octaves lower than normal and he spoke with quavering difficulty.

Hephaestion had Olympias' letters ready and gave them to Alexander. "I'm pleased that you are better," he said to his friend. "What else do you require?"

"Leave me alone, old friend," Alexander answered. "When I finish mother's letters, I want to read Antipater's dispatches. Separating them two years ago was a good idea. Mother needed a small, inconsequential kingdom to rule."

"Call for me if you need me," Hephaestion said as he left Alexander alone.

Alexander took a copy of Euripides' *Iphigenia in Aulis* from a bedside table. It had a large numeral four etched on its leather cover. It was the fourth of five works of Greek literature that the king and his mother had been using to encode and decode their private messages to each other.

Alexander repositioned his healing leg on some stuffed pillows and began decoding his mother's message. Although her writing ability had improved over the years, she still showed rudimentary, almost childlike skills in writing standard, Attic Greek. As a boy, he had resented Philip for never allowing his mother to become fully literate. Her writing skills would never get any better than they were now. When he finished decoding, Alexander read his mother's message for meaning.

'Alexander, Son of Zeus-Ammon, Beloved of the Gods,
Conqueror of the World, My Dearest Son:

I was furious with both you and Antipater when you sent me back to Epirus. I could have served you better in Pella, watching that monster you named Macedon's regent. But when my brother was killed fighting in Italy and I took over ruling my homeland, my life became better. I now rule here until my cousin, Aeacida, comes of age.

Antipater and I never speak nor write. He came here recently, but I shunned him. I know you trust him, but one day you will have to deal with his ambition. Although I dislike him, he is an able administrator and commander. Without him, you would have been forced to return to Macedonia to put down the rebellions. I do give him that.

His son, Cassander, is more dangerous than his father. Be careful of that snake. He supports you now, but he will turn on you when you are weak or threatened by your enemies.

I learned from the captain of a sailing ship that put in at Corcyra that you are in Afghanistan or Bactria. If my tracking of you is accurate, you have been there for over two years. What is taking you so long in that godless land?

I know you won't return to Macedonia until you take India. Aristotle put that awful dream in your mind. Why do you linger in the east? Have you found a woman or a new man that you love?

I don't want to grow old and die without ever seeing you again. Write me as soon as you get this letter. You must answer each of my questions. I am your mother and I gave you life. I deserve more than an occasional message about your military victories.

I continue to hear alarming reports about your drinking. You swore to me that you would never become your father, but your uncontrolled drinking is leading you to repeat his self-destructive patterns. If you cannot stop, at least have the good sense to dilute the wine — the way the Athenians do. Your mind is too great to destroy with drink.

Do you ever look at the lion's head birthmark on your thigh?

My love and devotion,

Yours,
Queen Mother Olympias

Alexander smiled but was exasperated with his mother. He decided to ignore most of her demands and insulting questions. Olympias had no idea what he had been facing for the last two years. She continued to charge high rent for the nine months that he had spent inside of her. He reached for a blank scroll and a writing instrument to begin a caustic answer to her questions. Then he had a better idea.

"Hephaestion!" he yelled.

His friend came quickly to his bedside. "What is it, Alexander?" he asked.

"Get four Afghan prisoners!" the king said. "Send them in chains to my mother in Epirus. Accompanying them must be a large container of Bactrian dirt. Don't send any written message other than the prisoners and

168

the dirt. She will understand. I hope future conquerors never get bogged down here the way I have."

≈

"These symposia are getting out of control," Callisthenes remarked to a young historian that he had been training since Alexander's expedition had begun. "Alexander uses them to test the allegiance of his men while they are drunk. He thinks it brings out their real character. Philip did it too.

"Eubulus described Dionysus' views on wine drinking," Callisthenes continued. "He urged that only three bowls be consumed. The first one is for health; the second should be used for love and pleasure; the third one should be taken to ensure sleep. Alexander never stops after three bowls, nor will he allow his guests to stop either.

"Eubulus said that the fourth bowl belongs to violence and fighting. The fifth bowl gives birth to uproar. The sixth generates drunken revel. The seventh produces black eyes. The eighth produces a call for the policemen; the ninth belongs to biliousness. At last, and this is the stage where Alexander now operates, the tenth bowl generates madness and furniture hurling."

Callisthenes' assistant had never heard the description of wine's effect in such a succinct series of aphorisms and was busy writing down details that he knew he would use later.

The admonitions about wine's effects described perfectly what was about to happen that hot summer evening in Maracanda.

≈

Black Cleitus was one of the last remaining commanders who had served Alexander's father. Still a powerful man, even though he was twenty years older than Alexander, he was the brother of Lanice, Alexander's wet-nurse during infancy. He had also been a wrestling companion and close friend of King Philip.

Alexander had just appointed him a satrap of Bactria and had invited him at the last moment to a royal symposium to honor his appointment.

Cleitus was both honored and troubled. The wily officer understood that Alexander was clearing out the army's old guard by assigning them to posts in remote provinces while the rest of his army proceeded eastward. He also knew that becoming governor of Bactria was filled with danger as well as opportunity.

As the drunken banquet wore on, Alexander motioned for a minor poet to recite and sing verses describing the Macedonians' near catastrophe at the hands of the Persian, Spitamenes, nearly a year ago. When the poet finished his verses, a group of Persians attending the banquet let out roars of ridicule and laughter. Cleitus and the army's old guard did not appreciate their behavior.

Well into stage five of wine's drunkenness, Cleitus stood up with a deadly frown on his enormous face. "I'm offended by these insulting jibes di ... di... directed at our Macedonian fighters," he stammered. "The weakest Macedonian is better than these wimpy Persians who find the poem so hilarious." His face grew redder with every word that he spoke.

Tension filled the banquet tent and an equally drunken Alexander allowed silence while he formulated his reaction. Then, with some difficulty in maintaining his balance, he rose to answer Cleitus. "You're trying to disguise Macedonian cowardice as misfortune, Cleitus. Are you pleading your own case?"

Cleitus, still standing, shot back an angry response. "We all know that it was my cowardice that saved your overeager ass at Granicus," he shouted. "You, who call yourself the son of god, needed my sword then. Great shame on you for disowning our Macedonians and your father. Ammon must be weeping!"

Alexander was furious. "You scum," he shouted. "Do you think you can stir up trouble among the Macedonians and continue to get away with it?"

Cleitus wasn't done. "Only the dead Macedonians are happy now," he shouted back. "They never lived to see us having to beg Persians for an audience with our own king."

Alexander paused in the escalating exchange and muttered an insulting jibe to some of his Greek courtiers that Cleitus could not hear. The fearful confrontation might have abated at this moment, but that was not to be.

"Speak up, so all of us can hear you," Cleitus roared sarcastically. "Otherwise, don't invite free men to your banquet who will not prostrate themselves before your white tunic and womanly Persian girdle."

Alexander quickly picked up an apple and threw it at Cleitus, hitting him in the chest. Then he reached for a dagger inside the tunic of one of his Royal Bodyguards and shouted for the emergency trumpet alarm to be sounded. Furniture, as in wine's tenth stage, began flying around the king's banquet table.

Alexander's companions, led by Ptolemy, stopped the sounding of the emergency alarm and quickly whisked Cleitus toward the tent's exit.

Cleitus, a crude man who nevertheless knew Euripides' *Andromache*, managed one last verbal shot at his king. 'It's a pity that only one man wielding a sword among ten thousand others received the credit for a victory on the battlefield.'

It was more than Alexander could take. He yanked a spear from a royal bodyguard's hands and thrust it deep into the chest of his nursemaid's brother. Cleitus' death was nearly instantaneous. He could only mutter "Betraying bastard" before he died and fell into the arms of Ptolemy. Another of the Macedonian army's conservative old guard was gone.

Alexander sobered immediately as he realized the gravity of his foolish action. "What atrocity have I done?" he cried. He pulled the spear from Cleitus' chest and started to turn its point, still red with Cleitus' lifeblood, toward his own chest. "I cannot live after this shameful act!" he shouted.

Only Ptolemy's quick action saved his king from suicide that day. He grasped the spear shaft with both of his strong hands, jerked it out of Alexander's hands and broke it over his knee. "Take him to his tent," he commanded the other bodyguards. "Great Zeus!" he uttered with exasperation. "All of this because of drunkenness."

≈

Alexander wept and sacrificed for Cleitus for a day and a half. He even prayed over his dead body in the privacy of his bedroom. None of this helped. He felt cursed by Dionysus and was resolved to die by starvation.

Callisthenes visited Alexander's bed and attempted a philosophical justification of the king's murderous action. However, his actions failed in helping Alexander accept the murder. The king continued to refuse both food and drink. Finally, at the end of the second day, a developing rival to Callisthenes went to Alexander and brought him back among the living.

"Get up and quit your whining about Cleitus," Anaxarchus said to his king. "You are now the world's Great King. Your actions are above all human laws. If you killed Cleitus, he deserved to die."

It was exactly what Alexander needed. From that day on, Callisthenes' influence over Alexander waned and Anaxarchus' increased. Things were done that way in Alexander's new world order.

≈

Later centuries would call it the campaign of the Soghdian Rock. The following early spring, after Spitamenes had been defeated and killed by his own men, Alexander was ready to resume his march toward India. However, one obstacle would have to be removed before he felt his already conquered lands safe enough to move still farther eastward.

The Soghdian Rock was the last fortress of a local baron named Oxyartes. It stood high above a rugged valley and its defenders thought it impregnable. "I offered them a peaceful return to their homes if they would surrender," Alexander said to his command staff. "Through a translator, they told me that unless our fighters could sprout wings, they would never surrender or fear us. Mountain snows last until late summer up there, and their water supply is not in question."

"The rock's walls are sheer on all sides," Craterus said. "Wings would help."

"I'll show them wings," Alexander shot back. "They'll learn that my spirit has wings. This afternoon I want to meet with any of our men who have experience as mountain climbers. I'll give the first man who climbs to the top of the rock twelve talents. The second man will get eleven and so on to the twelfth successful climber, who will get a single talent. They will climb all night; tomorrow the Soghdians will awake to find our forces standing above them. We'll then see how brave they are."

≈

Three hundred Macedonian mountain climbers volunteered for the dangerous mission scaling the vertical Soghdian rock face. After a long night of near-impossible climbing, when more than thirty fell to their deaths in the deep snows below, dawn found over two hundred of them on a high ridge, well above the forces of Oxyartes. They signaled Alexander in the valley below and then let out the mighty Macedonian war cry. It echoed and reverberated through the rock canyons that surrounded the high Soghdian citadel.

When the Soghdians heard the fearsome cry, they looked up and saw their enemy above them. Assuming them to represent a much larger enemy force, their collective shock caused immediate surrender. Most thought that the rumors of Alexander's godlike persona had allowed him to equip his men with the wings.

Captured without much bloodshed were Oxyartes' guerrilla army and many women and children. The richest prize was Oxyartes' daughter, Roxane. The teenage girl was said by all who saw her to be the most beautiful woman in Asia, except for the deceased wife of Darius. In time, she would become the only wife that Alexander ever took.

CHAPTER 17

ROXANE

Two of Alexander's Macedonian fighters walked outside the army's encampment, decrying what was happening to their king. Both had signed up as mercenaries when Alexander had made the too-attractive-to-be-turned-down offer to continue eastward with his new mercenary army. One man, an aging battalion commander, had fought with King Philip when he was a young man. The other soldier, ten years younger, had never known Philip but still revered him. In recent months, they had taken to complaining to each other about what was happening to the Macedonians during long walks far from the prying eyes and ears of the camp. Open complaining there would have been suicidal.

"If we survive the king's excesses, we'll be rich for the rest of our lives," the older man said. He was a tall, burly soldier with multiple battle scars on his face, arms, and legs. "There is a fertile estate in Orestis province that I have always wanted. The coming years will earn me enough to buy me it."

The younger soldier smiled and gave his friend a silent nod of his head. He was fond of the old man and admitted to modeling his fighting behavior after him. He also liked him because he saw situations fully. These were valuable qualities during a time when Macedonians were gradually being replaced by Persians and foreign mercenaries in Alexander's army. "Now that he has killed Callisthenes and the five Royal pages that were involved in the plot, few of us are safe," the younger soldier said.

"I'm sixty two and a half now, and I never thought Alexander would come to this," the older soldier lamented. "Aristotle may never talk to him again now that he has eliminated his nephew. Even his choice of women has shifted since he married Roxane. Barsine has been banished from court. The king is sending her back to Pergamum in three days. A friend of mine has been commanded to lead an escort to take her back."

"I hear she's pregnant with Alexander's child," the younger soldier said. "Is it true?"

The older man laughed and threw both of his arms into the air. "It's a false pregnancy," he said sarcastically. "She so wants Alexander's child, that her mind made her pregnant when she wasn't. I'll never understand how women function. A physician I know examined her yesterday in preparation for the difficult trip. He wasn't sure she could make it without losing the baby. From the appearance of her belly, she looks as if she is more than six months pregnant. The physician told me that he is certain that she isn't pregnant.

"Alexander knows the truth and is encouraging the rumor that she is with child. The king even allowed Barsine to name the phantom, unborn baby. She calls it Heracles. Alexander thinks it will help the Greeks think that he has finally sired a successor."

The younger man knew less about women than his friend, but this news was astonishing. How could she look pregnant but not be? "Great Zeus Almighty," he said.

"It's best she's out of here," he continued. "I saw Roxane when she was brought into camp after the capture of the Sogdain Rock. I also saw Darius' wife when we captured his harem. Roxane is nearly as beautiful as she was. Her name means Little Star."

"It seems that Alexander really loves her," the older soldier said. "When they married so quickly, I thought it was just to appease the local barbarians. We'll see if the king has enough spunk in his organ to impregnate her and produce a real heir."

"I'd be willing to help him," the younger man said. "I fathered a child when I was sixteen. Scores of my offspring are running around several villages that we conquered."

This talk was dangerous, even though the two men were far from camp and alone. "Let's return," the older soldier said with a frown. "Don't ever make that stupid remark again. You're not even drunk! Others would tell the king immediately. We would both be killed. I don't intend to have my bones strewn in this forlorn desert, so far from my family."

The younger man realized that his remark was dangerous and regretted saying it. Everyone knew that even close friends of Philotas had testified against him at his trial. He decided to guard his words more carefully

175

as they walked back to the camp. He also intended to sire many more children and bring his crude brand of Macedonian culture to the backward barbarians that he had been killing for so many years.

≈

Alexander was now twenty-nine; Roxane was just past her sixteenth birthday. Even though the king had mastered the main Persian language as a boy and parts of the provincial dialects during the long invasion, the local Afghanistan language that his new wife spoke was unintelligible to him. Therefore, the king found a Balkh woman who could translate for them. She had been married to a Greek mercenary in Darius' army and spoke both Roxane's dialect and average Greek. The Balkh woman's linguistics skills were strong enough that the king could converse with his stunning bride whenever he wanted.

"You have allowed me to love as a man at last," Alexander said to Roxane. "I never thought this would happen. It even frightens me at times." He waited for the Balkh translator to relate his sentiments to his wife.

Roxane listened to the translation and smiled demurely.

Alexander knew that she understood the effect that her charms had on him. Clearly, this knowledge pleased her. The king saw that it imbued in her a serene dignity and self-assurance that seemed to radiate from all around her.

Speaking through the translator, she answered her husband. "I will give you a successor, Alexander," she began. "Women in my line are immensely fertile. I will be pregnant in a month. I will let you know when my body is ripe."

Alexander waited for the translation and was pleased. He had started consuming less of the strong Macedonian wine since his marriage, attempting to increase his sexual potency. Although Barsine had made him furious with her cutting remark about his diminished virility due to drinking, he had come to believe that she was right. Lest he fail to heed Barsine's advice, Olympias had just written him again with the same warning.

He looked at Roxane and used the silence to examine her qualities. His first thought was that she resembled his father's last wife. However, she was far more exquisite and delicate than Cleopatra-Eurydice. Although not a Greek, her royal breeding was apparent to anyone seeing her. She would be perceived as a queen in any culture, in any time.

Roxane was a little taller than the smallish Alexander. Like Philip's last consort, she had pure-white-alabaster skin and large breasts. Her figure was womanly, with the tiniest waist that Alexander had ever seen. Her hips were full and in perfect proportion to the rest of her voluptuous body. Alexander thought about the ratio between her cinched waist and her full hips. He wondered if Pythagoras had ever considered this womanly physical characteristic. Without question, she was ready to grow his heir. Zeus-Ammon had chosen his true wife well, for which he was grateful.

"I am nearly ready to invade India," the king said changing the subject abruptly. "It is rare that I will speak to you of military or political matters. They are not the domain of women. There will be times, however, when I will want you to know what I am thinking. You may even be able to help me with matters that involve your countrymen." He waited for the translation and watched his wife's reaction to his words.

Roxane
~~Barsine~~ simply nodded her head and remained impassive.

"I have decided to take several thousand Afghan and Persian youths into protective custody," Alexander continued. "It's a common practice, both here and in Greece. My father was held in Thebes for nearly two years in his youth. There will be at least 30,000 of them. Their instruction will focus on Attic Greek, Hellenic culture, and our military tactics. When India is conquered and all of Asia is mine, they will help me rule the world. The son that you will soon produce will, in time, become their king." Alexander waited for translation.

Roxane, at first, showed no reaction to the king's message. Then, when the translator conveyed the number of youths that he intended to hold, Alexander saw that it produced a reaction. His wife sighed, and rolled her beautiful eyes. Clearly, she was deep in thought. Then, with deliberate and reasoned speech, she reacted to Alexander's intentions.

"You must ask my father, Oxyartes, to coordinate these efforts," she began. "He now supports you and understands your dreams. Your

Companion, Peucestas, also knows our language. Have them work together on this project.

"I know you want these boys to forget their heritage and become cosmopolitan Greeks, citizens and leaders of your new world," she continued. "However, don't erase their pasts—that would steal their souls. They will serve you better and grow into your new world men if you allow them to remember how far they have come. If you break their spirits, you will produce human shells. The entire project will fail."

Alexander waited for the Greek translation then smiled. His wife was wise beyond her years, he thought. He even partially agreed with her. Nevertheless, he knew that the captive youths would forget their diverse barbaric heritages in time. Inevitably, they would become a new breed of men. They would evolve and grow in every way, just as he had grown and evolved when Philip had sent him to study with Aristotle. Their souls and minds would far surpass the heritage of their limited, primitive cultures.

"I am grateful for your support and suggestions, Roxane," Alexander said. "We may discuss this more. Go to your quarters now. After I meet with Hephaestion, I want to bathe with you. I'm feeling sexual," he said with a hungry look on his face. "Our birthing efforts may begin this evening."

Roxane waited for the translation, and then smiled. She rose and walked to her husband, pausing to dismiss the Balkh translator with a wave of her hand. She took Alexander's left hand and placed it on her right buttock. Then she took his right hand and placed it inside her silky dress bodice. She moaned gently as Alexander began a slow manipulation of her erect nipple. Rapidly, the lovers' heat rose, and Roxane felt Alexander's organ rising strong against her leg.

None of these universally understood actions required a translator. Alexander picked up his wife and took her to Darius' expansive bed. His meeting with Hephaestion could wait.

≈

Hephaestion was not happy. "Is this how we end?" he asked his friend and lover. It was the first private time he and Alexander had shared since the king's marriage to Roxane. Hephaestion circled Alexander in an agitated state while the king remained seated on a chair in the center of his quarters.

"What makes you think this is our end?" Alexander asked. "Men must eventually marry a woman. Politics alone demands it."

"Do you love her?" Hephaestion asked.

"I love her the way a man loves a woman," Alexander answered. "But I love you the way a man loves a man. What is so hard about that to understand?"

Hephaestion calmed a bit, hearing Alexander's words.

Yet Alexander could see that he remained threatened in a way that he had never been since his relationship with him had started.

"How would you feel if I married a woman?" Hephaestion asked in an entrapping manner.

Alexander smiled, knowing that the bitchy question was coming. "Someday you will marry, Hephaestion," he answered. "I won't be troubled; it would not change anything between us. Is there a woman you are looking at, or is your diatribe just pique?"

Hephaestion wasn't sure what *pique* meant, but he pretended that he did. "Is the love of a man for a man deeper than the love of a man for a woman?" he asked, continuing his emotional attack on his lover.

"You're not known for such deep questions, Hephaestion," Alexander answered. "I must consider your question. I can't answer it now. Roxane and I are just beginning to love each other. Give me a year and I will tell you then. I can tell you now that our love is different. It's like comparing the taste of the finest Macedonian wine with the finest wine that we have found in Persia. Both may have admirable qualities that a cultured man like I am can learn to appreciate."

Alexander could see that Hephaestion hated being compared to a fine wine; his feelings were not being assuaged either.

"That's enough!" Hephaestion shouted. "I don't like what I'm hearing. Perhaps you will return to me when you tire of Roxane. I know your limited attention span. How you require new experiences. Only a man could ever provide that variety for you."

Alexander was tiring of this tedious exchange and let Hephaestion know it. "This talk is at an end!" he said abruptly. "I want my commanders to meet this evening. The logistical plan for our move over the Hindu Kush into India is ready. Trouble yourself with military matters and you will forget this silliness about men loving women. Our conquests are far more important than the love weaknesses that emasculate strong men. In time, you will learn that."

With those cutting remarks, the king dismissed Hephaestion without his usual embrace. He watched Hephaestion leave and experienced an immediate mental comparison between the physical characteristics of the two humans he loved most.

Women's bodies, especially Roxane's, were far more interesting and beautiful, he concluded. They had graceful, even maddening, curves that made men appear as stick figures. For the first time in his life, he understood why poets celebrated women's allures.

By comparison, men were physically boring. Their only unique feature was a penis. These thoughts amused Alexander, and, for a moment, he considered that he was becoming more heterosexual. It was all a new sensation.

At last, his thoughts leaped to his next goal: mysterious India. India was the mysterious land that both Aristotle and Herodotus had long described. Both scholars believed that is was just a small peninsula on the shores of the Great Eastern Ocean, a vast sea that extended farther than anyone knew. Aristotle had taught him that one could see the Great Eastern Ocean from the crest of the Hindu Kush. No land existed beyond India, his teacher maintained.

Greeks believed that Indian men had tails and the heads of dogs. They also believed that Indian archers fired their weapons using eight fingers on both hands. Incredibly, Greeks had heard rumors that far off India had enormous ants, ants that were as big as dogs. These dog-ants were supposed to be able to mine gold—gold that, for centuries had been sent to Persia's Great King.

Alexander finally decided that his coming military adventure was much more interesting to him than wasting valuable mental energy on how men and women are constructed or how they act when they are in love.

CHAPTER 18

INDIA & THE JHELUM

Alexander was in a foul mood when he, at last, entered India. The last four months had seen him split his army. Hephaestion and Perdiccas had followed their orders and were successful in taking the main force down the Kabul River, over the Khyber Pass and then to the Indus River valley of western India. The ruler of Taxila, a rajah named Ambhi, had come over to the Greeks and had served as their guide to his capitol. Hephaestion's orders were to build a pontoon bridge across the mighty Indus near Taxila and wait for Alexander.

However, for four months the king and Craterus had been fighting their way through the fierce mountain tribes that inhabited the hills of eastern Afghanistan, Bajaur, and Swat. Alexander led only lightly armed troops during these forays, and they were nearly annihilated more than once by the fierce fighters that opposed them. The king suffered an arrow shot in his shoulder and later was wounded slightly in his ankle during two of these bitter encounters.

Finally, his force entered Taxila where Ambhi hosted his main army. Alexander richly rewarded the rajah and allowed him to continue controlling his territory. However, Alexander also established a large Macedonian garrison in Taxila, just to keep his new ally honest.

Fatefully, Alexander decided to stay in Taxila for the next two months. His fighters needed rest, and he needed fresh intelligence about the eastern rajahs who would oppose him. India was still unknown territory and Alexander rarely initiated military activity without knowledge of what he might face. That policy was part of the reason for his phenomenal success. His divine heritage didn't hurt, either.

"Aristotle had his head up his ass when he spread those ridiculous stories about India," Alexander said to Hephaestion, Perdiccas, Craterus, and Ptolemy. "The only thing he got right was a partially accurate description of elephants. It's probable that India is huge. There may even be another continent beyond it. Almost certainly, the Great Eastern Sea lies far to the east of where we are now. Perdiccas, what have you learned while you waited?"

"There are three rajahs that are players in the coming contests," Perdiccas answered. "I think we can trust Ambhi here in Taxila, at least for now. He has long hated Porus and would do anything to topple him.

"Abisares is the rajah of Kashmir and a sometimes ally of Porus," Perdiccas continued. "He has already sent envoys to us here in Taxila months ago. I suspect that this is just a delaying strategy while he raises forces against us. It's likely that he will join Porus against us, if they can bury their old antagonisms."

"Tell me about Porus," Alexander directed, rubbing his sore, wounded shoulder. "He is the central figure that we must deal with before long. Has he sent emissaries?"

"None," answered Ptolemy. "He's a giant of a man, as tall as Darius. These Asian leaders all seem to be of great stature! Maybe they ate better than we did when growing up. We know little about his present disposition or if he intends to sue for peace or fight. His kingdom is vast; he will be a formidable enemy. Perhaps we should take the initiative and send out feelers to him."

"Do it today," Alexander commanded. "Inform him that I will meet him at the Jhelum River. It seems to be his western frontier and is a likely spot. Direct him to prepare a tribute to me as a token of his submission to my army. It will force the issue one way or the other."

Alexander left his commanders, after ordering them to develop details of the coming operations. Then he went to Ambhi's royal baths. He wanted to steam his weary body and get drunk. Roxane had just told him that she thought she was pregnant so there was no longer any need for him to avoid good wine. If her pregnancy were a false alarm, like pitiful Barsine's phony pregnancy, there would still be time for impregnation of his wife, after he stood on the shores of the Great Eastern Sea. Only then could he call himself the conqueror of Asia. Neither Heracles nor Dionysus was ever able to make that glorious claim.

≈

Porus frowned and answered Alexander's envoys immediately through his court translator. "I have heard that Alexander is short," he said contemptuously. "Tell him that I will meet him at the Jhelum, but I will be in full battle formation. Inform him further that I will have one of my court midgets fight him in a personal contest on the eastern shore of the river. No other Greek will ever set foot in our territory."

With a wave of his hand, he dismissed Alexander's startled representatives. Then he called an immediate war council to complete his plans to stop the barbarian from the west.

≈

"He underestimates the effect of the monsoon rains that will start soon," Porus said cunningly to his field generals. "The traitor Ambhi has, no doubt, told him about our wet season. Nevertheless, I know that Alexander has never directed field operations where it rains continuously for two or more months. Our monsoon will become our most effective weapon against him. The fool waited two months in Taxila while his men held poetry and athletic contests. I will use this folly against them when they try to cross the Indus in full flood."

Porus' generals laughed then stood and started shouting the Indian war chant to their god of war and killing. Each had heard of Alexander's great victories over the Persian Great King, but the barbarian invaders were about to confront real fighters and hundreds of Indian war elephants. Each of the Indians knew that their homeland would become the final resting place of the undersized Greek who knew so little about their beloved and vast India.

≈

"It can't rain for three straight months," Alexander said to his host and newest ally, Ambhi. "How can people live through that?"

Through a translator, Ambhi answered him. "Sometimes the monsoon lasts two months, sometimes three months. The rain is nearly incessant. During monsoon, we say that no man can see his shadow at midday."

The rains had just started and Alexander had been receiving disturbing reports that Porus was about to receive thousands of new Indian reinforcements. Nor did Alexander know what Abisares was going to do. Yesterday, Alexander's envoys had returned with Porus' answer to his request to meet him as a vassal. The envoys left out the insulting words about the rajah's intention of having a court midget fight him.

Alexander's intelligence officers also told him that he was likely to be up against 200 elephants, 300 war chariots, as many as 4,000 cavalry, and 50,000 infantry. Clearly, despite the deluge, his army must depart immediately. The invaders must encounter Porus before his strength could grow.

"My most critical problem is transport," the king said. "Coenus, get back to the Indus. Dismantle the pontoon bridge there. Cut the boats in half and load them on carts for the trip south. We will reassemble them on the banks of the Jhelum. I'll leave tomorrow via the Salt Range, at a pass that I think the locals call the Nandana. Our damn maps are almost useless here. We'll have to rely on Ambhi's scouts and what we can pick up along the way."

"There is a ford location at Haranpur," Ambhi offered. "It's the narrowest spot at that point in the river. However, I suspect that Porus already has his advanced forces waiting there on the eastern bank. This battle won't be easy in the torrential rains."

Alexander grimaced and dismissed everyone except Hephaestion and Ptolemy. "I've seen how our war horses act around the Indian elephants," he said. "Even Bucephalas fears them, and he fears nothing."

"I tried to condition our horses by walking them among the elephants that Ambhi gave us," Ptolemy said. "It's hopeless. We must use our horses far away from Porus' elephants or they will just get in the way."

"I know this," Alexander said with irritation. "My final battle plan will minimize but not eliminate the problem. Go to all of the units now; prepare them for departure at dawn. I want to be alone now. This battle is going to require my most resourceful tactics. My spiritual father and I will work it out. We have not come this far to be turned back. It's my destiny to see the end of the earth."

$\approx$

Hephaestion and Ptolemy started preparations to move the army south. Both knew that the future was secure as they discussed the grim look of determination they had seen on their king's face at the strategy session. Porus did not know it yet, but he was about to become just another ruler that the great Alexander would subdue. Both officers knew that their king was unstoppable.

≈

"How in the hell did Ambhi ever think we could ever ford here?" Alexander shouted. He was standing on the banks of swollen Jhelum River, watching the muddy sweep of water race from his left to his right. On the opposite bank, over four stadia away, was an entrenched and sizable force of Porus' fighters. Alexander grimaced when he saw a number of the enemy fighters wave their weapons at him. Beside the enemy soldiers were eighty-five elephants in the downpour. The great beasts paced nervously back and forth. Sharp flashes of lightning and the following thunder crashes filled the saturated, leaden skies and made the huge animals even more nervous.

"Our cavalry is useless here against their elephants," Alexander said. "The horses can smell them even from this distance. I've never seen Bucephalas so spooked." He walked over to the horse that his father had given him so many years ago and calmed him. The magnificent steed was one of the few living things that he dearly loved.

"I'm modifying our plans," he said at last to his commanders. Standing with him in the pouring rain was Hephaestion, Craterus, Ptolemy, and Perdiccas. "Craterus, stay here with most of the army. Establish the camp openly. I want the enemy to see everything that you are doing. Put my command tent in the middle, in clear sight of Porus and his spies.

"Get that double we've been training to dress and act like me. His uniform must be identical to the one that I wear before our battles. Have him walk up to that cliff there several times a day," Alexander said while pointing in the cliff's direction. "Several officers and bodyguards must accompany him. From a distance, Porus will be convinced that they are watching me."

Alexander's commanders smiled as they wiped rain from their faces. Each was rain-soaked down to his crotch. "I understand the ruse," Craterus said. "After camp is established, we will give them our war cry at regular intervals, just to rattle their asses. I'll also make several feints at crossing the river. They will think that our attack is imminent. It may focus most of their forces opposite me here."

"I'll start bringing in food supplies when the camp is set up," Ptolemy added. "We'll make them think that we believe a full-monsoon crossing is impossible. With luck, they'll think that we are waiting for the rain to end."

"Good," Alexander said. "I'm leaving with my scouts immediately. I must find the narrowest part of the river where we can cross with our cavalry. It has to be a place where our horses won't smell or hear their cursed elephants. Craterus, when you see me flanking the enemy on the other side, start your river crossing. Under no circumstances should you start before that. It would help if we could get a clear day to launch operations."

"The rains have just started," Hephaestion said. "It will be a difficult battle, but we have had many difficult battles. Do you want me to intercept Coenus and have him stop the boat transport until you have found a suitable ford site?"

"Yes, do it immediately," Alexander answered. "When I find a suitable ford, I'll send for you both. We'll get through this."

≈

"The locals call it a nala," Alexander said. "It's a deep valley cut right into the mountain. It will hold several thousand troops easily, without anyone seeing them from the other side of the river. There is a wooded island between the nala and the opposite shore. We shouldn't be spotted until it's too late. It's the perfect place for us to launch our attack."

With Alexander, one hundred and forty stadia northeast of Haranpur, were Hephaestion and Perdiccas. "What forces do you want here, Alexander?" Hephaestion asked.

"We'll assemble 5,000 cavalry and 4,000 of the infantry," Alexander answered. "They'll all be lightly armed. I want them to begin leaving Haranpur at darkness tonight. It will take most of the night with this incessant rain. When they are all here, the river crossing will begin. I've sent couriers reminding Craterus what he must do while we are advancing south toward Porus' main force. Coordinated timing will be everything."

≈

Alexander's plan worked perfectly, at the start of the operation. But well before dawn, in nearly total darkness, the unrelenting rains became even more intense. Scores of Alexander's men were struck by lightning and killed as they were getting into the large boats for the crossing. The cavalry's horses were terrified by lightning and thunder and they reared away from their riders and slipped into the muddy river embankment before entering the swift water of the river. Then, Alexander's forces were surprised by something that could not have been seen in the low visibility skies.

"This is only an island in mid-stream," Alexander shouted to his commanders in the following boats. "Make for the real embankment! Do it now! We are vulnerable here and can be picked off while we are being swept forward in this fucking muddy river." The king's shouts were barely audible amid the crashing thunder that surrounded his struggling fighters.

Some were able to make their way eastward, and they started to climb up the muddy embankment. Calvary riders were in the water, riding their choking and terrified horses from the unexpected island to the opposite bank. An enemy attack right now would annihilate them all.

Only iron will and battle hardened-discipline made it possible for most of the king's fighters to struggle to the river's eastern side. More than a hundred drowned, pulled under the muddy river by their heavy armor. As the rains continued unabated, Alexander helped his remaining men up the river embankment and directed them into their battle formations. Each looked like a wet rat. They were sodden, cold, angry and ready to take as many lives as they could.

The Indian defenders saw what was happening. Immediately, an Indian general dispatched a swift rider to Porus with the message that Alexander was crossing north of the Rajah's main forces. Porus' only chance now was to intercept Alexander and kill the Greeks before they could establish a foothold on the eastern shore. But he could not remove his entire southern army at Haranpur. That would give the Greeks opposing him there an unfettered opportunity to begin their river crossing. Porus sent his son racing north, while he remained with his main force opposite Craterus at Haranpur. He had been outmaneuvered; it was his only possible course of action.

Soon, the Macedonians and Indians met in combat. Porus' son was heavily outnumbered, and the chariots that most of his forces arrived in were quickly immobilized in the mud. The enemy swept them aside easily. Most were annihilated by the most battle-hardened veterans in Alexander's army. Four hundred Indians, including Porus' son, were killed. The rest retreated south to join Porus.

Waiting in reserve between Alexander and Craterus' main forces at Haranpur, were Meleager, Attalus, and Gorgias. Seeing Alexander's initial success, they forded the river and joined him to meet Porus. It was lighter now but the dark skies continued to empty their monsoon rains over the hard-charging Macedonians and mercenaries.

Porus was in a hopeless situation. If he turned to face Alexander, Craterus would ford the river, allowing thousands of enemy fighters to come at him from the rear. If he remained where he was, Alexander would attack him on his flank and rear.

"We will fight Alexander," he shouted to his commanders. "Leave most of the elephants here to block the river crossing. Everything depends on us taking out their king. There's a flat sandy area not far from here. It will give our cavalry and elephants a chance to maneuver. Sound the battle trumpets!"

The main battle was underway. Alexander conducted a series of cavalry charges that confounded the enemy and eventually pulled them into a trap. But Porus' elephants were devastating to Alexander's phalanx fighters. A hundred elephants charged the Greeks and began to stomp them into the ground. The screams of crushed men filled the air. The berserk elephants picked up other Macedonian fighters in their trunks and slung them high into the air. These attacks, made even more terrible by the elephants' wild trumpeting and slashing ivory tusks, continued without interruption.

Never had Alexander's fighters experienced such battlefield terror. For the first time since they had left Macedonia, battle fatalities mounted early and the battle's outcome was in doubt.

Stunned beyond effective fighting at first, the phalanx at last regained its discipline. They circled the elephants, called for archers to eliminate their handlers with arrows and then used their spears and javelins to penetrate the soft underbelly of the giant animals. Macedonians slashed at the elephants' trunks with their short swords while other fighters managed to chop at the huge creatures' feet, like a woodsman taking down a mighty tree. Chaos reigned and death was left, right, below, and above each fighter.

After a bloody ebb and flow of the battle lines, the Greeks and Macedonians slowly advanced on the Indians. The elephants, watching what was happening to the injured and dying animals, now escaped control of their handlers. They started a wild charge in every direction that took out as many Indians as Greeks and Macedonians.

Porus saw what was happening and led one last, vain charge. However, the tide of battle had changed.

Alexander ordered his phalanx to lock shields and mount the final charge. The rest was a bloodbath.

Craterus was now fully across the river and Porus was caught in the middle. The slaughter of his fighters was immediate and merciless. Twelve thousand Indian fighters soon lay dead or dying in the mud-mixed-with-blood goop that was the product of a massive battle. .

Porus lost most of his commanders and the last of his two sons. He attempted to flee the field, but a spear wound had injured him so badly that he had to get down from his war elephant and simply wait for capture. He was covered with blood, too weak to continue the fight.

≈

Macedonian officers held Porus for King Alexander while he wrapped up the battle. Then he and his personal bodyguards rode to meet the rajah of Paurava. His great courage and valor during the battle was obvious to every Macedonian. Alexander dismounted Bucephalas, who had been injured seriously in the battle, gave his stead to a handler for treatment, then walked to examine the man he had just defeated. He felt like a little boy approaching his tall father.

Through a translator he spoke. "You are my most ferocious opponent," he said in a soft, respectful voice. Torrential rain continued pelting both men as Alexander asked, "How to you wish to be treated?" Alexander asked.

"Like a king," Porus answered without thinking.

Alexander was struck with the nobility of his enemy's answer and was pleased. For the first time, he had finally met an honorable barbarian of great dignity. He smiled, then was startled by a lightning bolt that landed close to his group. It created a pungent smell that permeated the rain-swollen skies. "Isn't there anything else that you want for yourself?" he asked Porus.

Porus, sitting in the mud, waited for the translation. Then he wiped blood from his face with rainwater and answered the invader who had just defeated him. "Everything is contained in that one request," he replied.

"You are a great leader," Alexander said. "We will treat you as a king; you will like what I have in mind for you. My physicians will attend you and then we will talk."

Alexander turned on his heel, slipped in the mud and then made his way to inquire about Bucephalas.

Walking alone, with twelve bodyguards trailing behind, he was lost in private thoughts. A strange miasma came over him as he suddenly sank to the middle of his boots in Indian mud and nearly fell. Pulling free, he continued his trek in the storm.

How much longer can I continue these monumental battles, he asked himself. He had lost nearly four thousand of his fighters in this battle. His propagandists would suppress that figure and make it far less than it actually was. The real death numbers could never get back to Greece. But worse than the physical loss of so many of his best soldiers was the psychological impact of them dying so far from home.

India was his after only one battle. But how much longer could he expect his men to follow him? His electric mind was flashing with ideas that rivaled the fierce monsoon lightning and thunder that would not stop in his newly conquered land.

CHAPTER 19

EASTWARD TO THE BEAS

"Alexander has ordered thirty days rest," the aging battalion commander said to his young friend. "We need it. There is great unrest in the ranks. How much longer does he think that games and poetry competitions will keep us happy?"

His younger companion, a changed man after the Jhelum River battle, just leered at his friend. His rash confidence had nearly disappeared. With his left hand, he was holding his bandaged, arm-stump where his right hand used to be. One of Porus' war elephants had crushed it during the worst chaos of the Jhelum battle. Only the quick action of a fellow fighter, who had severed it at the wrist, had saved his life. "My nightmares are filled with elephants' trumpeting," the young soldier said. "I'll never get over it."

"Your stump looks awful," the older man said staring at the bandage. "Is that yellow liquid medicine or infection?"

"It's not medicine," the younger soldier answered. "In this heat and rain wounds won't heal like they do in colder climates. I have an infection. The physicians say they have used everything they have. I may lose the rest of my arm if things don't improve. What I wouldn't give for a cool day without rain."

The older soldier gave his friend a gentle rub on his head. He had also been badly injured in the Jhelum battle. His legs showed deep cuts, and he would probably never be able to run again. He too feared infection in India's unrelenting heat and humidity. "Mold grows on everything," he complained. "Even when I polish my sword and armor, rust forms in half a day. My leather straps are cracked and nearly useless."

His friend nodded his head in understanding. "Alexander still gazes eastward," he said. "He will ride to the sun on our backs."

"Let's return to camp," the older fighter said at last. "I want to talk with our comrades about our situation. For the first time we can complain publicly; everyone is doing it."

"Is action being considered?" the younger man asked. "Is an insurrection brewing?"

"Not yet," the older man answered. "But Alexander must be made aware of our weariness. Things can't continue like this. Returning home is the only thing that is going to calm things."

The two men walked back to camp in near silence. Both were devoted to Alexander and considered him a god. Nevertheless, their spirits were almost broken. If they could just make it back home, a life of semi-luxury awaited them. However, both knew that Alexander's pothos-driven wanderlust must be assuaged first. They also understood that more men would die before that would happen.

≈

"Bucephalas is dead," the king's stable physician announced. "It was a combination of two spear thrusts and old age. As mighty as he was, life left him. A noble spirit has left the earth."

Tears formed in Alexander's eyes and he sobbed openly. No one had ever seen him cry. Fighting a complete breakdown, he dismissed everyone but Hephaestion.

The two men had grown apart during the last weeks because of Alexander's apparent love for Roxane. Now Alexander needed his oldest friend to give him comfort.

"I know what he meant to you," Hephaestion said, hugging the king with one arm. "What kind of funeral do you want?"

Alexander, red-eyed, regained control and motioned for Hephaestion to sit on a nearby couch. "Bucephalas was twenty," he began. "I want a city established on the west bank of the Jhelum in his honor. His funeral will be an affair of state. I will name the city Bucephala. A dignified shrine will be built there of fine stone. No one must ever be allowed to forget my magnificent friend. After you, I loved him most."

Alexander observed that Hephaestion was pleased with his words. He knew that his friend would take the comment as an indication that their long period of personal animosity was over.

"Construction on both the city and the shrine will begin immediately," Hephaestion answered. "Do you want other commemoration sites honoring your victory over Porus?"

Alexander sighed, rubbed his eyes, and then acknowledged the importance of Hephaestion's question. "Yes, I want another city built where we conducted our Jhelum night-crossing. We'll name it Nicaea to honor the victory. Build both cities of that mud-brick these locals use. It won't last long in this cursed rain, but it will help establish my legend. That's all that matters in the great scheme of things."

"An appropriate action," Hephaestion answered. "What are our military plans? The men are restless; there is talk of returning home."

"I'll have none of that," Alexander shot back angrily. "India can't be that large, and we may be close to the Great Eastern Ocean. My soul will not rest until I stand on its shores.

"When you leave, send Craterus in here. I'll order him to coordinate the construction of the two new cities. I'll also order him to begin construction of a vast new fleet that will take us down the Jhelum, to the Indus, and out to the open sea. I need you with me as we move eastward. There is still a lot of mopping up around here before that can happen."

"What are you going to do with Porus?" Hephaestion asked. "He has nearly recovered from his wounds. It seems that he may support you. His treatment now could be critical for the success of the outpost that you want to establish here."

"I've decided to give him control of his former lands," Alexander said. He looked at Hephaestion and saw that he was surprised. "A garrison will be left here to keep him honest. But I don't want Ambhi taking control after we leave. Each of them will be allowed only enough power to counterbalance the other."

"How much of this do you want your commanders to know?" Hephaestion asked. "Their unrest is real. Some of the officers are already saying that the best way to gain control of a kingdom is to be defeated by Alexander."

Alexander smiled, recognizing the truth of Hephaestion's observation. "I'll give them a city to sack soon," Alexander answered. "That always calms any unrest in the ranks. I'll keep telling them that the Great Ocean is just beyond the next river or hill. It has worked for eight years and 141,000 stadia. They will follow where I lead."

"Their morale is the lowest it's ever been," Hephaestion answered. "Some are swearing that they will never fight elephants again. I must tell you, Alexander, this is serious."

"You trouble yourself with matters that are beyond your command level, my friend," the king said in a condescending voice. "Put it out of your mind! I'm on top of this. Go now and send for Craterus. I feel my pothos rising again. My adventure is not over."

Hephaestion left and Alexander was alone. He knew that Craterus was out of camp so it would take time for him to return. His mourning for Bucephalas was not complete. He would use this quiet time for final supplications. He got on his knees and prayed to Zeus-Ammon to take his mighty stead into whatever spirit world existed for animals. "Let it be a place where monsoon rains never fall, where he will never face angry war elephants again," he said. He raised his arms heavenward and chanted a simple prayer-song that his mother had taught him when he lost a dog to death. Slowly, the spirit of his sacred father descended upon him and his grief began to lessen.

Then he rose and went to a table to read the latest letter from Olympias. It had taken five months to reach him. Self-satisfied, even calm now, he was convinced that Asia had not heard the last of Alexander of Macedon.

≈

It was midsummer and the final days of the monsoon continued unabated. The deluge had filled all of the rivers and low-lying land, forcing most of the snakes in northwest India to seek higher ground. Every house and tent was infested with both poisonous and nonpoisonous snakes of every variety. Alexander's army could only cope with the slimy invasion by sleeping in open-air hammocks, strung between sturdy trees. Flimsy tents surrounded these makeshift arrangements but most soldiers were fearful of falling asleep in them. Despite these precautions, poisonous snakes hiding in their boots bit some men and they died painful deaths. Insurrection, like the unrelenting rains of India, was in the air.

"The bastards are ingrates," Alexander complained to Ptolemy. "I gave them a three-day sacking holiday and they still won't listen to me. When I spoke to them, there was just silence. To a man, they all want to go home with their plunder."

"This is your most serious crisis with the men, especially the Macedonians," Ptolemy answered. "They are unified and won't budge. Scores of them have told me that if you want to continue east, you must do it without the real leadership and power of your army. They know that the mercenaries and Persians don't have their fighting skills or experience. They are right."

"Are you siding with them, Ptolemy?" the king asked with a deadly look on his face.

"I'm not," Ptolemy answered. "But we are at an impasse. They look across the Beas River and see only the endless, level plains of India. Every man can see that the Great Eastern Ocean is nowhere in sight. You must do something quickly."

Alexander was furious and walked around his command tent in a tight circle. A large puddle was forming on the floor of the tent, beneath a rip in the top, caused by a sudden rainsquall. The king slipped in the water and almost fell. The mishap only made him angrier. "All right," he shouted. "Assemble my senior officers. I'll convince them and then we will deal with the men. This mutiny will not go any further!"

≈

"We have come this far and now the men, even some of you, have given up," the king began speaking to his top commanders. "The ridiculous claims of an even larger empire east of India are horse shit! There are no more wide rivers to ford, and we have learned how to fight the elephants. Where has your courage gone?"

Alexander had worked himself into an agitated state and quickly realized that his comments were bordering on being insulting. With great internal control, he calmed himself. The action was a trick that Aristotle had taught him as part of debating strategy. He lowered his voice and slowed his delivery.

"If we turn back now, everything we have worked for will be lost. Is that how you want our legend to end? Do you want it remembered that we were never whipped by a real foe, but dissipated by fatigue and wild rumors of a phantom army three times our size?"

Alexander's harangue came to an abrupt halt. He had said enough for now. *Let silence punctuate my points*, he decided. His logic had been overwhelming. His men, who had gone through so much with him, would not abandon him now. Awkwardly, he continued to manage the silence. Then he spread his arms, arched his eyebrows, and invited a response.

However, not one officer spoke. Most refused to even look at Alexander. The silence seemed interminable. Finally, the king could stand it no more. "Someone speak, damn it!" he yelled.

At last, an aging former son-in-law of Parmenio, Coenus, rose to answer his king. He was in the beginning stages of what his physicians had told him was a mortal illness. It was only because of his failing health that he was able to summon up his courage and speak. His words were aimed at a man who knew that he was the son of god.

"Alexander," he began, "the most courageous of the Macedonians, men who have taken us where we are today, are utterly exhausted. Their friends, men who grew up with them in Macedonia's provinces, are lame, broken or dead. Their vitality is sapped. They want to see their families again; they want to enjoy the wealth that you have brought them in what remains of their old age.

"King Alexander," Coenus continued, "I believe your wisest course is to return to Greece and Macedonia. From there, you can mount other expeditions with younger men. You can continue to have a conquering life ahead of you. But not with this group of worn-out fighters. You must understand that one mark of a great leader is knowing when to stop, knowing when enough is enough."

Coenus sat down and, for a brief time, silence reigned again. Then every officer in Alexander's top command structure rose and gave Coenus' remarks a thunderous roar of support. The message was clear: even Alexander's most loyal officers had turned against him.

"You miserable, fucking cowards," Alexander shouted. "If you won't continue with me, I'll lead the Persians and mercenaries eastward. My historians will record that you abandoned your king with his enemies at every side. But I will not stop!"

Alexander turned on his heel and strode arrogantly out of the command tent into the Indian rain.

Inside the tent, his commanders sat in silence. It was the worst crisis of the expedition. None of them knew if they would survive the next days, but their resolve was fixed. Like the common, fighting men, they would not go on.

≈

Alexander pouted in his private quarters for three days. Only Hephaestion saw him. Each time Hephaestion left the king, he spread the word that Alexander had not relented. He could not accept what he considered the ultimate betrayal.

Finally, Alexander called in his personal seer, Aristander. He had decided to leave it up to the gods. "Tomorrow I want you to sacrifice a thousand sheep and a thousand goats," he directed. "Even though I have insisted on continuing the expedition, I will abide by the omens. If the signs are favorable, I will cross the Beas with whatever fighters remain loyal to me. If the signs are unfavorable, I will turn back and lead the men home. This will show everyone that I am still a pious man. The final decision is out of my hands!"

≈

Aristander was not only skilled at delivering messages from the gods and interpreting omens and prophesies, he also knew a volatile leadership crisis when he saw one. The evening of the next day, he went to his king and told him the gods' wills. "My priests examined the entrails of every slaughtered animal," he began. "Ninety percent of the organs were black or gray. Even those without dark color showed organs that were not their normal red or pink. The gods' intentions are clear: the expedition must stop."

Alexander bowed his head. *So, this is how my destiny is to be thwarted,* he thought. *Not by Memnon, Darius, Spitamenes, or Porus.* No mortal human had been able to halt his great eastward movement. Now, the guts of sheep and goats had stopped the son of Zeus-Ammon.

A powerful surge of negative emotion swept over him. During the night, he had wrestled with the possibility of the omens going against him. By morning, he hoped that he would be able to recover from a possible humiliating affront and shortsighted limitation of his great abilities. Now, for the first time in his life, he doubted. He would lead his men back, but the journey would not be quick or easy. Neither would he ever forgive them.

"Tell my commanders that I will abide by the gods' intentions," he announced to Aristander. Leave me. I want to be alone."

Aristander left and Alexander started a solitary, all-night drinking session. Hephaestion found him at noon the next day asleep and soggy. He was unconscious. The king of the world's greatest empire lay oblivious to everything on a wet cot under the dripping tent. When Hephaestion finally awakened him from his drunken stupor, Alexander remembered what had happened. It had not been a nightmare, it was real. He had lost.

Nevertheless, final retribution was to be his. The journey home would provide opportunities to prove his worth as the son of god. Although shaken about his men's refusal to go on, he started to dream mighty dreams. Some of them involved northern Africa, Italy and a little-known, still inconsequential continent: Europe. His glorious life would continue but in a different direction.

CHAPTER 20

JALALPUR ON THE JHELUM TO PATTALA AT THE DELTA

Alexander walked among the enormous altars and fake artifacts that he and his army were leaving on the banks of the Beas River. Surrounding him were twelve tall altars, one to honor each of the Olympian gods. He climbed to the top of one and gave prayers for the gods' sponsorship. He also made supplication for their continued support during his army's arduous trip home.

Then he inspected enormous pieces of military equipment, bigger-than-needed earthen fortifications, absurdly long sleeping beds, and oversized dining couches. His armorers and construction corps had been building them for weeks. "Anyone looking at what we leave behind will think that they belonged to a mighty race of giants, three times our actual size," he said with smug satisfaction. "That's how I want these barbarians to remember us."

As he walked among the artifacts, scores of his men came up to him, thanking him for his decision to return home. He had never seen them so joyful and full of enthusiasm. Before long, his shoulders started to hurt from the friendly pounding that each gave him. Finally, he had to tell his bodyguards to stop the physical outpouring of gratitude. His men were overjoyed but he was not. It was not in his heart to forgive them, not ever.

"It's time to leave this miserable place," the king said at last to Ptolemy. "Write these events in that journal you're keeping. You understand all sides of what happened. Your record must be the last of this matter. We'll go back to the Jhelum River at Jalalpur tomorrow. Craterus has exceeded my command to build a fleet for our trip south. I'm told the flotilla is vast. I have ordered competitions and festivals there before we head south."

Ptolemy left and Alexander remained alone, except for ten of his bodyguards who stood at a distance. The king looked up and studied a tall, brass obelisk. It had been erected by pacified Indians on an embankment, high above the river. Written on its base in three languages was a terse, factual statement: Alexander stopped here. Nothing else. *Is this my zenith,* the king asked himself in a silent voice. *Just a brass monument that will rust to nothing in the perennial Indian rains?*

Anger rose in him, and with it a resolve was born to continue growing his legend. The East had seen enough of him. Other lands would meet the son of Zeus-Ammon. The last eight years had been only the opening chapter of his young life. He was barely thirty, yet he had he achieved so much. Already, he was greater than Philip or Dionysus, greater even than his ancestor, Heracles. Walking back to the army's main encampment, his mind raced with visionary dreams of more conquests. He was not done yet.

≈

Craterus and Nearchus of Crete stood proudly on the prow of Alexander's command boat and waited for their king to board. An enormous flotilla that both men had created was docked at Jalalpur on the Jhelum River. King Alexander boarded, followed by Ptolemy, Craterus, and Hephaestion. Craterus and Hephaestion glared at each other as they vied to be closest to Alexander. Their bitter hatred for each other had grown more intense in recent years.

Craterus raised his arms and began the presentation of the fleet to his king. "Alexander, you now command eighty, thirty-oar boats. There are two hundred galleys without decks. Eight thousand soldiers can be transported on these boats. The rest of the army will march at your direction. Eight hundred service ships will support us and serve as horse transports and supply vessels. There are also other smaller boats, too numerous to count. India has never seen anything like this."

Alexander smiled and was pleased. He looked around and saw brightly colored banners and battalion flags as far as the eye could see. His command vessel's sails were dyed bright, royal purple. Hundreds of temporarily friendly Indians lined the riverbank. Many played strange musical instruments. Everyone's mood was celebratory. If Alexander must return home, this departure had the style that his bruised ego needed.

"Craterus, march south with your force on the right bank," he shouted so that hundreds could hear him. "Leave immediately and make the way safe for our slower journey. Hephaestion, march on the left bank with the

201

main army. Two hundred elephants will accompany you. If danger is to come to us, it will be from the east. Leave now and pacify the territory as you move southeast. Nearchus is now my admiral and will command all vessels. He tells me that they total more than 1,800. I'll depart the command ship when I'm needed.

"With the 30,000 new infantry and 6,000 cavalry reinforcements that just arrived from Thrace, Greece, and Babylon we will be unstoppable. India will never forget that we came this way."

A mighty cheer emerged from all of his fighters who could hear him and the departure ceremonies were over. The king then gave sacrifices to Ammon, the Nereids, Poseidon and finally Amphitrite, the wife of Poseidon and Heracles, his ancestor. Also recognized with libations and sacrifices were the Jhelum, Chenab, and Indus river gods. Then the king ordered immediate departure.

Alexander's massive baggage train, hundreds of married and unmarried women, the expedition's scholars, historians, architects, geographers, mathematicians, botanists, zoologists, poets, and the thousands of noncombatants who supported his army followed at a slower pace. The number of humans that left northwestern India that day totaled more than 120,000.

≈

Beneath the main deck of Alexander's command vessel his wife rested. Two days earlier, Roxane had given birth prematurely. Sadly, the baby was born dead. The young queen had seen the infant's sex. It had been a boy. It was a terrible ordeal for the royal consort.

Roxane looked up and saw Alexander coming to her bedside as the ship started its gentle swaying movement in the water. Alexander paused, examined his wife to see if she was sleeping, and then walked to her side. Seeing her eyes open, he stroked her forehead and stretched out beside her.

Roxane managed a weak smile and snuggled next to her husband. She heard Alexander begin singing a simple song whose words she could not understand. She assumed that his tune was a love song and she was touched. With tears in her eyes, she buried her head deeper into his shoulder. When her massive vaginal tearing healed, she knew that she would become pregnant again. Now that Alexander had agreed to return home, she felt that there was less danger of him being killed in battle. All she needed was nine more months.

Roxane would learn much later that Alexander's song was about the sacrifices of motherhood. It ended with a blessing for women who give their husbands a son.

≈

The Malli were one of the two most powerful peoples that Alexander was to meet southeast of where the Jhelum and Chenab Rivers joined. Inspired and supported by the Brahmans—the Indian priestly, aristocratic class—the Malli were fierce fighters who defended their cities to the death. Soon, Alexander's fighters were again in the business of all out, even genocidal, war. Although no Indian force could resist Alexander's army and victories became commonplace, Macedonian morale, once again, fell in the ranks.

Deep in the southern Punjab was the ancient Malli city called Multan. Alexander's forces quickly surrounded it and began a half-hearted attack. It became apparent to the king that most of his Macedonians' fighting spirit was gone. Without energy or aggression, they were just going through the motions of a deadly ritual that they had done too many times.

Alexander watched his flagging fighters and realized that the final attack on Multan's citadel was in danger of failing. "What's wrong with you?" he screamed to several hundred of his sappers and shock troops. The Mallians had beaten them back several times and most were just standing idly by, out of arrow shot. Their ladders were horizontal at their sides.

Without thinking, the king pressed three of his officers into service. "Follow me," he ordered with anger in his voice. "I'll show the weak bastards how real Macedonians fight." The four grabbed two siege ladders and charged the citadel's main wall, dodging a barrage of Indian arrows as they ran. Alexander was the first to climb the ladder and stood high on the wall's parapet, a clear target for Indian archers. He shouted for the others to follow. Quickly, the officers joined him.

His heroic action spurred the rest of the Macedonians to launch their attack. Almost immediately, several of their ladders broke under their weight. Scores of Macedonian fighters fell in a heap at the wall's bottom. The king and his officers were now alone atop the wall and in deadly danger.

Alexander saw the ladders collapse and realized that his small group would soon be killed. "Jump inside the wall," he shouted to his men. Nearly in unison, they leaped down the inside of the wall and formed a meager defensive fighting group. However, they were hopelessly outnumbered; death appeared imminent.

The Mallians, yelling with bloodlust in their voices, saw their opportunity. They launched wave after wave of attacks and the fighting reached a point where it was just a matter of time before the Macedonians were overwhelmed. Nevertheless, the king and his brave fighters continued to kill every Indian fighter that came near them. "Hold out," Alexander shouted to his fighters as he dodged an enemy sword. "We are Macedonians. They cannot kill us. The rest of our army will rescue us!"

Suddenly, a Mallian archer shot a long Indian arrow that struck Alexander in his right breast. The tip of the arrow, barbed and shaped like a leaf, penetrated the king's cuirass, tore into his lung, and ended up lodged deep in an inner rib. Alexander was able to fight on briefly, but then fell back against the wall, a glazed look in his eyes. Blood covered his chest armor and a gurgling sound emerged from his throat.

Peucestas, the king's shieldbearer, straddled Alexander and used the king's shield of Achilles to cover him. Another Indian arrow struck Abreas, a young guards' officer, in the face and killed him instantly, while Leonnatus defended his king from the side. Only brave Peucestas, Leonnatus, and a near-mortally wounded Alexander remained. Another wave of Mallian fighters started to form, and the trio knew that their end was near.

By now, the Macedonians outside the wall realized that their king was in deadly danger, if not dead already. When the ladders collapsed, they rushed an enormous battering ram to the citadel's main gate and began to pound it relentlessly. Others used axes and began a frantic dismantling of the wall. Soon, the mud-brick that surrounded the gate gave way and the king's fighters began clawing and fighting their way into the city. Other

Macedonians used metal spikes to pound into the citadel's outer mud-brick wall, and they soon emerged atop the parapet.

The Mallians attacking Peucestas, Leonnatus, and Alexander withdrew and rushed to help their fellow fighters stop the Macedonians' incursion into the city. But they were too late. Thousands of blood-seeking Macedonians surged throughout the citadel; before long, not one Mallian man, woman, or child was left alive.

≈

"Get Critobulus," Alexander muttered as he revived briefly. He grasped the arrow shaft in his chest and continued to choke on his own blood. "He fixed Philip's eye soc—" he stammered, and then passed out. His officers put him on his great shield from Troy, lashed his lower body to it with leather thongs, then started a wild run toward the king's royal tent, two stadia from Multan. Each of the body carriers had a frightened look on his face as he ran, screaming for the way to be cleared.

Thousands of Alexander's fighters, both Macedonian and mercenaries alike, saw the ashen-faced body of their king as he was rushed back to camp. Even before Alexander had been placed in his royal bedroom, hundreds of his soldiers knew of the king's devastating wound. By sunset, rumor had it that he was dead and that his top officers were withholding the news for fear of losing control. Dread and fear hung in the air like the suffocating, South Punjab humidity.

≈

"How in the hell will we ever get back?" one young Macedonian who had just joined the army asked. "Only Alexander has that ability. We're doomed to die in this miserable place." He was close to tears.

The aging battalion commander walked up to him and slapped him viciously with the back of his battle-scarred hand. "Stop sniveling, you little worm," he snapped. "I could lead us back alone. Don't make matters worse with your cowardice."

The old commander limp-walked away from the worrisome group of soldiers, a group that was intent on fanning the dangerous flames of rumor. He muttered invectives against them to himself, and then decided to walk to the army's main camp and inquire about the king's condition. If Alexander were dead, he would begin to take actions that would preserve his life. The moment was dangerous and he needed knowledge before taking action. His well-honed, practical understanding of how things worked in Alexander's army, coupled with his life-shrewdness, had saved his life more than once during the last eight years.

He still intended to enjoy a long retirement in Macedonia. What had happened to Alexander today might end that dream. Unlike his young friend who had died of arm amputation and blood poisoning weeks ago, he refused let his life fly away uselessly so far from his beloved homeland.

$$\approx$$

"It's the closest he has been to death," Ptolemy said to Hephaestion. "We may still lose him."

Hephaestion's face was dour. For the moment, he ignored Ptolemy's morbid evaluation of Alexander's condition. He had stood over his friend while Critobulos had cut open his chest to remove the deadly arrow and shaft. He had been at his bedside for over a week, sleeping fitfully on a cot beside the king's bed. He let out a mournful sigh, and then acknowledged Ptolemy's comment. "He hasn't said a word. His eyes have only opened twice. But he's going to make it. Death has never met such an opponent."

Ptolemy smiled a half smile and agreed. "Either one of us would be dead by now. Nevertheless, despite our assurances that he lives, his men think him dead. Only when they see him will they believe us. Insurrection is in the air again. Many of our first-rate Macedonian fighters have told me that they will return home without us soon if they're not allowed to see Alexander alive."

"He can't be moved yet," Hephaestion snapped. "That would kill him. Meet with the senior commanders and tell them, once again, that the king lives and that he is recovering. I want all but a small force to move south to where the Ravi and Chenab rivers join. Establish camp there and wait for us. I hope that in a few days we can join you by boat. Perhaps then, I can let the men see him. Not before that! I don't want to be asked again about this. It's your job to convince everyone that this is how it is going to be."

Ptolemy nodded and left Hephaestion alone. The king's intimate friend then kneeled beside his wounded companion's bed and started a mournful prayer to all of the Greek gods. "One day he will join you on Mount Olympus," he began. "But it's too early in his life. Other worlds await his conquering and all-knowing guidance. He is your representative on earth and cannot be taken. Heal this great man. He's a true son of Zeus-Ammon. Touch him with your spirit and give him continuing life."

As never before, Hephaestion meant every word in his prayer. "If a life is needed in his place, take mine," he lamented. "I will gladly die before he does. In the name of Zeus-Ammon, I make this supplication."

Hephaestion had tears in his eyes by now. Sobbing, his arose and touched the fevered brow of Alexander. His temperature was still alarmingly high. He went to a bowl of cold water beside the bed and dipped a soft chamois in it. Alexander himself had killed the beautiful animal that had produced the skin. He wrung out most of the water, then wiped Alexander's face and forehead.

The king breathed deeply as the soothing coolness reacted with his clammy skin. Then he moaned and was silent. Hephaestion quickly put his ear next to Alexander's heart and was reassured to feel and hear a strong beat. His friend just needed time; he knew that Alexander would recover.

≈

Four days later, the king was conscious and talking for brief periods. Hephaestion explained what had happened and told Alexander that his army was in great distress over his condition.

"Begin the move south in the boat," Alexander whispered. "The journey must be slow. My insides are almost gone. The slightest jarring causes me great pain."

"We'll leave as you command," Hephaestion answered. "How do you want the men to see you? I hate to ask this of you, but it's important right now."

Alexander grimaced, then managed an insipid smile. "Lash another boat to my command vessel," he commanded with a weak voice. "It will make both vessels more stable. When we approach the main army encampment, have my bed carried to the main deck. Build a platform between the two boats. Make it high enough so that I can be seen. The men will then be reassured."

Hephaestion left Alexander with Critobulos and began preparations for departure. Soon, all would be well. Although still gravely ill, Alexander was recovering. His legend would grow when his men saw that he had cheated death, Hephaestion thought. The crisis was nearly over.

≈

Four days later the king's ship slowly approached the first of his men waiting quietly on both banks of the Indus. A great hush fell on the rugged fighters as the ship passed. Many of them took off their helmets and dipped their weapons in the king's direction as a sign of respect. Alexander, visible on an elevated platform in the middle of the two ships, could only move his head in the direction of the men.

"He's dead," a surly Macedonian soldier shouted. "I know him; if he was alive he would have at least raised a hand saluting us. It's a trick. He's dead, I tell you!"

Before Alexander's boat docked in the middle of the army's encampment, wild rumors had preceded him. Although thousands of his men had seen him, it wasn't enough. "It's just the theatrics of his commanders," a young Macedonian said who had just joined the army in India. Anger, unrest and renewed talk of returning home without their officers once again swept the camp.

≈

"It didn't work, Alexander," Hephaestion said. "They won't believe that you are alive unless you walk among them. I can do no more."

Alexander knew what he must do. "Get me up," he commanded in a quiet but firm voice. "Dress me in my most colorful uniform. Wrap me in my cloak, the one with the eight-pointed Macedonian star on it. I'll walk from the boat on my own. Then I'll get on a horse. I won't be able to mount alone. Have some men available to lift me onto the saddle blanket. It must be done."

Seeing Alexander among them that day was the only thing that saved massive desertions and premature departure for Macedonia. Shouts of "He's alive!" and "Zeus saved his son!" were heard amid shouts of joy and tears. The king's men still had great affection for him, as long as he led them back to their homeland.

Another crisis had passed.

≈

It took weeks of slow recuperation for the king to recover. Then, more months of continued pacification of the ever-aggressive Indian armies to the east was necessary. But Alexander's life and his precarious empire had been preserved.

Predictably, an uncontrolled rumor that Alexander was dead swept through his conquered lands. It caused the revolt of 3,000 Greek mercenary-settlers in several provinces. Reports started to come in that groups of mercenaries were returning to Greece.

Finally, nine months after they had left Jalalpur, Alexander's naval and land forces arrived at Pattala. The grubby city was on the delta of the great Indus River. It was from here that he and his army would start their fateful trek west. Almost nine years had elapsed since the start of the invasion.

CHAPTER 21

THE GEDROSIAN DESERT

Craterus' mission turned out to be the easiest of the army's return westward. His king had ordered him to lead home the siege and baggage trains, all of the army's sick and wounded, 10,000 time-expired veterans, two hundred elephants, and three support battalions totaling 20,000 fighting men. Queen Roxane, Thais, and hundreds of other women and children who had followed Alexander's expedition for years also went with him.

Craterus' mixed force left the Indus Valley well before Alexander's departure because of the slow movement that was inevitable with so many noncombatants. "We'll cross the mountains via the Bolan Pass," Craterus said as he sat in his command tent with his second in command, Polyperchon. A large map of the entire Hindu Kush mountain range was spread out before them. Other regional maps of the territories they would pass through were scattered on a large field table. "Our final destination is in Carmania province, at this location. It's called Salmous.

"I'm in awe of these maps and their details," Craterus continued. "Alexander's surveyors and scientists are the best an army ever had. We would be lost so far from home without them."

"Some of the details come from our eastward conquests," Polyperchon remarked. "But much of this return journey will be new to us. How the geographers got so much information is a marvel."

Craterus nodded agreement, folded the maps and went outside with his second in command. "I'm glad to get out of Hephaestion's sight," he said with a scornful look on his face. "Alexander warned us both that our bickering must end. He even threatened to execute the next one who starts something. That's how I ended up in command of these noncombatants. Any glory that emerges from the Gedrosian Desert crossing will go to Alexander, Hephaestion and Nearchus. I'm seething about it."

"Our scouts have already reported rebellions in the territories beyond the mountains," Polyperchon said. "It may not be as easy as you think. Three battalions may not be enough if these reports are true."

"Winning difficult victories with less than the full army will help build my reputation," Craterus said arrogantly. "Every battalion fighter with us is a seasoned veteran; we will not be defeated. I'll establish a new city along the way and name it after Alexander. That may help me get back in his good graces."

Polyperchon smiled and agreed with his commander. "You know there will be intrigues once we reach Babylon," he added. "Alexander is extraordinary in war. But I don't know what he will be like as Great King, with no more worlds to conquer."

Craterus flashed a cruel look at Polyperchon. "Don't talk like that," he snapped. "Your words border on insubordination. I'm aware of what might happen, and I am prepared. I know too that I will never advance in the king's designs as long as Hephaestion remains his darling. But I don't ever want to hear you discussing this again. These are deadly challenges; amateurs like you can only muddle the situation. Do you understand me?"

Polyperchon, humbled by Craterus' upbraiding, answered quickly. "I'll never speak of it again. I leave now to brief our commanders on our journey. Is there anything else?"

"Leave me," Craterus said, still miffed at Polyperchon rash words.

Alone, he ruminated on Polyperchon's remark. He knew that his second in command was neither a fool nor wrong in his assessment of what could happen when the return was complete. Clearly, Alexander had enormous trust in him or he would not have turned over command of 20,000 of his best fighters. It was the first time that the king had done that.

Yet, the problem of Hephaestion remained. Craterus knew that he could never advance to higher positions as long as Hephaestion continued to poison his relationship with Alexander. He could only wait and perform his duties without failure. His high ability and devotion to Alexander would eventually pay off. Hephaestion was pretty, but he wasn't Craterus.

≈

Thais, Ptolemy's mistress, was exhausted. She had just given birth and now had the responsibility of an infant daughter, along with her two other sons sired by Ptolemy. "I had a good life in Athens," she complained to another hetairai, a woman who was the mistress of a young officer in Alexander's Companion Cavalry. "I love Ptolemy, but it hasn't been worth all of these years I gave him. Now, we have to follow Craterus over those damned mountains again. I almost lost my feet to the cold the last time. I'll look like a sixty-year-old woman by the time we get back to Greece."

Her lament was genuine and shared by most of the women who had accompanied the expedition for the last nine years. Both women knew their social rank in the mass of noncombatants that began their second traverse of the Hindu Kush mountains.

Roxane occupied the top of the social pyramid, and only her ladies in waiting and women slaves ever saw her. The aloof Bactrian cared nothing for common women and children below her exalted status as Alexander's wife and queen.

Next in the social order were the wives and mistresses of Alexander's top officers. Thais occupied this level, along with nearly two hundred other women. Some of these women were Greek or Macedonian; most had been picked up from among native women during the last years of the expedition. Many could not speak the other women's languages. It made for a lonely and difficult life.

The lowest social level was women who were common prostitutes. No one other than Alexander's ordinary fighters ever associated with these unfortunate souls. Their lives were short and brutal. Most died early of malnutrition or sexually transmitted diseases. While they lived, they trailed after the army wherever it went.

The other hetairai made a feeble attempt to rearrange her unkempt hair out of her face and agreed with Thais. "I'm only twenty nine and I look older than my mother," she said. "Do you think they will ever marry us?"

"We all hope that," Thais answered. "But few do. When they get back to their homeland, most will discard us. We're as expendable as one of the king's broken siege engines. I thought that when Ptolemy named our first son after his father that he would marry me and legitimize our relationship. But time is passing. I know that he has other dreams in other lands."

The other hetairai hung her head and agreed. "If we make it to Babylon, that's where they will dump us. Rumor has it that Alexander wants his officers to marry royal Persian women there. You know where that will leave us."

Thais had heard the rumor too. Yet, she felt that Ptolemy would never reject her. He might take a wife, but she would remain his mistress. He valued her sexual prowess too much. Despite all of the uncertainties, she knew that he loved her.

She walked to her friend, stroked her birdnest hair, and gave her a comforting gift. "Ptolemy bought me a slave hairdresser and I will share her with you," she said. "Our hair is our glory; if we stay beautiful, we will survive. Use her as much as you want."

Thais walked away from her friend and rejoined her children. She would struggle to keep herself attractive, but the toils of the coming trip were sure to cause her aching body to deteriorate even more. She prayed to an obscure Athenian deity that after she reached Babylon, she could regain her stunning looks. It was her only hope.

≈

Alexander remained in Pattala in the middle of the brutally hot Indian summer. Still weak from his near-fatal injury, he directed plans for the pacification of south India and heard reports of an enormous half-a-million-man army that was being raised against him in central India. Intelligence reports told him that the new enemy force had over five-thousand war elephants. The chance to fight a monumental battle and die gloriously in combat caused his pothos-driven personality to dream impossible dreams. However, he had promised his men that he would return and he would keep his promise.

Each night his sleep was interrupted as his subconscious struggled with opposing emotions. He both loved and hated the fighters that had brought him this far. His love for them was obvious in the way that he enjoyed being in their company. However, they had betrayed him at the revolt on the Beas. Some symbolic action was necessary to repay that rejection.

The last weeks had seen him meeting with Indian Brahmin wise men and philosophers. Many of them never wore clothes. He could not wait to tell his countrymen about these naked philosophers.

Through translators, Alexander debated with them about the meaning of life, his greatness, and how their worldview compared to Aristotle's. He finally concluded that their belief system was similar to the Greek Cynic, Diogenes.

Gradually, his wound healed and he grew stronger. At last, he decided to begin his journey westward. He called for Hephaestion and issued commands that would stabilize his rearward position and allow for the return to Babylon. "Stay in Pattala and construct docks and a seaport," he began. "It will become an important trade center after I return to Babylon.

"When I have explored the two arms of the Indus Delta, I'll take the rest of the noncombatants and some of our fighters across the great Gedrosian Desert. If they won't let me continue east, I'll conquer an impossible desert with a large army. Two Iranian rulers tried to invade India across the Gedrosian and failed. Both returned with less than twenty survivors."

"Why don't you wait until the port is completed and let me return with you?" Hephaestion asked. He too had heard stories of the aborted Iranian invasions across the dreaded Gedrosian and knew what his friend was attempting.

"No, I have made up my mind," Alexander shot back. "Nearchus has agreed to command the navy flotilla and take most of the army back on ships. His will be a fearful voyage, the most dangerous of any of our commanders' journeys."

"Do you trust the maps that we have gotten from these Indians?" Hephaestion asked. "You know that they have also heard the stories. They could be sending you into a death trap!"

"I've thought of that," Alexander answered. "Our maps come from a variety of sources, not just the Indians. Everything has been coordinated with Nearchus. He will sail along the coastline and leave water and food at predetermined supply dumps. I will leave enough for you and your men when you leave Patalla. You worry too much."

≈

After only a few days, Alexander's Gedrosian expedition turned into a disaster. The desert was a nearly waterless moonscape and the heat was greater than anything the Macedonians had ever experienced. Everywhere Alexander looked, he saw only sand dunes, salt flats, and wind-scoured cliffs. Soon, his army was forced to march only at night and then find what shade they could for sleep before the relentless sun returned.

When they found map-marked wells on their maps, they discovered that most were brackish. This didn't prevent soldiers and noncombatants alike from rushing headlong to the well and drinking polluted water. Within hours, many died from gulping down the foul water. Others who did not drink died of heat stroke. Troops began breaking into sealed stores that were intended for Hephaestion's soldiers and killing pack animals and horses for food.

≈

Weeks passed. For some reason that Alexander did not understand, Nearchus did not appear on the coast as planned. Had his entire naval force been lost in a storm? Yet the king would not turn back. It was the beginning of a two-month hell across the Gedrosian.

One night, most of the noncombatants and the king's entire baggage train camped in a dry wadi. Hundreds of stadia north of the wadi an intense rainstorm raged. It produced a raging wall of water that raced southward through the night, following the random system of dry wadis that spread throughout the Gedrosian like a spider's web.

No one heard the water coming until it was too late. It swept through the encampment taking everything with it. Over five thousand women, children, and pack animals drowned. Many of the bodies were never found.

Few of Alexander's tough Macedonian fighters were killed in the wadi flood. Yet death took scores of them each day for other reasons. Many died of thirst and lack of food. Some lost their minds in the relentless heat and just wandered alone into the desert to die. The Gedrosian was an enemy that they had never met and they were being defeated.

≈

The aging battalion commander had somehow managed to remain alive for over thirty days. His wounded legs had never healed, and they were now bleeding from new sores that oozed a watery substance that he had never seen before. After a long night's march, he and a friend found a sleeping place beneath a large rock outcropping. It would provide some shade from the sun's relentless attack.

"Your legs look awful," his friend said. "What are those black things in the wounds?"

The aging commander was surprised with the question and propped up his legs on a rock to examine them. Tiny sand bugs had infested his leg wounds and they were busy burrowing into his raw flesh. "Son-of-a-bitch!" the old man cried out. "Now this! How much more can I take?" he cried out as he started to dig out the bugs with dirty fingernails.

He managed to dig out most of the visible bugs but knew that many had burrowed deep into his skin. Exhausted and fearing more infection, he finally gave up the removal effort and rolled over on his side to get some sleep. "I hope Alexander knows what I have sacrificed for him," he said in a quiet voice to his friend. "I've never had the chance to talk with him after all of these years. I'll seek him out tomorrow and ask if his personal physician can look at my legs. The king has done it for other men. He owes me that."

He closed his eyes and dreamed of the farmland that he would purchase in Orestis Province when he got back to Macedonia. Before he died that day, his dream was of his wife and now-grown-up children. In the dream, he and his extended family were busy getting in the harvest of an abundant crop that would be sold at market. A crop would increase his wealth more than it already was. His body's last action was an unseen smile. He was at peace at last.

≈

Sixty days after they had started, only 25,000 of Alexander's men stumbled, nearly dead, into fertile Bampur. The Gedrosian crossing had resulted in the loss of mostly noncombatants. However, even Alexander's elite Royal Companion Cavalry had been reduced from 1,700 to just fewer than 1,000. Each man's face was sunburned almost black and their lips had ugly sores on them. Most had lost a fifth of their body weight.

"Where in the hell was my support from Harpalus and the provincial governors while we were staggering across the Gedrosian?" Alexander shouted to a local chieftain in Bampur. "I had nothing. I still don't know where Nearchus is. Craterus has yet to arrive. Things are falling apart! Heads will roll before I'm done!"

The local official cowered before Alexander but had no answers for the furious king. He told him that emissaries would be sent immediately to the governors of Gedrosia, Susiana, Paraetecene, and Carmania informing them of the king's anger. He made it clear that he had not failed Alexander and that the blame lay elsewhere.

That night, the local official fled to the south and boarded a small boat for Arabia. He would never return to his homeland as long as Alexander lived. Self-preservation was a strong trait of his family.

≈

A month later Hephaestion and his men limped into Bampur. Their losses had been even greater than Alexander's. They were fortunate that anyone survived the hellish journey. It was only because of the few supplies that Alexander had left for them that had allowed them to make it. Hephaestion had never seen Nearchus during his journey across the desert.

"We'll slowly make our way toward Salmous while we wait for Nearchus and Craterus to arrive," Alexander said to Hephaestion. He looked at his friend and realized that he was lucky to be alive. Hephaestion had lost thirty percent of his body weight, and his usually beautiful, fair skin was covered with sun-generated sores and blisters. Strangely, his abundant, thick hair had started to fall out after the journey across the Gedrosian. None of the king's other men had experienced this.

Alexander put Hephaestion's appearance out of his mind and then continued. "I've ordered a week of Dionysiac revelries that will help our men forget the terrible experiences that we have all gone through," he announced. "It always works for them to get drunk and rape a few local women."

"Yes," Hephaestion said without elaboration. "But keep Craterus away from me when he joins us. You must soon make a decision about us. We both love you in different ways. But don't think that we can coexist now that the major fighting is over."

"I've already made a decision on this, Hephaestion," Alexander answered. "Craterus will be sent home to Macedonia with our retired fighters. Mother has convinced me that Antipater has outlived his usefulness in Pella. She wrote me that he is white on the outside but purple on the inside. Craterus will take over as my regent in Macedonia and Greece."

Hephaestion's face showed his surprise. "It will get him away from me and, for that, I am pleased," he said.

Then Hephaestion changed the subject abruptly. "Our Gedrosian crossing has nearly destroyed your image, Alexander. King's live and die on what other think about their invincibility. Now, among what remains of our army and among these provincial governors, dangerous talk is being heard. It's said that Alexander has finally experienced defeat. You cannot allow this vicious story to spread."

"Do you think that I have grown stupid, Hephaestion?" Alexander asked contemptuously. "I hear the same talk, and I have already started actions to counter the rumors. When all the elements of my army are reunited, a purge of the traitorous governors will begin. Harpalus had better have a good excuse why he didn't send bullion when I needed it so desperately. A massive reorganization of my new empire will begin once our forces are united."

"Good," Hephaestion answered. "Let me know what role you want me to play."

"When you leave, send for Eumenes," Alexander directed. "He and I will write a positive account of the Gedrosian crossing. I'll have him attribute our losses to enemies that we encountered along the way. I won't have a desert defeat me, not when I have conquered every human enemy that I faced.

"Get some rest, Hephaestion. You look awful. We will get through this. Soon we'll rule the greatest empire the world has ever known. Both of our legends will grow, and people everywhere will see us as gods. A long life awaits us both. After our many sacrifices, we will both deserve what we get."

CHAPTER 22
PERSEPOLIS TO SUSA

"That gimpy little bastard," Alexander shouted. His fury over his Royal Treasurer, Harpalus, was more violent than any of his inner circle had ever seen. "I ordered him here to Salmous and he knew what he would get. He's on his way to Athens with six thousand mercenaries and five thousand talents of my silver. I'm fortunate that he didn't steal my entire treasury."

Ptolemy, Perdiccas, and Lysimachus listened and knew the gravity of the situation. At last, Perdiccas spoke up and offered his king a suggestion. "You must order all of the central kingdom generals and satraps to disband their mercenaries immediately. Harpalus' actions were probably the beginning of a plot against you."

Alexander, still weak from the Gedrosian crossing and his shoulder wound that would not fully heal, stood up and gazed into space. In recent days, his drinking had increased. Drinking bouts that used to last a single night now stretched into two and three day drunken, Dionysiac orgies. His nose was always red and had a bulb at its end.

The silence in the command tent was palpable. Alexander's face was etched with a vindictive scorn as he started a walk around the tent. Everyone present knew that complete silence was mandatory when the king started his circuit. He had picked up the habit from Aristotle.

"I'll make a list of those who will be executed," the king said at last. "Cleander and Sitacles will be eliminated after a trial tomorrow. Anyone even remotely responsible for our supply failure in the Gedrosian will either be deposed or killed. Never again will I allow those serving me to make me vulnerable. It's clear than an insurrection was well into the planning stages."

"Hephaestion and Craterus will be kept apart from now on as well," Alexander continued. "Yesterday, both had their swords drawn in their latest squabble. I've ordered Hephaestion to take the coastal road to Persepolis and Susa. With him will be our baggage train, all of the elephants, and most of the army. Craterus and I will move overland with the Companion

Cavalry. Nearchus will continue commanding our fleet and meet us south of Susa."

Ptolemy waited for the king's edicts to sink in, then brought news of importance to everyone gathered in the tent. "A courier arrived this morning with news. The 30,000 youths you ordered trained in our language and military tactics are ready for presentation to you. Where do you want them to meet us?"

Alexander was pleased with the news and his anger lessened. It had been three years since he had established the youthful cadre. If he liked the outcome of the youths' training and indoctrination, they would become his model of the new fighting men of his empire. "Have them meet us in Susa," he answered. "I want this conspiratorial mess cleaned up before we charge them with their duties. If they are as good as I hope they are, I will no longer have need of Greeks and Macedonians questioning every command decision I make."

Alexander knew the impact that his last statement had on his officers in the tent. Each was a Macedonian. He looked each bodyguard in the eye, and then ordered them to leave. He had more drinking to do with a teenage eunuch that had just been presented to him.

In three days, he would leave and everything would be different. He was becoming a different man; his vast empire would have to learn to accommodate these changes. World civilization would soon bear the imprint of the son of great Zeus-Ammon.

≈

At Persepolis again,
six years after I left it

Olympias:

I walked today through the charred desolation that the Persians called the most beautiful city in the world. I now regret burning it.

Inside, I feel like the city's blackened expanse. When we first came here, I was full of hope and confidence, imitating proud Persepolis herself. All of that has changed.

221

I have prayed and offered countless supplications to Zeus-Ammon, but my spirit continues its descent. Conspiracies are all around me. I eliminate those whom I know are plotting, but there are more. I trust no one.

Lately, I have even had difficulty confiding in Hephaestion. He and Craterus quarrel constantly. I give them command responsibilities that keep them apart. My heart weeps because of this. They are the two that I loved and trusted most.

My health is poor. My shoulder wound that I received in India will not heal properly. I fear that my arm strength will never return. This is an ominous condition for the fighting king that I have always been. Our crossing of the Gedrosian Desert sapped my energy further.

I find comfort only in our Macedonian wine. As you feared, mother, I have lost control of my drinking. In that regard, I have become Philip.

I tried to write a poem about all of this, but nothing came out. I often long for my childhood days, when poems flowed from me like the winter melt of the Hindu Kush. When I grow old, I know that I will become a prolific poet again. But not now.

I need information about Antipater's activities. I received reports that you and my sister are challenging him in Macedonia and Epirus. Continue these activities. When I reach Babylon, I will replace him. There may be others in Greece and our homeland who are plotting with him. Spy on his son, Cassander, and keep me informed on his actions.

When you decode and read this message, burn it. The thoughts contained here are for you alone.

I may bring you to Babylon once I solve all of these problems. An Indian philosopher helped me understand that I should rule my empire from there. The longer you and Cleopatra stay in Epirus and Macedonia, the more danger you both will experience.

I go now to bathe in Darius' tub. Only boiling water helps me relax and think with clarity. I'll get through these difficulties, as I always have.

Please go to the Dodona temple that we visited when I was a boy. Offer prayers and sacrifices for me there that I may continue to fulfill my destiny. I need the support of our ancient gods as my life proceeds.

Your troubled son,
Alexander

≈

"Look at them," Alexander said as he sat in the royal reviewing stand in Susa. He was dressed in full Persian regalia that featured a long Persian pleated robe and mantle. He wore multicolored trousers made of the finest pure silk from an eastern land that he had never reached. On his feet were boots with high heels. They made him appear much taller than he really was. His ears seemed heavy because of six golden earrings, each one studded with precious stones and gems. He knew that most of his Macedonian soldiers and officers hated his dress. That knowledge gave him a perverse pleasure.

In the reviewing box with him were all seven of his Royal Bodyguards. For most of the morning, they had been watching the 30,000 Iranian youths that Alexander had commissioned years earlier.

"By my edict, they will be called the Royal Successors," the king announced. "Each is fluent in Attic Greek and is expert in our Macedonian battle tactics. From their ranks will come my empire's future governors and field generals. I've spoken to over a hundred. Each one is a zealot and completely devoted to me. They doubt nothing and burn with ambition to serve their king. Their successful training and presence here is the best news that I have had in years."

Alexander was aware that these teenage boys presented a substantial threat to his inner circle of bodyguards. That also gave him pleasure. As devoted as each of his bodyguards were to him, each man would have to develop an understanding that a new day was approaching when unquestioning devotion, even worship, of him would become the measure of whether they remained alive or not. The past was the past. He was now the Great King of Persia, who used to be a Macedonian. If the old guard Macedonians were to follow him to new conquests in Northern Africa and Europe, a new level of kingly service was required. This was to be the beginning of his new world order.

The last marching formation of Royal Successors — a group that Alexander had been told was the elite of the elite, approached the reviewing stand, and Alexander stood to salute them. Their squadron resembled the vaunted Macedonian phalanx, with sixteen rows and sixteen columns. All two hundred and fifty-six of the youths carried the long Macedonian pike, the sarissa.

Seeing the king stand to salute them, the group's commander gave a sharp verbal command. Every youth in the formation simultaneously and effortlessly lowered his pike at a right angle to their march's direction. The moving, human mass projected two and a half hundred spears directly toward Alexander. It was a scene high with theatrical drama.

Then, without an audible command, they started singing a chant that extolled and glorified their king. Their marching boots created a deep, percussion accompaniment as the song's words reached Alexander's ears.

> A living god — trained us well.
> For Great Alexander — we'll march into Hell.
>
> Our language is his — we speak like our King.
> We fight as he does — great victories we'll bring.
>
> Ask the impossible — we'll soon win the day.
> Successors we are — leading the way.

The youths then brought their pikes to vertical and started singing the song again. At last, with the sound of their voices fading, they marched away to join the rest of the Successors in a distant camp established just for them. The impression that they had made was enormous.

"They make all of the sacrifices I have made worth it," the king said with a broad smile on his face. "Let it be known that everything will change because of their superiority. They are my model of the Great King's fighters and leaders. Everyone around me either will emulate their behavior or suffer elimination. Those are the choices."

The king then left the reviewing stand to ride to the Successors' encampment, followed by his personal guards. He wanted to hear the song again and speak to as many of the youths as he could. He didn't want to be around his old guard at a moment like this. He would handle them later.

≈

Alexander and Hephaestion were alone. Their meeting was a reconciliation, a much-needed one after the king had nearly killed his friend because of his juvenile attitude toward Craterus. However, he couldn't shut out Hephaestion any longer. Alexander smiled at Hephaestion and knew that what he was about to announce to his life-long companion would please him as never before.

"I've planned mass marriages for nearly a hundred of our top commanders and Bodyguards," he began. "Ten thousand of our soldiers will also marry Persians. I will take two royal wives myself: the daughter of Darius and the daughter of Artaxerxes Ochus. Philip would be proud of me. This will give me three royal wives. That's more than enough to produce a male successor."

Hephaestion's face was impassive. Alexander knew that his friend thought that this was the final act of him being cut out of the king's life. "What is to happen to me?" he asked. "Is this my end?"

Alexander grinned and walked over to his lover and gave him a warm embrace. "It is not," he answered. "I want you to marry Darius' other daughter. It will make any children we sire nephews and nieces. This will bond us to each other for the rest of our lives."

Hephaestion's face brightened. Then an ominous scowl swept over the same face. "Is that all?" he asked. "Have I not earned more?"

"Don't jump to conclusions," Alexander shot back. "Let me finish! After the weddings, I'm naming you Grand Vizier. You will own the official title of the Great King's second in command. If anything happens to me, you will be my official successor if I haven't produced a son." Alexander stopped and let his announcement sink in. It had just the effect that he knew it would.

"You honor me greatly, Alexander," Hephaestion said with pride. "I thought that I was to be removed from you for life. My heart soars with love and devotion for you. I won't disappoint you."

"You will also become the sole commander of the Companion Cavalry," Alexander added. "Craterus will also marry a Persian, but not one of royal Achaemenian lineage. That isn't the message I want to send. Only you and I will marry high Persian royalty. Do you understand what I am announcing with these actions?"

"It's clear," Hephaestion answered. "What else do you intend for Craterus?"

"He and Polyperchon will continue west, leading 11,500 Macedonian veterans home. I will make him supreme commander of all Macedonian forces in Europe. As I told you, he will replace Antipater. This is all delicate, so keep quiet about everything until we reach Babylon. However, when our men see the marriage ceremonies, everything will become apparent."

"You don't ever intend to rule from Macedonia or Greece, do you?" asked Hephaestion.

"Never!" Alexander answered quickly. "Except for future expeditions to North Africa and unknown Europe, I will live and die in Babylon. The marriages will be the start of my new world order. The development of a new, cosmopolitan man will result. The best of our blood and the best of the Persian and Mede blood will become the basis of a superior human in time. Aristotle gave me private teaching on this. The only thing I want from Greece now is for them to worship me as a god. Efforts are already under way for that to happen."

"Your vision amazes me, Alexander," Hephaestion said. "No one is history has ever thought this way. You are the only one of Aristotle's students who could make this happen."

Alexander smiled and knew that his friend spoke ultimate truth. "Leave me now, Hephaestion," he commanded. "The wedding ceremonies will last five days, and I want to be involved in the planning. I've learned how important symbols are in the lives of kings. You will see powerful symbols in the ceremonies that will become legend for hundreds, perhaps thousands, of years."

Alexander handed Hephaestion a sealed scroll. "Go to the Companion Cavalry and read them this royal degree announcing your command. It bears my ring seal, so no one will question it." He handed Hephaestion the scroll and gave him a strong pat on the back with his good arm. "Our life adventure continues, and more glories await us both. Everything that happened before this is merely prelude. You and I will set a standard in the decades ahead that no man will ever reach. That thought gives me more pleasure than you can imagine."

Hephaestion left and Alexander called for his personal guard. "Get Eumenes and Anaxarchus in here," he commanded. He had neglected historical recording of his legend in recent weeks. He wanted to make sure that the vision that Hephaestion had spoken of would not be lost. Ultimately, that was the most important thing in his life.

He poured a large kantharos of Macedonian wine and waited for his royal secretary and chief propagandist. Life was becoming good again.

ARISTOTLE'S REFLECTIONS FROM A SPIRIT WORLD

3

Callisthenes' murder marked the turning point for me. My nephew was difficult and had an independent mind, but he didn't deserve to be killed for that. Why didn't Alexander just send him home? Grief, then anger about his death burned inside me for years.

It was apparent that Antipater was next. During Alexander's years in the east, I had met often with the Macedonian regent and we had become friends. He was prudent, wise, and a great leader in Alexander's absence. Gradually, his letters to me began to express alarm about Alexander's return to Babylon. News of the king's purges of his provincial governors and veteran generals at Susa was especially troubling to Antipater.

Alexander's pretensions to divinity galled both Antipater and me. Greeks and Macedonians would never accept this sacrilege or any of the other grandiose, Persian practices that Alexander adopted. We both knew that if we ever saw Alexander again, he would demand that we perform the ridiculous proskynesis. Antipater wrote me that he would laugh in Alexander's face before he groveled on the floor like some effeminate, eastern sycophant.

More than all of this, however, was my hurt that resulted from Alexander's intellectual betrayal of both my teaching and me. He had been a brilliant student, the best I ever had. At Mieza, I had been convinced that he accepted my thesis that the best ruler of men was an enlightened, supremely educated king. He was supremely educated, but any semblance of enlightenment had vanished years before.

I agonized for months, and then a plan started to emerge in my troubled mind. Your historians may call it a plot; I prefer to call it a plan. My decision was the result of a series of actions that Alexander had already implemented or would soon put in place. I dared not commit any of this to writing at the time, but decided to make another trip to Pella. Private words with Antipater were the only way to set in motion what must be done.

≈

Antipater, then in his middle seventies, listened to my proposal with respect and silence. At last, he told me that I was right. "Without direct intervention to stop Alexander and Hephaestion, both of our lives are in danger," he said. I had not thought of Hephaestion's role in the total scheme, but news of his appointment as Alexander's Grand Vizier proved Antipater's point. A careful, coordinated plan to remove them both was required.

The second day of my Pella visit, I met with Cassander, Antipater's son. His father had informed him of our previous day's conversation. Cassander told me that getting to the king was almost impossible. He was insistent that Hephaestion must be removed first. "He loves Hephaestion so much, that his death might be the end of Alexander by itself," he said. I had not understood that the two of them were still that close. I accepted Cassander's reasoning.

Antipater and Cassander left the method of their elimination to me. The day I left Pella for Athens, Antipater told me that the event that must set our plan in motion would be when Alexander summoned him to Babylon. He related that he would refuse to go and would send his son in his place for negotiations. I had that much time to develop a removal plan. It would not be simple.

≈

During the years preceding my Pella visit, I had started to study chemicals. When I arrived back at the Lyceum, I put my mind to the subject with a deadly purpose. I allowed none of my students to work with me on this. Future gods will hold me alone responsible for what happened.

Weeks later, I was successful. I discovered a secretion that came from a sea creature that was tasteless, colorless, and odorless. Several of my laboratory animals and a slave died during the testing process. One drop of the fluid in a rhyton of wine would slowly kill anyone who ingested it. Death would be unhurried, often taking days. The poison's effects were easily mistaken for a variety of other natural illnesses. The toxic liquid fit our needs perfectly.

I made a final trip to Pella to deliver enough of the fluid to accomplish our plan. That was the extent of my involvement. I was the prime mover, but I left it to the conspiratorial designs of Antipater and Cassander to complete the final acts.

While I waited for news of Alexander's return to Babylon, I worked in Athens to build support for Antipater. He would become vulnerable after Alexander's elimination and the Greeks loved to take advantage of a political and military vacuum. I lost sleep over my actions, but after I had given the matter my best thinking, normal, restful patterns returned. Even now, in this spirit world, I do not regret my actions.

I always taught my students that moral virtue is a mean between two less desirable extremes. This is what I did with Alexander. I pray to the gods that I may encounter when I leave here that they will forgive me for any flaws in my logic.

CHAPTER 23

ECBATANA

Ecbatana, high in the Zagros Mountains, was the Persian Great King's traditional summer retreat. It was also his northernmost capital. Ecbatana was the royal refuge during the intolerable heat of summer that made the Great King's more southern and lower elevation capitols uninhabitable.

In Ecbatana, Alexander held a multi-day festival honoring Dionysus. The festivities featured symbolic plays honoring the spirit of Dionysus, numerous athletic contests, grand musical productions, and poetry readings. Three thousand Greek actors, magicians, and orators infused the festival's events with themes of Hellenic culture. It was the grandest, wildest, most drunken festival that Alexander had ever hosted.

Practically every evening, the king held marathon drinking parties. At one of these, with slurred speech, Alexander and Hephaestion discussed the success of the festival. Clearly, there would be many more like this one. "At times like this, I re… realize how good my life has been," Alexander said. "All of our travails and sacrifices have been worth it. After my Macedonian and Greek problems are solved, I will expand my empire."

"It doesn't get any better than this," Hephaestion answered vacuously. "Both of us will shake the world even more in the coming years. I'm so pleased that you made me your second in command. You know that this will make many enemies for you, both in Persia and Macedonia."

"I've always handled threats," Alexander answered as he spilled red wine down the front of his Persian-style, linen blouse. "Cassander should already be in Babylon waiting for me. When I get there, we will begin negotiations about Antipater. I'm still furious that he refused my command to come to Babylon. I'll order him to go back and tell his father that he must come east immediately. Otherwise, I will send army units to get him. That will be the extent of our negotiations!"

Hephaestion wiped wine from his lips and was quiet. Then he responded to his friend's plan in the usual way. "It's your only course of action. The two of them represent great danger to both of us."

Then he changed the subject to one that Alexander knew obsessed him. "What of Craterus?" he asked.

"He is disconsolate that I have placed you above him," Alexander answered. "However, he has other orders and missions that will occupy him. He will never interact with you again. Does that please you?"

Hephaestion smiled and grasped Alexander by the shoulder. He was nearly as drunk as Alexander and carelessly waved his rhyton in the air. As he made the gesture, he spilled blood-red wine on both of them.

Three slaves appeared immediately to clean up the mess. Another one trotted out of the banquet hall to fetch new clothing for the king and his closest friend.

"I wondered who would be the first to dump a full rhyton," Alexander said good-naturedly. "It shows that Dionysus attends our party. Let's drink until sunrise. We can sleep for days, now that matters are in hand. You're even with me now, but I wager one thousand talents that I can drink you under the table."

"I accept your bet," Hephaestion answered. "You are the world's greatest king, but my body can hold twice the wine that yours can. Let the contest begin."

Alexander's Royal Cupbearer, Iolaus, stood nearby and heard Alexander's challenge. Quickly, he fetched two new rhytons of wine to the king's table. He presented a solid gold one to the king. He gave a lavishly decorated, pure silver one to Hephaestion.

Alexander and Hephaestion waited for Iolaus to pour a small test-sample of both wines and drink first. However, both were so intoxicated that they did not notice that Iolaus merely feigned drinking from Hephaestion's rhyton. Unaware, Hephaestion started the contest, and the party continued.

That simple action changed everything.

≈

Early the next morning Hephaestion collapsed. He was unconscious and barely breathing.

Alexander sobered up as much as he could, then examined his friend. He decided that the poor man just couldn't keep up with him in drinking. As a precaution, however, he ordered Hephaestion taken to his royal bedroom, where his personal physician would examine him and treat him if necessary.

The king had seen countless men pass out from drink before; he was not overly concerned. Self-pleased that he had won the contest, he stumbled out of the banquet hall to a nearby bedroom and collapsed onto a bed. His last muddled thought was that Hephaestion would sleep it off. The king then passed out and slept for a day and a half.

≈

Hephaestion finally revived. However, he was lethargic and had a low-grade fever. He had not left the king's royal bed where the slaves had placed him.

When Alexander finally awoke, he walked, with some difficulty, to his royal bedroom at the other end of the palace to visit Hephaestion. He spotted his friend still in bed and was alarmed. Hephaestion looked awful. His usually clear skin was ashen and his facial features were sunken. "You look like Darius when we caught him," Alexander said with brutal honesty. He gently stroked Hephaestion's brow. "But they tell me that you are better. My physician prescribes a strict diet for you with no drinking for a while."

Hephaestion flashed his eyes at Alexander but was unable to speak.

"I've recovered enough from the drinking, and I want to watch my Successors compete in the stadium tomorrow," Alexander continued. "I'll check on you from time to time. You're strong and will get through this."

The king ruffled Hephaestion's thinning hair, then turned to leave the bedroom. Something caused him to pause and look back at his friend. He gave him a half-wave, clenched his left fist before his chest, and then left.

Hephaestion couldn't and didn't return the gestures.

≈

The next day Hephaestion grew stronger. Still weak, he was ravenous. Against his physician's orders, he ordered and ate a whole, boiled chicken. Then, continuing to honor Dionysus, he ordered Iolaus to bring him wine to settle his stomach.

Before the morning was over, Hephaestion fell into unconsciousness again. Alexander, three stadia away watching his boys compete, was summoned to his friend's side. But he arrived too late.

Hephaestion died alone, soon after wolfing down a forbidden meal and resuming his uncontrolled consumption of wine.

The most important person in Alexander's life was gone.

≈

"Get away from me!" Alexander screamed. "I'll tell you when to return." He lay on Hephaestion's dead corpse, sobbing and retching. None of his Royal Bodyguards had ever seen him like this.

The king of the world's greatest empire stayed next to Hephaestion's cold body for a day and a half. At last, still alone in his bedroom, he sat up. He wiped layers of tears from his face and began speaking to a dead person. The last time he did this was after his father's assassination so many years ago.

"You were the one great love of my life, Hephaestion," he began. "Countless times, I was so angry with you that I nearly ordered your death. You were vain, vainer than I am. You acted like a child most of your life.

"You were also dull. I'm surprised that I ever found any value in you. You easily could have become just another of my boyhood friends.

"Yet I never doubted your loyalty and unwavering love for me. Life without you is going to be empty.

"You will be honored with a grand funeral in Babylon. I'll preside over your embalming personally. When I recover from your loss, I'll request your deification from the priests at Siwah. The governor of Egypt and the priests there owe me. You deserve it for your long service to the son of Zeus-Ammon.

"Your funeral will be the grandest a human has ever had. When I am old, these last, private moments and your funeral will be all that I have. I want the memory of you to stay with humankind and me forever.

"All of this will be done."

Alexander, overcome with continued grief, sobbed openly. Finally, he regained superficial control and continued his diatribe to the dead. "If one of your wives is pregnant, though I doubt that either is, I will care for your son or daughter. They will become royalty and great leaders. This, and more, I promise you."

Alexander then stood, exuded his last sobs, and walked to the door of his bedroom. "Get in here," he shouted. "I'm ready to return to the world of the living."

Perdiccas entered first and awaited his king's orders.

"I've cut off all of my hair to honor Hephaestion, just as Achilles did for Patroclus," he said to Perdiccas. "It is the least I could do for my friend. Order all of our horses' tails sheared as well. When that is done, execute that miserable physician who killed Hephaestion."

≈

Nearing the end of his mourning, Alexander commissioned a magnificent, monumental lion honoring Hephaestion and ordered it placed in Ecbatana.

But Alexander's life had to go on. He accepted Ptolemy's view that the cause of Hephaestion's death was the result of excessive drinking and an inept physician. The tragedy also caused him, for a few months, to reduce his own reckless consumption of wine.

His friend's death also caused him to reconsider his mortality. Two weeks after Hephaestion's death, a period that he thought was sufficient for his body to cleanse itself of alcohol, Alexander summoned Roxane to his personal quarters.

"I am ready to give you a son," he began speaking through the translator. "I know that I have ignored you. I also know that you understand my continuing grief over Hephaestion's death. However, life continues despite our tragedies. The gods always have their way with us.

"What I rejected before I left Pella, the siring of a male, royal offspring, I now accept and understand. If I should die without a son, my empire would disintegrate. The strongest, most vicious of my generals would win what I sacrificed so much for. The rest would wage civil wars for decades. That would negate my entire life."

Roxane waited for the translation, then smiled. Regally, she swept back her full head of hair from around her eyes and then gave Alexander a simple answer. "When do you want to begin?"

Alexander chuckled, and then walked nervously in a tight circle around the room. "Your eagerness is intimidating," he said after completing his miniature circuit. Then he recovered his composure. "You once told me of a special diet women in your country eat if they must have a male baby. Is that true?"

"It never fails, Alexander," Roxane answered. "You must eat it too and stop all drinking until I am pregnant. If we both stay on the diet for a month and make love every day, a royal son will result."

"Then it is settled," Alexander answered. "I am ready to become a father."

≈

Roxane's diet worked. A month after Hephaestion's death she was pregnant. Pleased with his strong heterosexual performance, Alexander resumed his drinking, but not at the intense, binge level as before. Within days of Roxane's pregnancy announcement, he started bragging to his Royal Companions about his fatherhood. He was as virile as any of them.

Slowly, the enervating pain of Hephaestion's death lessened in Alexander. The king found solace in the action that he did best: military conquest. He led his fighters southwest of Ecbatana and encountered mountain tribesmen who had always received exorbitant annuities from the Great King just for passing through their territory.

Alexander's transferred his grief into violent, aggressive action against the tribesmen: in just five weeks, they were eliminated. The king knew that the tribesmen's ancestors would never again get tribute for an army to pass through their territory. That knowledge gave him great pleasure.

Alexander's last actions in Ecbatana found him ordering an expedition north to the Caspian Sea. He ordered his officers to investigate the quality of the local forests there and determine if the trees could be used for shipbuilding. The next stage of the king's conquests would involve more than land armies. Stout, Greek fighting and transport ships would become necessary in the years ahead.

At last, pleased that initial plans for invasions of North Africa and Carthage, Italy, and Spain were in place, the king and his army prepared for departure from Ecbatana. Before leaving, he visited the memorial site of Hephaestion. Local sculptors were in the initial stages of revealing a lion that lay hidden inside a huge block of granite.

"Good-bye, old friend," he said reverentially to the incomplete lion. "We came a long way from Mieza to here. After North Africa and Europe, I will return to see your completed lion. I drew the image for the sculptors myself. I know that you will be pleased when you look down on it from your spirit world. I will see you there when we meet again. Perhaps we will conquer that place too. He smiled at the thoughts of that victory, then tucked it away for another day, perhaps one filled with drink and loneliness."

Alexander then mounted his horse and rode southwest with his Royal Companions toward Babylon. It would be good to see the city again after seven years. He would make it the most beautiful city the world had ever seen, worthy of Alexander's capitol.

Riding amid a cloud of dust, he was pensive but satisfied. The rest of his life lay ahead of him. His spiritual father continued to protect him. Things would be better before long.

CHAPTER 24

BABYLON

Alexander and his army neared Babylon and encountered a group of Chaldaean astrologers just after they crossed the Tigris River. The priests, earthly representatives of the Persian god, Bel-Marduk, had left their temple complex to meet Alexander before he entered his new capitol.

"We beg you, Great King," their chief priest said, speaking in near-perfect Greek. "Our god issued a clear warning; the signs are unmistakable. You must not enter Babylon through the eastern gate, the Gate of Bel. It will be fatal for you if you do. Entering through the Gate of Bel means you would be facing the setting sun. You and your army must enter the city from the west, marching through the Royal Gate. It is imperative that your army march facing the rising sun."

The priests had left the Esagila early that morning. That religious complex, thousands of years old, was in the center of Babylon. Just north of the Esagila was the Foundation of Heaven on Earth. This ziggurat was later called the Tower of Babel in a holy book of the Jews.

Alexander rubbed his eyes and frowned. *This is just what I need*, he thought. *Another group of priests telling me what I can and cannot do.* Yet, he could not dismiss their warnings, for the Chaldaeans were famous for the accuracy of their predictions. When he was in Babylon seven years ago, he had examined their archival record of Persian events and predictions. Their *Astronomical Diary* recorded realized prophesies that went back over thirty-three hundred years. Alexander could not ignore them.

Alexander issued orders that stopped his army's march.

"I can't bring the army in from the east," the king said to Bel-Marduk's chief priest. "My scouts already warned me that the approach is unsuitable for a force as great as ours.

He walked away from the Chaldaeans, irritated, and shouted an order to a Royal Bodyguard. "Get me Anaxarchus. I want a Greek interpretation of this."

Anaxarchus soon arrived, and he listened to Alexander's explanation of the Chaldaeans' warning. "Do you have another entry choice, considering your huge army?" he asked.

"Entry from the west would be difficult, perhaps impossible," Alexander answered. "The swamps and marshes there are extensive; the terrain is difficult. I won't have our fighters entering Babylon covered in mud."

"Then ignore their superstitious prattle," Anaxarchus told him. "Enter from the east. Facing the sun doesn't have anything to do with your greatness."

Alexander, still troubled, finally made up his mind. This Persian superstition was too much. He issued orders for the army to enter Babylon through the Gate of Bel, facing the setting sun.

Walking away from Anaxarchus, he turned to him and said, "Prophets are best who make the truest guess." Then he left to ride to the head of his massive forces. The matter was resolved.

≈

At a supreme leadership council meeting in Babylon's royal palace, Alexander met with his top officers and Royal Bodyguards. His army's entry into Babylon had been uneventful. It was now time for long-term plans.

"Hephaestion's funeral arrangements are my first priority," he said with a mournful look on his face. "His pyre alone will cost 10,000 talents. His funeral will reduce my royal treasury by five times that amount. Nevertheless, I promised his dead body that I would honor him as no man has ever been honored. All funeral events will take place in the northeast quarter of the city. Even the nervous Chaldaeans agree that the site is propitious.

"Perdiccas, you are in charge of the final arrangements. The Siwah priests won't allow his deification. However, they indicated that Hephaestion could be worshiped as a hero. Build his revered status into the funeral ceremony."

"I will," Perdiccas answered tersely.

"Enough of the sad past, then," Alexander said. "I must start meeting with the delegations that are waiting. Each insists on seeing me personally. It wasn't this way the first time we were in Babylon. Eumenes tells me that envoys are here from the Corinthian League, Carthage, Libya, Southern Italy, and Rome. Even Iberians and Celts are here. I'll have to learn a new set of maps just to deal with their issues."

≈

Alexander spent the next days in tedious meetings with the lackeys that called themselves national leaders and diplomats. They honored him with their gifts and obsequious remarks, but he was bored with their self-serving praise and requests. At last, he could stand no more and ordered Perdiccas to meet with them and commit to nothing. His pothos-driven wanderlust was rising and he was intent on additional conquest. It was the reason that Zeus-Ammon had given him life.

≈

"All right," Alexander said. "Here is our priority list, from most important to the least important." The king stated each objective forcefully, as if emphasizing its order would increase the likelihood of it happening.

"One: Nearchus will leave soon with our new ships to reconnoiter Arabia and Africa. If his reports back are positive, I will join him to circumnavigate the continent and find where the unknown western sea opens into the Mediterranean. That is supposed to be at the Pillars of Hercules. We will then sail east and meet our main army after it completes a road across Northern Africa. Our combined naval and land forces will then take Libya and Carthage.

"Two: After Libya and Carthage fall, we will sail to Spain and create outposts there. This campaign will be exploratory, until we find what forces are there to oppose us.

"Three: I will then sail to Epirus, the land of my mother's birth. I'm eager to see her again. I must see the great temple at Dodona again.

"Four: We will give thanks to the gods in appreciation for our successes. I want seven new temples built: three in Greece, three in Macedonia, and one magnificent one to Athena at Troy. Each will become one of the world's greatest wonders.

"Five: If an enemy arrow hasn't killed me by then, I will return to Aegae and construct a pyramid for Philip that is greater than Cheops' Giza monument. I have surpassed Philip, but he made all of this possible.

"Does anyone have any questions?"

His men knew only vaguely the scope of their king's dreams, but having him state them all at once was staggering to each officer.

Finally, Ptolemy spoke up. "Let me lead the army across Northern Africa," he asked. "I understand Egypt and speak their language. It will aid the road construction and pacification effort."

Alexander looked at his half-brother and smiled. "I agree," he said. "I think you covet Egypt, Ptolemy. I may make you my satrap there when everything is done. Would you like that?"

"I would," Ptolemy answered honestly. "However, I exist now only to serve you, Alexander."

Alexander glared at Ptolemy, then stood up. He pointed to the door, signaling that the meeting was over. "There is a departure party for Nearchus in a few days," he shouted to the exiting officers. "I want all of you there. It will symbolize our solidarity and launch our new conquests. Our glory continues!"

≈

"You are more beautiful now than when you were not with child," Alexander said to Roxane. His wife was eight months pregnant and Alexander saw a warm glow of expectant motherhood that radiated from her. "I give you my word; I will be a good father to the son that you are growing inside you," he said with pride.

Roxane could only understand half of what Alexander said without a translator present but decided to surprise her husband. "Words are nice

…" Roxane answered. It was her first attempt at speaking a little, halting Greek. "Pregnancy were easy; it won't be long time."

Alexander, pleased with his wife's attempt to speak his language, walked closer, and raised Roxane's blouse so that her bare, protruding stomach was open to his touch. Then he began to stroke the skin covering his unborn baby.

"Oh!" he said, startled. "He moved! Does he know the king is here?"

Roxane smiled and walked to the doorway, summoning her Balkh translator. She had uttered as much Greek as she knew. When the translator entered the room, she motioned for Alexander to repeat his last question for translation. Then she answered her husband.

"He moves nearly all of the time. He will have as much energy as you do. You will be proud to give him your empire when you grow old."

Grow old? Alexander thought. He had never considered the idea. It was a novel notion. "I have much to do before that," he answered. "Know that I love you more than before, Roxane. I am so proud of you and my son.

"Come, walk with me in the Royal Gardens. I'm going duck hunting in the swamp tomorrow. Then, we will honor Nearchus with a banquet. I may not be able to see you again before we depart for Africa."

Roxane put her head on Alexander's shoulder and they entered the gardens of Babylon. It was a tranquil time and the two held hands as they strolled into a mellow, early-summer evening. They heard the Esagila temple priests in the distance calling worshipers to their evening prayers. Both sensed that their lives were at a crossroads.

Persian gardens had brought out these emotions in people for centuries. The gardens continued to provide a much-needed refuge from life's uncertain ways.

Two adults and an unborn child slowly disappeared into the evening mist, absorbing peace and serenity from the special place.

≈

"His weakness is wine," Perdiccas said. "It has always been so." One of Alexander's greatest commanders, Perdiccas, did not look at the other plotters. It was only his relegation to a lower status in the king's command structure that had brought him to this meeting.

"Yes, but it won't be as easy as it was with Hephaestion," Iolaus cautioned. "His lightning mind would detect the slight of hand that I used on his beloved. He seems suspicious of me. As never before, he watches me drink his wine before he drinks after me. I can no longer fake it."

Cassander spoke up and provided the answer the plotters needed. "Someone else must administer the liquid, someone he trusts. Aristotle told me that Alexander must get multiple doses, over a long time. It would work better if he were tired, ill, or coming off several days of binging. It must done in this manner."

Medius, the secret lover of Iolaus, finally spoke. "I'm in the king's favor now. He and I have had many drinking bouts. If I'm careful about the timing, I might have an opportunity."

"Then you will be the agent of his demise, Medius," Cassander said. "I would do it, but I can't get near him, not after the incident when I laughed out loud at that Persian giving him proskynesis. The king leaped off his throne and beat my head against the wall. I should have killed him then and there."

Perdiccas had seen the event. At the time, he was surprised that Alexander had not ordered one of his guards to kill Cassander. "He is going duck hunting in the swamp tomorrow," Perdiccas offered. "He never drinks wine during hunts. He feels it deadens his aim with the bow. It will have to be done after that."

"We'll wait our time during and after Nearchus' party," Iolaus said. "Each of us will have a small vial of the liquid. Tighten the cork, then put it inside your buttocks in case he has us searched. A little shit on the vial will be the least of his problems!"

Each plotter smiled an uneasy smile. They were committed. Everyone knew that everything in the Greek and Mediterranean world would soon change.

"May the gods and future generations understand why we had to act," Perdiccas said as he stood up to leave. "Pray to whatever deity that you believe in that we do not turn out as Alexander did. It occurs to me that we may just be scripted actors in the second act of a very long play by Euripides." The senior general paused to let the insightful comment sink in.

"I killed Philip's assassin at the theatre in Pella," Perdiccas continued. "It seemed to make perfect sense then. I'm older now. Somehow, everything is less logical.

"I'll support each of you when this is over," he offered. "But you are never to speak to anyone about what we are about to do. If anyone speaks or writes of our actions, I will eliminate him. Does everyone understand that?"

Each plotter stared at Perdiccas and knew that he meant his stern words. To a man, each nodded his head and the secret meeting broke up.

That night, Perdiccas prayed to Dionysus that the god's inebriating power would be strong enough to help bring down the greatest man who ever lived.

CHAPTER 25

DIONYSUS' EMPTY MASK

"Is your fever so high that we must cancel the banquet for Nearchus?" Eumenes asked Alexander.

"I don't think so," Alexander answered feebly. "I feel flushed around my face and neck, but that is common when I'm ill, especially after a night of drinking."

"A Persian told me that they call the condition swamp fever," Eumenes said. "You were in the marshes all day yesterday. Something there probably caused your fever. It is supposed to last three to five days, most sufferers have recurring, high-fever episodes at about the same time each day."

"I've heard the same story," Alexander said. "A Chaldaean priest told me that it comes from mosquito bites. We were in a swarm most of the morning. I'm covered with bites. I can't stop scratching them."

"Tell me what to do about the banquet," Eumenes asked a second time.

"Continue with the plans," Alexander answered irritably. "I won't send Nearchus to explore Africa without honoring him. I may never see him again."

Alexander dismissed his secretary and went to the Royal Baths. His chamberlain had prepared a steaming oil and myrrh bath that was supposed to help heal his bites. Afterwards, he planned to sleep until the banquet. A celebratory night of drinking with his most intimate friends was all that he needed to get well.

≈

Twenty of the king's closest friends attended Nearchus' farewell banquet. Included were Ptolemy, Eumenes, Perdiccas, Iolaus, Peucestas, Medius, Philip (Alexander's personal physician), Philip (the king's royal engineer) and twelve others.

Slaves served wine with the first eating course. More than once, Iolaus tried to serve wine to his king. However, Alexander rebuffed him each time. The king had selected a new wine taster.

Alexander spent the first part of the evening reclining next to his newest court favorite, Medius. Amid meaningless gossip and Alexander's bragging about past military feats, Medius continued to pour Alexander kantharos after kantharos of the mind-destroying gift of Dionysus.

Well after the midnight watch changed, Alexander left the main banquet and led a small group of his friends to Medius' quarters. A new table of food awaited them and another round of drinking ensued. When everyone had reclined on their couches, the king rose to propose the night's fifth toast. "To the hero of the day, Nearchus," he said with mumbled speech. "Greeks will learn more about Auh … Arabia and Africa in the coming months than we have known in the last thou … thousand years. If he doesn't fall off the edge of the world, his explorations will open new vis… vistas for all civilized peoples. To Nearchus!"

The group stood and raised their cups toward Nearchus. "To Nearchus!" they all shouted.

Alexander, now completing his fourth kantharos, grasped the cup with both hands, tilted his head back, and opened his throat to receive its contents. The king had saved the rich, unmixed wine that his father had named Philip Red for this elite gathering of his closest friends. It was Alexander's favorite, grown in Macedonia's Gardens of Midas and shipped to him in Babylon.

Halfway through the gurgling drink, Alexander stopped and dropped his kantharos. His eyes were transfixed on an invisible object, three arm-lengths in front of him. His wine spilled out of the kantharos and down the front of his Persian robe. It then crashed onto the table and splattered onto the marble floor.

"Ahhhhh! Ahhhhh!" Alexander shouted with a guttural utterance of pain. Both of his hands went to the lower-left abdomen, and he slowly fell to his knees. "God," he gasped. "I've never felt such pain." Then he fell to the floor.

Five of his friends were beside him in an instant.

"What is wrong?" Ptolemy asked with concern. "Is it something that you ate?" Ptolemy looked around suspiciously, already making assumptions about what might have happened.

Alexander continued making rasping sounds and could not answer him.

"Take him to his bedroom," Perdiccas commanded in a strong voice. "Put a double security guard around him. Get the slaves in here that prepared his meal. I want his new wine taster in here, now!"

Alexander's physician, Philip, ordered several of the men to carry him to his room. "Don't touch his stomach," Philip said. "That is the source of his pain."

Ptolemy and Eumenes slid their arms under Alexander's back and lifted him off the floor. Nearchus and Medius did the same under his legs.

The group half-ran to the king's quarters, all but one fearing the worst. Each had seen Alexander wounded in battle more than once, but this was ominous. Already, the king's face was losing its color; then suddenly, he started vomiting. His body temperature was hot even through his clothes. It had all happened so quickly.

≈

Alexander had only ten days left to live. The day after the banquet, his fever continued unabated. He took several cooling baths to lower his temperature with no success. However, he was well enough to dine alone with Medius that evening. Fatefully, his consumption of wine never stopped.

The next day he played dice with several of his bodyguards and seemed to rally. A scroll arrived from Olympias, but he was too ill to read it. "Put it beside my bed," he told Eumenes. "I'll read it when I'm better." The following day he spent his waking hours in the bathhouse attempting to lower his raging fever.

On the fifth day, he rallied and was able to speak at length with Nearchus about his ocean voyage around the Gedrosian and his coming explorations of Arabia and Africa. Nearchus reminisced at length with Alexander, then left his bedroom, encouraged that he would survive.

The following day, Alexander realized that he was critically, perhaps mortally, ill. "Put all of my senior officers and officials on notice," he said feebly to Eumenes and Philip. "I want them near me if I should start to fail."

A week after the banquet he called for Perdiccas. The man who had aided Alexander in the plot to eliminate his father's assassin sat close to the king and, with difficulty, heard him speak in a feeble, whisper-voice. "This ... this is my end," he stammered. "Take my ring. I name you my successor, Perdiccas. Others will ... challenge this. Get ready."

Perdiccas took the ring, but did not put in on his finger, not while Alexander was alive. "What else would you have me do?" Perdiccas asked.

Alexander started to answer, but a deep cough rattled his lungs and stopped his words. His face contorted in pain, his lips trembled uncontrollably. Then, with a weak left hand, he motioned for Perdiccas to leave. It was all that he was capable of doing.

≈

The king's Macedonian fighters heard only wild rumors about what was happening to Alexander. After a week of waiting in the dark, they took action. Several hundred of them surrounded the palace and demanded to see their monarch. When Perdiccas refused them entry, fifty of them ran to an exterior wall opposite the king's bedroom and broke a hole in it with a battering ram. More than five hundred men then lined up quietly and filed into the bedroom to see if Alexander were alive.

Alexander heard the crashing of stone and mortar and knew what was happening. He was pleased, but could do little to show his appreciation of his men's direct action.

Soon a long line of his fighters began to file past his bed. Some dipped their heads to Alexander, others got on their knees briefly. More than a few wept openly when they saw their king's condition. He was alive, but just barely.

Alexander's mind was still functioning even though his body was shutting down. All he could do to recognize his men's presence was to raise an index finger and flash his brown and blue eyes toward them. He knew that they saw the actions and that they understood. He realized too that, despite everything that he had put them through, they still loved him.

≈

The ninth night of Alexander's illness, all of the king's Royal Bodyguards went to Babylon's Bel-Marduk Temple and started a prayer vigil. Many wanted to bring Alexander to the temple to receive the god's personal blessing. However, the temple priests intervened and informed the Bodyguards that Bel-Marduk forbade it. The supreme god himself had let them know that Alexander was too ill to be moved.

Early in the morning of the tenth day, Ptolemy, Perdiccas, Leonnatus, Lysimachus, and Peucestas went to Alexander's bedchamber. They joined Philip, his physician, who had not left his side for three days.

Alexander was either asleep or in a coma, so they waited. In the middle of the night, the king awakened and looked over the group. A pathetic, half-smile appeared on his face, and he whispered a question "What do you want?"

Ptolemy, with tears in his eyes, bent over his half-brother and said, "Who should inherit your kingdom, Alexander?" Everyone in the group moved closer to Alexander to hear his answer.

Alexander attempted a deep breath but could not reach it and coughed harshly. Then he made a second, successful attempt at air and was able to speak, just above an inaudible whisper. "It must go … It must go … to the strongest. There will be a great funeral contest over me."

The king of the greatest empire that the world had ever seen then attempted another breath, but the effort failed. Each man there heard his death rattle, then silence. Alexander of Macedon was dead. It was fourteen years after he became king.

≈

Peter Messmore

Later, a Chaldaean priest-astrologer wrote a terse entry in the *Astronomical Diary* for the Persian year 3337. It read, "29 Aiaru The king died. Clouds were in the sky."

ARISTOTLE'S REFLECTIONS FROM A SPIRIT WORLD
4

Alexander and Hephaestion had to be eliminated. My involvement in their deaths, albeit only at the beginning of the plot, was a near refutation of my life's work. Yet, given the chance to do it again, I would. My time in this spirit world has taught me that.

I now understand the excesses of Alexander's megalomania. He never could have ruled a world empire. Nevertheless, that was his ultimate dream. That vision obsessed him during his tempestuous life.

Macedonia's strong wine would have killed him anyway.

My action saved countless humans from losing their individual and national identities. Now, after centuries here, I know that I was wrong in thinking that Persians and other eastern peoples were inherently slaves and barbarians. Alexander's many letters to me during the campaign, especially the last ones, convinced me that theirs was an advanced civilization. He should never have destroyed them. Greeks could have learned much from their high culture.

Within weeks of Alexander's death, Athens was in a near state of rebellion. Demades made a speech and doubted the authenticity of Alexander's death report. "Alexander dead?" he shouted. "Impossible; the whole world would stink of his corpse." It was a pithy, rhetorical remark that I know that Demosthenes wished he had made.

Alexander's generals lingered in Babylon and the nearby territories. Each busied himself, trying to carve up major pieces of his empire. All of them wanted to become a king in their own right. Their contests developed into a bloody mess before a single ruler emerged.

Olympias fled to her homeland in Epirus. Her grief over Alexander's death was only exceeded by her determination to strike back at those who killed him. I doubt that she ever knew of my involvement in her son's elimination. She wanted to become the first woman to rule Macedon. I find it curious that she outlived both Philip and Alexander. It was only the gods themselves that saved the Greek world from the vindictive fury of Olympias.

The year after Alexander's death saw a vast and expensive funeral being held and a stunning funeral monument begun. During that last year of my life, I learned that it resembled an enormous, royal wagon, complete with statues and columns. His generals intended to bring it to Pella, where a pyramid greater than Cheops' was planned. However, Ptolemy stole the body and fled with it to Alexandria in Egypt. As you know, he and his line formed a great dynasty there.

Roxanne delivered a male baby after Alexander's death. She named him Alexander the Fourth. The infant was Alexander's only legitimate heir. The child's name alone was laden with dynastic ambition.

Antipater ordered the former queen and her infant to return to Pella. They remained safe there for a while. That changed, as the so-called successor-generals divided Alexander's empire.

Athens' leaders saw me, understandably so, as a Macedonian sympathizer, one who could not be trusted by real Greeks. My life was in danger and I had to leave my beloved Lyceum. I went to my family estate on the island of Euboea to begin my exile. It was there that I died of old age and being too involved in the life of one of the most enigmatic men who ever lived.

≈

Yet, I feel that I acted with honor during Alexander's short life. Had he followed my teaching, everything would have turned out differently. Immediately after my death, I doubted that he would ever be anything more than a footnote in history. I naively thought that it was great ideas, concepts, and scientific principles, endeavors in which I made serious contributions, that would form the basis of altering civilization, giving humans a chance to improve their condition. Observing your history over the millennia, I know now that I was wrong.

Alexander is not here, nor has he ever been here. I cannot understand why I ended up here and he did not. I often fear, if there is an afterlife beyond this spirit world, that I will meet Alexander there. I will give that possibility some thought. I have always been good at thought.

CHARACTERS, GEOGRAPHIC LOCATIONS
AND UNIQUE TERMS
USED IN

ALEXANDER THE KING

Abuleites: Persian satrap of Susa

Abydos: Persian seaport near the Hellespont

Achaemenid: Royal line of Persian Great Kings

Aegae: The ancient, spiritual capitol of Macedonian kings.

Aeorpus: Provincial ruler of Lyncestis in Macedonia

Aetolia: A Greek city-state

Agatho: Alexander's phalanx commander; left behind in Media

Agis: King of Sparta; planned revolt against Alexander

Agrianians: Soldiers from a province in northwest Macedonia. Their king, Langarus, led them. He gave Alexander "some of his toughest and most reliable" light-armed fighters.

Ahura Mazda: The Persian supreme god.

Akitu: Persian new year's festival

Altious: Olympias' priest conspirator and accomplice

Amanic: The Gate (pass) where Great King Darius descended on Alexander at Issus

Ammon Ra: The supreme god of Egypt. Ammon's oracle resided at the desert oasis in Siwah.

Amphipolis: City in Thrace, ten days march east of Pella

Amyntas: Phalanx commander in Alexander's army

Anaxarchus: Advisor/propagandist to Alexander; rival of Callisthenes

Antipater: Regent of Macedon during Alexander's conquests; quarreled with Olympias

Apadana: The Persian Great King's central audience chamber in the Royal Palace at Persepolis (Parsa)

Arbela: Ancient Persian city northwest of Babylon; near the battle site of Gaugamela

Archon: A high Athenian government official elected annually

Ariobarzanes: Persian satrap who opposed Alexander

Aristander: Alexander's seer during the Persian expedition

Arrhabaeus: Alexander's commander of Lancers and Paeonians

Arridaeus (Philip Arridaeus): Half-brother of Alexander; made mentally defective in childhood by Olympias

Aristotle: Scientist, philosopher, teacher; Founded the Mieza School in northwest Macedonia where Alexander and the Royal Pages were taught. Later founded the famous Lyceum in Athens.

Arses: Young son of Persian Great King Artaxerxes Ochus; he was poisoned by Bagoas, the Grand Vizier

Artabazus: Father of Barsine; former Persian satrap of Phrygia; initially fought with Darius; a later ally and supporter of Alexander

Artaxerxes Ochus: Persian Great King during most of Philip's reign; poisoned by Bagoas.

Attalus: One of Philip's leading generals; killed by Alexander's orders at the start of his reign

andrapodismos: Total elimination of a polis through razing and selling its inhabitants into lifelong slavery.

Bactria: Persian province governed by Bessus

Bagoas: Grand Vizier of Persian Great King Artaxerxes Ochus

also

Bagoas: Beautiful boy-eunuch; lover of both Great King Darius and Alexander

Barsine: Daughter of Artabazus; wife of Memnon; Alexander's first female lover

also

Barsine/Stateira: Daughter of Persian Great King Darius and Stateira. Her birth name was Barsine. Alexander renamed her Stateira when he married her during the mass marriages in Susa.

Bel Marduk: Local Babylonian god (called Marduk by pious Babylonian Persians)

Bessus: Persian provincial governor of Bactria; killed Darius and led the remnants of Persia's army

Boeotia: City state in central Greece

Bosporus: A strait or narrow sea connecting two seas or connecting a lake and a sea

Bucephalas: Alexander's famous horse

Byblos: Persian city

Boule: The council of 500 that directed Athens' government

Cadmea: Thebes' high citadel

Calas: Alexander's officer; son of Harpalus

Callisthenes: Nephew of Aristotle; scholar who accompanied Alexander on much of his Persian invasion.

Callixeina: Athenian courtesan who tried (unsuccessfully) to initiate Alexander sexually

Caranus: Baby son of Cleopatra-Eurydice and Philip II

Cassander: Son of Antipater

Cebalinus: Young man who revealed the possible plot against Alexander's life

Chaeronea: Site of Philip's great victory over the allied Greeks in south central Greece

Chaldaeans: Babylonian priests versed in astrology and sooth saying

Cheops: Greek term for the Great Pyramid on the Giza plateau. Egyptians called it Khufu's Pyramid

Chios: Island off the Persian cost of Lydia

chiton: A tunic worn next to the skin by both sexes

Cilicia: The region south of Cappadocia; today, called the Turkish Riviera.

Cleander: Parmenio's second in command; murdered Parmenio

Cleopatra-Eurydice: Last wife of Philip II; mother of Europa and Caranus

Clearchus: Officer who commanded the Agrianian archers

Codomannus: Name of Darius before he became Great King of Persia

Coenus: Parmenio's son-in-law; commanded 1/6 of the phalanx battalion on the extreme right.

Craterus: Commanded a phalanx battalion; appointed a "friend of the king"; hated Hephaestion

Crenides: Grimy mining settlement near Mount Pangaeus

Cunaxa: Persian city on the Euphrates, sixty miles northwest of Babylon.

cuirass: body armor made of metal plates

Daric: Persian coin of the realm

Deinocrates: Architect who laid out Alexandria in Egypt

Demosthenes: Athenian orator and legislator; hated adversary of Philip II and Alexander

Didyma: Site of Apollo's oracle near Miletus in Persian Caria.

Dodona: Site of oracle in Epirus. The Dodona oracle was revered by Olympias and Alexander

Drangiana: Persian province, west of the Hindu Kush mountains.

Dymnus: A young plotter in the plot to murder Alexander

Ecbatana: The Persian Great King's summer capitol in Media

Elis: A Greek city-state.

Erigyius: One of Alexander's oldest and most trusted friends; officer and inner circle member

Esagila: The temple complex in the center of Babylon

Euboea: Greek island north of Athens

Eubulus: Athens' minister of finance

Eumenes: Alexander's personal secretary and propagandist

Europa: Daughter of Cleopatra-Eurydice and Philip II

Gaugamela: Site of the third and last major battle between the Macedonians/Greeks and the Persians

Gedrosian: The great desert across the southern tip of modern-day Afghanistan

Gordium: Ancient Persian city and location of the famous Gordian Knot

Granicus River: Site of Alexander's first victory over the Persians in modern day Turkey

Halicarnassus: Persian seaport city in Caria

Halys: River in Persia that flows north into the Black Sea; near modern-day Ankara, Turkey

Harpalus: Alexander's treasurer and boyhood friend

Hecataeus: Macedonian officer & early supporter of Alexander

Heliopolis: City in northern Egypt

Hellespont: The narrow strait between Thrace and Persia (modern day Europe and Turkey). An invading army had to enter Persia across this historic sea passage.

Hephaestion: Friend and lover of Alexander.

Heracles: Alexander's ancestor; Roman name was Hercules

hegemon: The supreme political leader in Greece and the Corinthian League. Philip first held this title, then Alexander.

Hindu Kush: The high mountain range in eastern Persia (Bactria).

hypaspists: Military unit created to protect the phalanx flank; also to maintain contact with Alexander's cavalry.

Illyria: The extreme northwestern territory in Philip and Alexander's homeland empire. The coastal region toward today's Adriatic.

Iolaus: Alexander's food and wine taster

Ishtar: Beautiful gate at the end of the Processional Way in Babylon. Remnants and a reproduction of the Gate are now in Berlin at the Pergamum Museum.

Issus: Site of Alexander's second victory over Persian Great King Darius

kantharos: A Macedonian, two-handed drinking cup.

Lampsacus: Persian city near the Hellespont.

Laomedon: Young officer who served Alexander; He had estates near Amphipolis and spoke Persian.

Leonidas: Leader of the Spartans at Thermopylae.

Leonnatus: Alexander's boyhood friend and Macedonian aristocrat from Orestis. He helped save Alexander's life in India.

Lesbos: Island off the coast of Aegean Persia (today off Turkey).

Lycia: Persian region immediately north of the Mediterranean Sea; northwest of the island of Cyprus

Lyncestis: Western and northwestern region in the highlands of Macedonia

larnax: An ornate burial chest for cremated bones.

Magi: Persian astrologers and priestly caste

Maimakterion: Attic Greek month (roughly equivalent to modern November)

Marathus: Persian seaport east of the island of Cyprus

Mazaeus: Persian satrap of Babylon

Medius: Thessalian friend of Alexander; hosted drinking party where Alexander was stricken

Meleager: Alexander's trusted companion and battalion commander

Memnon: Greek soldier of fortune and mercenary who fought for Persian King Darius; husband of Barsine until his death

Mieza: Location of Aristotle's Royal Pages School in western Macedonia. It was in the eastern foothills of the Bermius mountain range, near the ancient Gardens of Midas. Today, near the northern Greek city of Naoussa.. The region is famous for its red wine today.

Miletus: Persian seaport on the Aegean Sea; north of Halicarnassus

Mosul: Persian city on the Tigris River, north of Babylon/Baghdad

Nabarzanes: Persian heavy cavalry commander

Naghsh-e-Rostam: Traditional, rock-faced burial site of Persian Great Kings

Nearchus: Alexander's boyhood friend and later, his admiral

Nicanor: The secönd of Parmenio's sons who commanded a guards' brigade. He fell ill and died.

Ochus (Artaxerxes) Persian Great King prior to Darius

Olympias: Wife of Philip of Macedon; mother of Alexander the Great and Cleopatra.

Oncestus: Greek city-state near Thebes

Orestis: Western, highland region in central Macedonia

Orontobates: Persian commander of Halicarnassus

Osiris: Egyptian deity

Ossa: Mountain in central Greece. Alexander cut steps up the seaward side of Mt. Ossa. These steps can still be seen today and are known as Alexander's Ladder.

Oxyartes: Provincial official of the Soghdian Rock; father of Roxane; later supporter of Alexander

Paeonians: Primitive region north of Pella; near the River Vardar

Paiko: A small Macedonian city a half day's travel from Pella. It was the site where Olympias established a religious convent and a school for young girls.

Pamphylia: Persian region immediately north of the Mediterranean Sea; northwest of the island of Cyprus

Pangaeus: Mountain mining site in Thrace, east of Macedonia; source of King Philip's silver and gold. The mines were nearly depleted when Alexander became king.

Parmenio: King Philip's leading general. Father of Philotas; Alexander's second in command until his death.

Parsa: Persian name for Persepolis

Pasargadae: The old Persian capitol, fifty miles north of Persepolis

Patroclus: Lover of Achilles. Alexander visited both of their tombs when the Persian invasion began.

Patronius: Macedonian garrison commander killed at Thebes

Pausanius: Assassin who killed Philip II at Aegae

Peloponnese: Region of southernmost Greece

Pelusium: City in northern Egypt

Peneus: River in Thessaly, in central Greece

Perdiccas: Alexander friend & aristocrat from Orestis province in Macedonia; one of Alexander's leading generals

Persepolis: Greek name for Parsa; Persian city that was burned by Alexander

Peucestas: Alexander's Shield Bearer & Royal Bodyguard; saved Alexander's life in India

Philotas: Parmenio's son; brilliant Companion Cavalry commander

Philoxenus: Alexander officer; obtained surrender of Susa

Phrygia: Persian province

Pinarus: A small river separating the Macedonians/Greeks and Persians at the Battle of Issus

Pindar: Great Greek poet from Thebes

Polydamas: One of Alexander's Royal Companions; delivered Parmenio's death warrant

Ptolemy: The rumored bastard half brother of Alexander and one of his leading officers. Ptolemy formed his own dynasty in Egypt after Alexander's death. History's famous Cleopatra was a distant descendent of Ptolemy's line.

peplos: A robe made of cotton or wool; worn by Greek and Macedonian women.

peristyle courtyard: The heart of the Macedonian royal palace in Pella. The courtyard was surrounded by grand statuary.

polis: A Greek city-state (plural is poleis)

pothos: A mood or yearning to accomplish the difficult or impossible. The term was attributed uniquely to Alexander in ancient times

proskynesis: the Persian greeting gesture that entailed either prostrating oneself, kneeling before someone, bowing or blowing a kiss. The specific action was based on the social rank of the individuals greeting each other. Greeks and Macedonians abhorred the practice, a practice that Alexander tried to introduce into his court.

Rhodian: An inhabitant from the island of Rhodes

rhyton: An ornate container used to hold wine; it was often in the shape of an animal

sarissa: The variable length Macedonian infantry spear/pike used by the phalanx satrap: A Persian provincial governor

Scythians: Inhabitants of a region where the River Danube empties into the Black Sea, far to the north of the Hellespont. Once subdued by King Philip, they became fierce fighters and archers in Alexander's army.

Seistan: A large Persian lake

Seleucus: A general in Alexander's inner circle. He ruled a great kingdom from Babylon after Alexander's death

Sidon: Persian Mediterranean seaport north of Tyre

Sisygambis: Persian Queen Mother

Siwa: The oasis shrine in the great desert of western Egypt (today in Libya)

Sogdain Rock: Mountain citadel of Oxyartes, father of Roxane.

Stateira: Wife & full sister of Persian Great King Darius

Susa: One of the Persian Great King's capitols

shabraque: ('sha brak) A saddlecloth, often in the skin of an animal.

stadia: Unit of Greek/Macedonian distance measurement; one English mile = 8.33 stadia

Thapsacus: Persian city on the Euphrates River

Thermaic Gulf: Body of water in the northwest Aegean closest to Macedonia

Thermopylae (Hot Gates): Historic invasion route into central Greece

Thessaly: Greek region south of Macedonia

Triballians: Primitive people in the region north of Thrace, toward the Danube

Troad: The area in northwestern Asia Minor near the city of Troy. In Persian times, the area was known by its provincial name, Phrygia.

Tyre: The powerful Mediterranean city/seaport located on an island during ancient times. Alexander besieged and eventually conquered the city. Tyre is in modern Lebanon today.

Vardar: River in Paeonia and Macedonia that flows south into the Thermaic Gulf.

Xanthos: Persian city and oracular site with an underground hot spring. A tablet there was inscribed with ancient symbols. Aristander, Alexander's seer, used the tablet to prophesy that Greeks would destroy the Persian empire.

Xenophon: Greek invader of Persia before Alexander

Zagros: High mountain range lying between Susa in Persia and two provinces of Iran. The highest mountains in this range reach 15,000 feet.

ziggurat: Babylon's Temple of the Foundation of Heaven on Earth; it was later called the Tower of Babel by the Jews in their holy book.

About The Author

Peter Messmore is a professor, teacher, poet, and author of historical fiction. He retired as a professor of higher education in 2004. He now devotes his time to teaching, consulting, writing, and travel.

Dr. Messmore's first work of historical fiction was *Philip and Olympias: A Novel of Ancient Macedon.*

Alexander the King is the second book in a trilogy of books by Peter Messmore about the ancient world at the time of Alexander the Great. The third book has a working title *Ptolemy of Egypt.*

The author conducted research in many of the historic sites depicted in his historical novels. These sites include the modern day countries of Italy, Greece (Macedonia), Turkey, Israel, and Egypt.

Printed in the United States
22662LVS00004B/25-33

9 781418 450373